S0-AYG-072

Esteban Morales Domínguez (born in Matanzas, Cuba, 1942) has been an active participant in the Cuban revolutionary project for the past fifty years and is one of Cuba's most prominent Afro-Cuban intellectuals. He is a member of the Cuban Academy of Sciences, has held numerous academic posts, and has been awarded three times by both the Cuban Academy of Sciences and the Ministry of Higher Education. He is the principal or co-author of fifteen books and has published more than a hundred theoretical articles; his 2007 book, *Desafíos de la problemáticas racial en Cuba* (Challenges of the Racial Question in Cuba) was the first book-length academic publication on this subject by a scholar based in Cuba since the 1959 revolution.

Gary Prevost is Professor of Political Science at St. John's University and the College of St. Benedict in Minnesota. He has published numerous books and articles on revolutionary parties and social movements in Spain, Latin America, and South Africa, including *Social Movements and Leftist Governments in Latin America: Confrontation or Co-optation?*; *Cuban-Latin American Relations in a Changing Hemisphere*; *United States-Cuban Relations: A Critical History*; and *Politics in Latin America: The Power Game.*

August Nimtz, Jr. is Professor of Political Science at the University of Minnesota. He is the author of *Marx, Tocqueville, and Race in America: The "Absolute Democracy" or "Defiled Republic"*; *Marx and Engels: Their Contribution to the Democratic Breakthrough*; and *Islam and Politics in East Africa: the Sufi Order in Tanzania.*

# Race in Cuba

*Essays on the Revolution and Racial Inequality*

*by* ESTEBAN MORALES DOMÍNGUEZ

*Edited and translated under the direction of*
Gary Prevost *and* August Nimtz

MONTHLY REVIEW PRESS
*New York*

*To all those that suffered the crime of the slave trade and slavery
and those who struggle for a better world*

Copyright © 2013 by Esteban Morales Domínguez
All Rights Reserved

Library of Congress Cataloging-in-Publication Data

Morales Dommnguez, Esteban.
  [Problematica racial en Cuba. English]
  Race in Cuba : essays on the Revolution and racial inequality / by Esteban
Morales Dommnguez ; edited and translated under the direction of Gary
Prevost and August Nimtz.
     pages cm
  ISBN 978-1-58367-320-1 (paper : alkaline paper) — ISBN 978-1-58367-321-8
(cloth : alkaline paper) 1. Cuba—Race relations. 2. Blacks—Cuba. 3.
Racism—Cuba. 4. Race discrimination—Cuba. 5. Cuba—History—Revolution,
1959—Influence. I. Prevost, Gary. II. Nimtz, August H. III. Title.
  F1789.A1M6913 2012
  305.80097291—dc23
                          2012036819

Cover image: © María E. Haya (Marucha) / Pareja de Bailadores
en la Herreria de Sirique

Monthly Review Press
146 West 29th Street, Suite 6W
New York, New York 10001

www.monthlyreview.org

5  4  3  2  1

# Contents

# Foreword

Toward the end of 2009 sixty African Americans, some quite prominent, signed a letter to "draw attention to the conditions of racism and racial discrimination in Cuba that have hitherto been ignored." The signatories accused the Cuban government of "increased violations of civil and human rights for those black activists in Cuba who dare raise their voices against the island's racial system. . . . Racism in Cuba . . . is unacceptable and must be confronted!" Some of us, African Americans and others, who have long defended the Cuban Revolution, countered these charges with the facts of the Revolution both at home and abroad.[1]

But perhaps nothing refutes these accusations better than the publication of Professor Esteban Morales's new book by one of Cuba's most prestigious publishers. Its very existence gives the lie to the claims of the sixty. *Desafíos de la problemática racial en Cuba II* (Challenges of the Racial Problem in Cuba II) is, as the title suggests, the sequel to an earlier book published in 2007, so coveted that it is virtually impossible to find a copy for purchase. It was the first book published on the question of race on the island of Cuba in more than four decades. The charge, therefore, of the sixty that "racial discrimination has hitherto been ignored" in Cuba might have some merit had it been made before the publication of

the first book. But that too would ignore Morales's prior publications on
the topic which are, fortunately, included here.

In a speech in New York City in September 2000 to a largely African
American and Latino audience, *Comandante en Jefe* Fidel Castro said:

> I am not claiming that our country is a perfect model of equality and
> justice. We believed at the beginning that when we established the fullest
> equality before the law and complete intolerance for any demonstration
> of sexual discrimination in the case of women, or racial discrimination
> in the case of ethnic minorities, these phenomena would vanish from
> our society. It was some time before we discovered that marginality and
> racial discrimination with it are not something that one gets rid of with
> a law or even with ten laws, and we have not managed to eliminate them
> completely in forty years.

Those of us who had the privilege of being there to hear what he said
and who had some sense of the Revolution's history and what it was
being subjected to at the time felt a sense of relief. For defenders of the
Revolution from within the proverbial "belly of the beast," it was reas-
suring to hear Fidel acknowledge what we all suspected to one degree
or another. The worst economic crisis in modern Cuban history, the
"Special Period," had taken a disproportionate toll on black and mestizo
Cubans, revealing just what Fidel admitted. His honesty made it easier
for us to defend a project, a work still in progress, that advanced, unlike
any ever before, the status of blacks not only in Cuba but elsewhere,
especially in Africa.

As a young African American on the picket lines in New Orleans
demanding the end of the Jim Crow system of racial segregation, I was
won forever to the Cuban Revolution when I learned that within months
of the triumph of the Revolution in January 1959 the new government
ended almost immediately the kinds of practices we protested against.
I hung on to every snippet of news about the Revolution and cheered
with every indication that it was surviving. I'll never forget the joy of visiting the Cuban Pavilion at the World Exposition in Montreal in 1967.
The facility lacked the flashiness of the other exhibits, which for me only

added to the credibility of the Revolution; the very graphic slogans and texts about the process on its stark walls livened up by Cuban musicians, *congris,* and, of course, Havana Club rum sealed my fate. That would be my initial physical contact with the Revolution but not the last.

The first major international attack on the Revolution for its alleged failings in regard to racial equality was made in 1972 by Carlos Moore, a black Cuban.[2] I was fortunate to have been living in Dar es Salaam, Tanzania's capital, because it was the virtual headquarters for the southern African liberation movement at the time. And exactly because of Cuba's well-known assistance to it, Moore's allegations fell on deaf ears of those within and around the various movements housed there. This was especially important for African Americans of my generation who were inspired by the African revolution but who tended to look at politics solely through the lens of race and skin color, as does Moore. To hear the movement's leaders and leading supporters, such as the Afro-Guyanese revolutionary Walter Rodney, denounce Moore was instructive.

Yet we were still vulnerable to Moore's charges, especially the one about the racial composition of the Cuban Revolution's leadership; that is, the underrepresentation of blacks and mestizos. And when we began to visit Cuba—my first visit was in 1983—it was almost impossible to find any books, journals, et cetera, that provided an analysis of the race question. The "silence" after 1962 that Morales speaks of was all so evident. At the same time, it was clear—provided one had historical perspective— that black and mestizo Cubans had made tremendous advances after 1959. Conversations with those who were born long before then provided confirmatory evidence.[3] We could, therefore, suspend judgment about the "silence" as long as the advances continued. Most encouraging was Fidel's report to the Third Party Congress in 1986 that called for the recruitment of more blacks and mestizos, along with women and youth, into the party leadership—"affirmative action," as it was then called in the United States. Three years later the Revolution was responsible for the most important advance in the global struggle for racial equality in the last quarter of the twentieth century, the defeat of the South African army in Cuito Cuanavale, Angola, which paved the way to the end of the apartheid regime in 1994. Thus, three decades after the overthrow of the U.S.-

backed Batista dictatorship, defenders of the Cuban Revolution could rightly feel confident that racial equality in Cuba was within grasp. But then came the Special Period and the consequences that Fidel's admission in 2000 alluded to.

Morales's writings are in many ways a very detailed analytical elaboration of Fidel's 2000 comments in New York City. They also address, even more importantly, "What is to be done?" His earliest essay in this collection, "Un modelo para el análisis de la problemática racial cubana contemporánea" (A Model for the Analysis of the Racial Problem in Contemporary Cuba), was written in the second half of 2002. For those of us who had the opportunity to read various drafts of it, we realized that there was—perhaps for the first time—a serious discussion under way in Cuba on the race question, one that had begun in the Cuban National Union of Artists and Writers (UNEAC) in 1998 with the participation of Fidel. His comment in New York City reflected, I suspect, that discussion. If the signatories of the letter of the sixty were apparently unaware of it, their counterparts in Cuba certainly were not. Morales was an active participant in these initial deliberations. What motivated the discussion was the increasing racial disparity in economic opportunities that came with the openings to capitalist penetration via tourism and international trade that Cuba was forced to allow in order to survive the very excruciating economic crisis of the 1990s. Unless this new development was addressed and confronted, it threatened to undermine a key bulwark of the Revolution, the support of blacks and mestizos.[4]

Morales is very frank, elaborating on the admission that Fidel made in 2000 that "we have not managed to eliminate [marginality and racial discrimination] completely in forty years." From the overrepresentation of blacks and mestizos in prisons to their underrepresentation on television or in administrative posts, he speaks the truth. At the heart of the problem, he argues, is the lack of consciousness about how not only race but skin color relate to such issues. The most recent census, 2002, he notes, typifies this shortcoming. Though an advance over the 1981 census it failed in this regard to ask the necessary questions to fully get at the problem and therefore provide an evidentiary basis for solutions. Some defenders of the Cuban Revolution abroad may be uncomfortable with these admissions. But what Morales does is salutary. He teaches us that we don't have to be cheerleaders, overlooking its shortcomings, to defend the Revolution.

Morales leaves no doubt that despite what it still has yet to achieve the Cuban Revolution constitutes a real advance for its black and mestizo denizens: "In spite of the racism that still exists in Cuban society, we can argue that the black and mulatto population on the island is the most educated and healthy group of African descendants in this hemisphere, and that no other country has done so much to eliminate racial injustice and discrimination as has Cuba." He reiterates this insight in the all-important interview in the December 2009 *Trabajadores*—the most widely read publication on the island after *Granma* and *Juventud Rebelde*—in response to the charge of the sixty: "Cuba is the only country in the world in which blacks and mestizos have the state and the government as their ally. If there had not been a revolution, blacks would have had to make one in order to reach the level that more than a few of us have achieved."

Morales does not exaggerate about "this hemisphere." No better evidence for his claim is what happened in the aftermath of Hurricane Katrina in New Orleans and environs in 2005—a tragedy and crime that impacted my own family. The more than 1,600 individuals who lost their lives, disproportionately African Americans and in stark contrast to the handful of Cubans of similar race and skin color who suffer a similar fate when even more powerful hurricanes strike, speaks volumes about what a difference a revolution makes. The post-Katrina social crisis revealed exactly what African Americans lack and what their sisters and brethren in Cuba have, which is "the state and government as their ally." What Morales correctly calls for is more conscious use of those instruments on behalf of Cuban blacks and mestizos for achieving full equality.

Though the discussion Morales is helping to lead is primarily for Cuban eyes and ears, its significance goes far beyond the shores of the island. The larger context for this ongoing discussion, it must be emphasized, is the global crisis of capitalism from which Cuba is not immune. Evidence continues to mount that the crisis, the deepest since the Great Depression, is still in its initial stages. Defenders of capitalism admit the seriousness of the crisis but argue that whatever toll it takes on the world's toilers there is no viable alternative to the market system. Hasn't history shown, they claim, that the socialist option has failed? It is precisely this question that makes what takes place in Cuba, the only country in the world whose leadership and working masses in their vast majority are still committed to a non-capitalist world, so important. And nothing, I argue, is as crucial to the fulfillment of that commitment as the race question. It is true that in order for Cuba to survive the crisis, its economy will have to grow, and that the measures its leadership are instituting to that end are most significant. But growing the economy requires in the long run a society in which all workers see themselves as equal participants in all the decisions to advance the socialist project. The "what is to be done" that Morales advocates will go a long way to make that effort a reality.

In the United States no segment of the working class will be as interested in the outcome of this effort as—to use the language of Marx and Engels—"workers in black skin." Despite the skin color of the present occupant of the White House, African Americans continue to shoulder the worst features of everything from unemployment to the mortgage crisis, deteriorating health, and diminishing educational opportunities. Black workers in the United States also have a long history—as is true in Cuba—of resistance and revolutionary action. "From the Civil War until today. . . the vanguard role and weight of workers who are black in broad, proletarian-led social and political struggles in the United States. . . is amazing."[5] There is no reason to assume that history is an interesting artifact of the past, given the still and increasingly oppressive reality that blacks face. They will not only be less willing to dismiss the socialist alternative as capitalism's defenders would hope but be more open to it *if* it can be shown that a socialist revolution actually opens up the possibility of full racial equality—not just in the electoral arena—for the first time in the history of the United States.

If what I say is accurate, that the achievement of racial equality in Cuba would enhance the socialist alternative for the United States, the implications for the future of the Cuban Revolution are more than obvious. The destiny of the revolutionary process in both countries—from the overthrow of slavery in the United States in 1865 to the taking of state power by the working class in Cuba between 1959 and 1961—has always been intertwined, the dialectic of geographical accident. Thus what Morales is helping to lead has immeasurable significance. I am honored to have been asked to reflect on his contributions to so momentous a discussion.

—AUGUST NIMTZ

# *Preface*

This book is the record of an intervention in a growing discussion in Cuba—a discussion due in part to the writings of our author. Esteban Morales Domínguez, Professor Emeritus of Political Economy of the University of Havana, a cadre in Cuba's Communist Party, and black, has been at the center of *la problemática racial,* or the race question, since its revival at the end of the twentieth century. The collapse of the former Soviet Union and the regimes it was allied with in Eastern Europe at the beginning of the last decade of the twentieth century had major consequences for Cuba. The Revolution experienced its gravest crisis since its inauguration in 1959 and in the process exposed the unfinished business of the quest for racial equality on the island. This provoked a discussion, initiated in part by Fidel Castro, to which Morales was a key witness and participant.

This is a translation of most of Morales's writings and pronouncements on the subject from his earliest in 2002 to the most recent when the manuscript was completed in March 2012—the most current book-length presentation of his ideas in any language.[1] One of the chapters, "Challenges of the Racial Question in Cuba," summarizes Morales's first book on the topic in 2007, *Desafíos de la probemática racial en Cuba* (Editorial de Ciencias Sociales, La Habana). The reader, therefore, is treated to the opportunity of seeing how the discussion has evolved for over a decade. To a large degree this is a continuation of his 2010 book, *La problemática racial en Cuba: algunos de sus desafíos* (Editorial José Martí, La Habana) because it reproduces most of its chapters with three additional ones. As the record of an intervention there is an understandable degree of repetition of the key themes in Morales's arguments—reiterated for different venues. Our goal is fidelity to his voice to insure that it comes through loud and clear even at the risk of repetition—a work in progress in the best sense of the term.

There are a number of names, terms, and events, familiar to Cuban readers, whose meaning and significance are not explained in the original text. So as not to clutter the translation with notes beyond those in the original, readers should turn to the glossary for clarification. One term or set of terms that requires special attention here are "*mestizo*" and "*mulato*." For readers who may be familiar with the different ways in which these terms are employed and distinguished in other settings in Latin America and the Caribbean—the United States as well—it is important to note Morales's usage. "My references to *mulatos*," he explains, "can all be used when speaking about *mestizos*, which is the largest category in Cuba. There are too many types of *mulatos*, which involves numerous classifications. Therefore, the best thing is to speak of *mestizos* in Cuba—which implies a large mixture that includes Europeans, mainly Iberians, Indians and blacks from Africa and the West Indies, and also Chinese. That's what I call *mestizo*—a mixture of physical features and colors that Fernando Ortiz calls the *ajiaco* or stew."

Without the voluntary labor of Bruce Campbell, Franklin Curbelo, Enrique Sacerio-Gari, and the team of Walter Lippman, the translators, this book could not have been published. Recognizing the importance of the project, they were always willing to pitch in when needed. We are also appreciative of the editorial work provided by Monthly Review Press and the timely way in which the book has come into print.

Since the publication of Morales's 2010 book there have been a number of developments—not necessarily reflected in this book—that register, in his opinion, the progress being made in Cuba on this issue. "Although," for example, "the race question eluded *Bohemia* [Cuba's most popular weekly] for a long time, it finally published a long interview [with Morales and others who've been addressing the question] in its June 4, 2010, issue." Most important following that breakthrough was the election of the new Central Committee of the Cuban Communist Party at its Sixth Congress in April 2011. Quoting Raúl Castro, "[it] remains made up of 115 members of which 48 are women, 41.7 percent, tripling the proportion reached in the prior congress, which was 13.3 percent. There are 36 blacks and mestizos, a ten percent increase in representation, reaching now to 31.3 percent [of the Central Committee]"—the highest ever.

As a member of the Aponte Commission to Combat Racism and Racial Discrimination of the National Union of Cuban Writers and Artists (UNEAC), Morales was involved in creating and promoting a variety of programs for 2011, the United Nations–declared International Year of People of African Descent, and 2012, such as:

- Closely coordinated work for two major commemorations: the 1812 rebellion of José Aponte and the 1912 uprising of the Independent Party of Color—two transcendent moments for the topic of race in Cuba.

- A day dedicated to the memory of General of the Army Antonio Maceo.

- A day dedicated to Mariana Grajales—the mother of Antonio Maceo.

- Provincial Hearings, in every province, on the race topic with all of the contributing political, cultural, higher educational, institutional and *Poder Popular* influences.

- Regular assemblies of the Aponte Commission of [UNEAC].

- A meeting in Cuba of the Regional Articulation for the Left Movement of People of African Descent in Latin America, the Caribbean and the Diaspora (ARA), September 20–21, 2012.

- Participation in conferences of People of African Descent in Venezuela, Panama, Brazil, and South Africa.

- Discussion and formulation of a political agenda of the topic for presentation to the political leadership of the country and to the National Assembly.

- Regularization of scientific work on the race question at all levels in coordination with the Academy of Sciences and the Ministries of Education.

- Casa de las Americas [Cuba's leading literary body] sponsored a competition for a Special Prize for the African Presence in Latin America and the Caribbean.

- Elaboration of a national agenda for the extension of the Year of People of African Descent as recently proposed by the United Nations.

In the context of these activities, this book, Morales says, "is not just one more on the topic but rather an expression of the struggle that has been opened in Cuba for the definitive elimination of racism and racial discrimination. Articulated systematically at the national level, the struggle has mobilized all of the potentialities of personalities, governmental, state, political and civil society institutions deemed necessary for the definitive social offensive against racism in Cuba."

—AUGUST H. NIMTZ
—GARY PREVOST

# 1—Challenges of the Racial Question in Cuba

There are very few contemporary writings on the subject of race in this country, and those that do exist are by and large found in journals, especially *Temas* and *Catauro*.[1] Abroad, there have been more publications dealing with the subject on a contemporary basis. Aline Helg, Alejandro de la Fuente, and Carlos Moore are noteworthy for their extensive research. But none of them share the vicissitudes of daily life in Cuba with us, and this can be seen in their writings. Even though we might not share some of their opinions, they make notable contributions.

This situation tells us that in addition to the difficulties associated with this subject within present-day Cuban society—something we will deal with later—we have in effect handed over to others the task of analyzing a problem of vital importance in this country's life. The resultant danger is that—in response—we find ourselves having to clarify matters about which we have still not been able to have a scientific discussion of our own. Therefore, it is of prime importance that we try to work out our own vision, from the island, of the racial question in Cuban society in these complex times.

This objective encompasses a desire to examine the existence of this problem within present-day Cuban reality, making clear that it is not simply a case of inherited burdens, but rather a problem that our society is still capable of generating. We must also call attention to the danger that racism and discrimination could again take root in the macro-consciousness of today's society.

The fundamental problems that we run up against regarding the subject of race include ignorance about it, continual avoidance of the topic, as well as insufficient treatment of the subject. Many people feel that it is not worth talking about this topic.

In *Desafíos de la problematica racial en Cuba*,[2] which this essay summarizes, my aim was to develop a model for studying and researching this subject—fulfilling the need to theorize about it—and examining the scope and form in which many phenomena of the problem are studied at present. In reality, with the exception of some of the investigative works of the Anthropology Center of CITMA [Ministry of Science, Technology, and Environment], which are still unpublished,[3] we did not find earlier studies that are worthy of mention regarding either of those two aims. The vast majority of the Anthropology Center studies are the fruit of praiseworthy research that has gotten caught up in the whirlwind of bureaucracy, ignorance, and fear of publicizing the findings.[4]

It might have seemed that racism and discrimination had disappeared from Cuban society. At least that is what many believed. But the economic crisis at the end of the 1980s and beginning of the 1990s, with its strong undercurrent of social crisis, caused racism to resurface with the virulence that can be expected from a problem that, having been seen as solved, in fact was not. To imagine it had been solved was an example of the worst kind of pure idealism.

Racism and racial discrimination was eliminated from the institutional frameworks of the state and the government with the triumph of the Revolution in 1959. But the phenomenon maintained a toehold in the family, individual attitudes, and some institutions, and today there is the danger of its reestablishment in the macro-consciousness of Cuban society. This could take place through mechanisms that inject prejudice and negative racial stereotypes into the population, as well as through the dynamics of the relations between the formal institutions and the informal networks of power.[5]

Therefore, we need to take stock of this phenomenon. We need to examine the mechanisms through which racism spreads and how we can help to design tools that allow us fight it. In this regard I begin with a series of premises.

Racism arose from slavery. In the Americas slavery took the form of color. Blacks, most of the time poor, were brought in the slave ships from the west coast of Africa and turned into slaves. It did not take long for the enslavement of these human beings to be justified on the basis of their being black.

For generations, blacks and their descendants occupied the lowest rung in Cuban society—first colonial and then neo-colonial society. We cannot expect that in a little less than a half-century since its triumph the Revolution could fully lift them out of their situation of inferiority. All the more so if we consider that owing to certain historic vicissitudes, the racial question, of all the social problems that the Revolution tackled since 1959, may have been the theme on which there has been the least progress.

We should not confuse the degree of social justice achieved by the many racial groups that make up our society today with the disappearance of racism, because racism is a complex multidimensional and multi-causal matter that does not disappear solely through achievement of higher levels of social justice. Cuba is a tangible example of this.

In the years immediately following the triumph of the Revolution, social, economic, and political conditions emerged that practically made "color" disappear from the considerations of the typical Cuban. New political conditions, in turn, encouraged an idealistic view on the part of the political leadership as well as the majority of the citizenry—including the vast majority of blacks—that it was possible to forget about racism.

In 1959, the chief of the Revolution had frontally and forcefully attacked the existing racial discrimination, which had been a direct inheritance from Republican Cuba. However, not long afterward, the language changed; the case was seen as closed, and in 1962 the matter was declared solved in the Second Declaration of Havana. After that a long period of silence ensued.

In practice, the subject of racism was no longer spoken of, until it reappeared in the second half of the 1980s, when the political leadership itself raised it. The complex conditions that had encouraged silence concerning the subject of race gave way to the economic and political shockwaves at the end of the 1980s, giving rise to a more realistic vision about what had actually occurred with racism, which encouraged a more objective and critical analysis of the situation.

Proclaimed at a mass meeting in 1962 that the problem of racial discrimination and racism had been solved was an error of idealism and wishful thinking. As a direct result, the subject of race has become the most avoided and ignored topic in our social reality. A significant segment of our intelligentsia pays it no attention, does not even deem it worthy of consideration, and thus there are major differences among our intellectuals over where we stand in terms of the consolidation of the nation and its culture. However, speaking scientifically, there cannot be the slightest doubt that when we talk about "race" in Cuba—even though this is a social invention—we are talking about culture and nation.

Moreover, making the subject taboo, removing it from all social and political arenas, gave rise to a social environment that made it more difficult to refer to racism. Those who brought it up were ideologically and politically repressed. In the sphere of culture the subject of race was still broached to a degree, but from the standpoint of the sciences it was impossible to do research on it, and especially to write about it. According to the prevailing view after 1962, in the midst of the political confrontation of those years, anyone who critically analyzed racism was playing into the hands of those who wanted to socially divide Cubans, and it earned that person the epithet of being a racist or a divider, or both.

If you don't deal with "skin color" as what it is, a historical variable of social differentiation among Cubans, you could forget that blacks, whites, and mestizos did not start from the same place in taking advantage of the opportunities the Revolution provided. So it was overlooked that many of the poor were black, which represents an additional disadvantage, even within present-day Cuban society.

Color exerted its influence and even though blacks and mestizos were treated in exactly the same manner as poor whites, they remained at a greater disadvantage. Later it was shown that it was not enough to be born in the same hospital, to attend the same school and same recreation center, if some children return to a tenement, to a marginal neighborhood, while others had a substantial house, parents earning good salaries in much better living conditions, conditions that do not characterize the immense majority of non-whites, and especially blacks. The neighborhoods are different, as are the families and their living standards.

Black and white children might have the same opportunities, but this does not mean that they all will be equally capable of overcoming the historic starting points bequeathed by their families, living conditions, neighborhood, etc. Unfortunately, social policies at the time of the triumph of the Revolution did not take skin color into account, with consequences that must now be corrected.

Certain subjects are useful for exploring the series of problems that seriously affect the racial balance in the social, educational, and cultural spheres. In the early years of the Revolution, in the context of the needs of the struggle against imperialism, excessive priority was given to questions related to the national identity, and matters of cultural identity were often given short shrift. Racism and discrimination were also fed by the stereotypes and prejudices against cultures originating from Africa. The upshot of this was that the dominance of "white Hispanicism" still retained its hold on our culture, despite the efforts made to reemphasize the values of the African presence within the national culture. Although we see a high degree of integration in our culture, racism and white dominance still leave their mark upon it. This type of situation can reflect a strong component of prejudices and negative stereotypes regarding the value of cultures coming from Africa; although there is also a significant economic component, given that virtually all the African countries are poor.

In addition, unfortunately, an ideopolitical atmosphere developed in Cuba wherein defining oneself racially is frowned upon. This affected the dynamics of personal identity, which must function as an integrated system whose components, valued individually, are important in fighting social perversions such as racism. A person must first know who he is before he can have the possibility of being part of some other thing. The consciousness of each individual cannot be subsumed within the national consciousness; all people make up an integrated system in which the whole does not function without the parts.

But this view implicitly implies a strong respect for diversity, which has been lacking in Cuban society. Diversity is the objective, one with which we grapple every day. Unity is an unrealizable goal if it is not built within the context of diversity.

Blacks and mestizos in Cuba, with very rare exceptions, do not have a genealogical tree and cannot trace their surnames to Africa or to Spain. In particular, the identity of blacks has always been under strong assault. Blacks have had to navigate a road mined by racial discrimination and nonrecognition of their values. Even when the economic level of a black person might have been similar to that of a white person, it did not save him from being racially discriminated against. This indicates that we are not simply dealing with an economic question.

With a certain amount of help the white person can escape from poverty and his color helps him escape being discriminated against for being poor. However, the other one carries the color of his skin with him. Therefore, even though he might escape poverty, he would continue to be excluded. What adaptation would allow the black person to leave discrimination behind; under what color could he hide? Although pulling him out of poverty might be difficult, achieving the conditions so that he is not discriminated against is even more difficult. These conditions are not just economic. They go much further.

Adding to the problems of the identity of blacks is that they tend not to have a recognized history. We have not been able to get beyond a version of our written history in which the black and the mestizo, especially the black, are scarcely mentioned. With very few exceptions, found in independent works, we almost completely lack a social history of blacks and mestizos in Cuba that would be comparable with the one that exists for the white population. This situation affects all of Cuban society, which is unable to develop an integral, realistic view of its historic development and therefore not infrequently muddles along with a distorted image of the true role that each racial group played in the formation of the culture and the nation.

The way power is distributed in present-day Cuban society does not go beyond what existed prior to 1959; within society white dominance is still forcefully expressed, especially at the level of what is called the "new economy." This is especially evident in the absence of blacks in the upper leadership levels of the state, government, and institutions of civil society in general, although not in the party structure. A recent example is that there is not one single black among the fourteen provincial chairs of People's Power.

This is in complete contradiction to the leadership policy put forward by the party in 1985, which is a long way from being realized in terms of racial representation. The matter is certainly much more complicated than the question of whether there might be blacks and mestizos in all the positions, but undoubtedly what is happening seriously affects the participation of non-whites in the structures of power.

The problems related to "whitening" still exist within our societal reality. What else would explain why so many people who are not white are unwilling to identify themselves that way? This distorts the census figures and moves the question of race into a realm of deception and hypocrisy, making it absurd to think that mestizism might be the solution, when what should be mixed are various forms of consciousness to create a consciousness that makes color disappear. So that, as Nicolás Guillén says, we come to "Cuban color." The attitude of many black or mestizo people toward their own pigmentation indicates that they do not find it advantageous to identify themselves as such.

Other aspects that are part of how present-day Cuban society presents itself ideologically are also affected, and these spheres also suffer from the imbalance in racial representation. We have a prime example in national television, where the number of blacks and mestizos in front of the cameras is very low. It is seen in the nearly total absence of blacks or mestizos in leading positions on our educational channels. Confronting racism requires that there be a balanced representation, especially on television, which has such an influence in providing role models and requires that all racial groups be represented.

The subject of race is not dealt with in school. This can result in a profound and dangerous dichotomy between scholastic education and social reality. We are not preparing our young people to deal with what they will later find when they go out into the streets. Things do not pass into the culture unless they are introduced in the schools, and this is an important flaw in our education regarding a subject of vital importance. Our curricula and educational programs are still characterized by full-blown "Occidentalism." African and Asian cultures are basically absent from the curriculum. As a result, students do not receive an integral and balanced education as members of a mono-ethnic and multiracial society, so when they leave the classroom we cannot be sure that they understand the roots of Cuban culture, much less the nation's real history. In the majority of cases they have a Manichean and stereotyped vision of the most important aspects of that history. Not to mention that they ought to know who Aponte was, the history of the so-called Little War of 1912, and the Party of the Independents of Color.

As I said earlier, Cuban scientific work has barely begun to focus on the question of race. In the course of these nearly fifty years of the revolutionary process, almost all of the most important intellectual work on this subject, from the perspective of the social and human sciences, has been done outside Cuba.[6] This is a weakness because we have almost totally handed over a vital aspect of our reality, with the resulting dangers that ensue for our scientific and cultural development and for the political and ideological struggle in defense of our social goals. Today in Cuba we have various challenges regarding this subject, which we must seriously confront.

Trying to gain a fundamental understanding of the context of this problem—which has for so long been ignored, swept under the rug, forgotten, neglected, and even repressed—has given rise to a very complicated situation in the framework of political policies. There is no well-rounded understanding of the situation by the institutions, social and political organizations, or leading sectors of the state apparatus. At times there is not even an acceptance that the problem exists. Instead, we see resistance. As a result it is virtually impossible to predict the reactions that dealing with it openly might generate. We see attitudes that run the gamut from a totally cynical approach to fear and ignorance, all the way to the most heavy-handed denial of the existence of a racial problem.

Not dealing with a problem of such importance would continue to engender bewilderment, ignorance, and social discomfort in those who suffer from discrimination, whether directly or as a result of not having acquired an anti-discriminatory ethic. Avoidance of the issue would lead to a level of social hypocrisy that would turn the racial problem into an endemic ill, with consequences for societal coexistence, the nation, and Cuban culture. This problem is something we must not leave to future generations. What kind of a basic overall culture can we have in a society that retains negative racial stereotypes, discrimination based on skin color, and racism? Society must come up with an integrated strategy to struggle against negative racial stereotypes, discrimination, and racism in today's Cuba.

We must not deal with social phenomena solely on the basis of classifying the population according to sex and age while passing over skin color. Cuba is not Sweden or Holland. Skin color has historically been—and continues to be—a factor of social differentiation within the Cuban population. Race or skin color, class and gender, go hand in hand in the country's history. Skin color, social differences, poverty, imbalances in the distribution of power, discrimination, lack of empowerment, negative racial stereotypes, and racism have always gone together in the island's history. What country are we talking about if we do not consider color as a fundamental trait of our population? What democracy do we speak of if one segment of our population continues being discriminated against because of skin color? This is a problem for all of society, not solely for blacks and mestizos; it is something everyone has to solve. To do that, to lay out an effective working strategy, people must be made conscious that the problem exists. They need to fundamentally understand the place that history reserved for each racial group; to realize that there is racism on the part of whites as well as blacks; a racism that stresses assigning each "their rightful place" flowing from a structure of class and power that allows some to discriminate against others. They need to understand that the response to these differences cannot be to maintain a social dynamic based on prejudice, stereotypes, mutual discrimination and poverty. Rather, it must be based on an understanding of history and on an attitude of melding consciousness in order to uproot these evils from our culture and the Cuban way of life.

Only by openly dealing with the question of race can we put an end to the ignorance, cynicism, and hypocrisy that still lie below the surface when race is discussed. Dealing with it openly can also help to develop an atmosphere in which it would be impossible to withdraw into some private social space to practice racial discrimination. Certainly the subject of race implicitly contains a strong element of social division, but the only way to achieve a solid, integrated national culture is to recognize race. That is the only way we can build a culture within present-day Cuban society in which all the forms of dominance that were spawned by the racist culture inherited from colonialism and capitalism can be overcome, a culture in which each racial group has its place.

We must no longer acquiesce in avoiding the subject of race in order to maintain a form of harmonious social coexistence. That only creates false harmony, riddled with hypocrisy and prone to making concessions to racism and discrimination, as well as a context in which those who choose to maintain their prejudices and discrimination will always be able to find a place to do so.

Nor should we accept the idea that attacking racism and discrimination weakens Cuban society. Rather, it is the complete opposite. Not fighting this evil is what divides society, weakens its culture, affects the national identity, and places the Revolution's social goals at serious risk, goals that must encompass nothing less than unity forged within diversity. The subject must be forcefully brought back into public discourse, it must be publicized, and it must be taken up in the political and mass organizations, so that it becomes what it should be and in fact is: a fundamental aspect of the already launched Battle of Ideas.

# 2—Race and the Republic

There is no such thing as a scientific concept of race; it is just a social construction. That is, unless you ask any honest citizen who happen to live in the Republic of Cuba. These issues cannot be overlooked these days, especially when it comes to digging up our past, because behind our back they can affect our present and shape our future. The exploitative classes removed from power by our victorious 1959 revolution have tried hard to change Cuban history, as evidenced by the praise heaped on March 10, 1952, in a biography of Fulgencio Batista that is by no means reflective of the dictator we knew on our island.[1]

Cuba proved to be a key setting to bring together the old and new world. It played a crucial part in the rise of a social model that gave us the new without losing the forms of exploitation developed by the old. Consequently, the so-called new world was in many respects more backward than the old one, as clearly shown in the long time it took to replace slave with wage labor in sugar production and Spain's remarkable reluctance to give up what it called "the always faithful island of Cuba."

All the prejudice, negative stereotyping, and discrimination against non-white and, particularly, black people moved unhindered from the colony to the Republic, despite their notable role in the bloody battles of the independence war. To be sure, blacks were already suffering from marginalization by the time the Republic was founded, among other reasons because racists from both sides of the Florida Straits had joined forces to that effect, especially in the wake of U.S. intervention. In order to understand Cuba's racial issue, it is necessary, if not indispensable, that we take into account three highly significant factors: first, slavery and its many psychological and other consequences; second, racism's economic, political, social, cultural, ideological, and even demographic effects—the "black scare" syndrome left by the Haitian Revolution; and third, the length of time that went by before slavery was abolished in 1886, making Cuba the second-to-last country to do so in the Western Hemisphere. This particular fact had a significant short- and long-term impact on the status of Cuba's black population and the racist culture they inherited.

Furthermore, the ill-fated transition from a colony to a republic was marked by the fact that it was not the pro-independence progressive and revolutionary forces but the U.S. interventionists and their allies who brought down the curtain on the conflict in Cuba and laid the foundations of the new establishment, imposed in 1902. The protectorate years leading up to the Republic served to ideologically convert most of the radical political forces and launch what proved to be Yankee imperialism's first neocolonial experiment in our hemisphere, a longed-for model of representative democracy that they strove to develop until 1958.

Such was the United States' plan when it commanded Spain to let go of the island: use its so-called autonomy to set up the protectorate that would "shape" Cuba until the time was ripe to take control of it. In this way they put on hold everything that whites, blacks, and mestizos alike had done for the sake of Martí's idea of a republic forged "with all and for the good of all." Since Cuban blacks and mestizos had no other source of inspiration but the liberation project led by Martí, Gómez, and Maceo, they saw their expectations smashed to pieces. Unlike blacks in the United States, blacks in Cuba had always fought for what they considered their homeland. They had no intention of going back to Africa, though they were fully aware they would still have to fight tooth and nail to be recognized as Cuban, or else risk being sent back anyway.

Racism and discrimination gained momentum following the Yankee intervention in 1898, and not even the powerful members of the *criollo* bourgeoisie could escape their effects, since by American standards they were mixed race, and therefore non-whites. Leonard Wood wrote to President McKinley: "We're dealing with a race which has been decimated for hundreds of years and must be taught a new life, new principles and new ways to do things."[2] As Wood said, it was the only way, because "after being swamped for centuries by the castoffs of Spanish society, there's too much 'mixed blood' in the Island to join successfully the group of civilized nations."[3] Accordingly, Cuba could only be accepted for membership at the United States' behest and only after being "whitened." To Charles Davenport, a famed geneticist of the time, "The mulattos combined ambition with intellectual deficiencies, which makes them unfortunate hybrids prone to alter society's harmonic order."[4] This appraisal was the racists' warning to the mulattos that for all their closeness to whites they were also blacks and hence unreliable. Even many of those whose views on the island's population were not so negative agreed that the Cubans were lazy, childish, incompetent, and encumbered by an acute sense of inferiority. Small surprise then that the teachers sent to Harvard University in 1901 for training on how to shore up the "American way of life" in Cuba were seen as "grown-up children unable to grasp the meaning of what they saw"; in other words, nearly stupid.[5]

As stated in Article 11, Section IV, of the Constitution of the Republic, blacks were granted citizen status as of 1901, but in practice this right was at odds with the still prevailing class interests and racial prejudice of the colonial period. Ergo, the non-whites, who accounted for the poorest and lowest strata of Cuban society, remained markedly ostracized by the emerging bourgeois capitalistic society. The foreign masters and the ruling Cuban whites used racism to subjugate and repress the blacks and mestizos while striving to twist, manipulate, and eradicate the glorious past and its myth of racial equality that had brought them together during the war. On top of that, those who had sided with the U.S. military intervention were not really sure that Cuba, freed from Spain, could become by itself a sovereign independent nation, which made the new masters' ideological work easier because local bourgeoisie were willing to settle for a protectorate.

It was thus very difficult for non-whites and especially blacks to voice their frustration and make their white countrymen understand that their outcry over their situation did not mean they were racist, anti-white, anti-patriotic, or enemies of the nation. They were just claiming their right to enjoy white Cuba's power, wealth, and job opportunities on equal terms, which was highly unlikely in a context where the social elite treated the smallest complaint as an assault on the atmosphere of peace and racial coexistence they advocated.

Based as it was on the Anglo-Saxon notion of white supremacy, this approach to the Cubans lived on in the Republic as a major hallmark of the way the United States treated Cuba. It is perhaps the reason why American diplomats in Havana once referred to the Cuban politicians who shared the administration of the island with them like this: "They have the superficial charm of astute children pampered by nature and geography, but beneath the surface they combine the worst traits of the unfortunate mixture of Spanish and African culture, laziness, cruelty, fickleness, lack of responsibility and innate dishonesty."[6] All of the above highlights the reasons why Cuba and particularly its black population had to submit to the new Republic's white power structure, acting as a perfect complement to the cultural, economic, and political order that the United States imposed on the island with the help of their local subordinates.

The controversial racial issue has always drawn the attention of black, mestizo, and white intellectuals who wrote about it in the media, although many journalists leveled fierce criticism on the efforts of this group to bring blacks and mestizos into the mainstream of Cuban society. A good example of this fight was the angry campaign launched by media between 1908 and 1912 against the Independent Party of Color and blacks in general, and a massacre of their members took place that latter year.

At its turn, the U.S. occupation and interference in Cuba's internal affairs paved the way for the inculcation of American "scientific" ideas about race, based on the concept of "biological racism" and its so-called laws of heredity. Sterilization programs were seen as the only viable solution to a growing crime rate ascribed, of course, to non-whites and blacks, your typical "witches" fond of human sacrifices and raping white girls. The smear campaign was so intense that not a few innocent blacks paid for it with their lives, and the concept soon became part of conventional wisdom.

Only through selective immigration could the desired radical change in the Cuban people's racial composition be achieved, whereas the low birthrate among the black population was expected to lead eventually to their "natural" disappearance. Then, as in José A. Saco's time, blacks had no place on the island and were somehow expected to pass out of sight so that the overall population could get whiter. Paradoxically, the survival of the blacks and mestizos who had been willing to die for Cuban independence was often threatened by the same people they had fought against during the war. As planned, the long-awaited arrival of white and Catholic immigrants from Spain was steadily stripping them of land and the best-paid jobs.

It was only under pressure from U.S. sugar companies that the Cuban government agreed to take in seasonal farm laborers from the Antilles. After all, business is business, and cynicism suits its purposes fine. Indeed, as far as many whites were concerned, what was at stake with regard to the "racial issue" was nothing less than Cuba's social and cultural future, though in their view the great tragedy was the island's increasing "Africanization." Thus all things African, a major source of sustenance to our identity, had to be culturally and physically removed from Cuba.

Two features that the ruling powers ascribed to non-whites ultimately justified their contempt for West Indian immigrants: their alleged criminal nature and primeval religious beliefs. It was racism at its worst. President Gerardo Machado's speeches often referred to the Cuban "fraternity" of races. He signed a bill declaring December 7 a day of mourning in commemoration of Antonio Maceo's death; honored Juan Gualberto Gómez with the Order Carlos Manuel de Céspedes, Cuba's highest; and decreed the disbandment of a Ku Klu Klan chapter in the province of Camagüey. Nothing but clever steps, in collusion with the domestic non-white middle class and with the support of Club Atenas, to pass for a president who sympathized with the blacks.

On September 5, 1928, representatives of 186 "color societies" across Cuba gathered at Teatro Nacional to hail the president while popular opposition was on the rise. The outcome was an alliance of all parties that gave further recognition to an increasingly authoritarian regime. It was all a sham: other than a certain political visibility blacks remained poorly represented in the power structure, could only hold limited positions in civil service, were shut off from private companies, and seldom found a job in industry because Machado never really did anything for black people. While he was being honored by Club Atenas on the eve of the Wall Street Crash of 1929, most blacks were going to great lengths to cope with deprivation, as they were hardest hit by the Great Depression and the Hawley-Smoot Tariff of 1930, when the Cuban economy nose-dived and the country's social problems piled sky-high. What followed was a wave of protests spurred by a new political front ready to overturn the status quo and whose actions put an end to Machado's tyranny.

By then the racial issue had grown such deep roots that it could hardly go unnoticed in the 1940s. Barring a few cases on both sides, black people were banned from whites-only public places, and vice versa, whereas some societies were solely for mestizos. On the other hand, the famous Havana Yacht Club was for the exclusive use of upper-class whites, and Club Atenas was only for the well-off and prestigious, be they black, mestizo, or white. Elitist societies were where social and class problems between—and among—whites and non-whites were more patently obvious. Yet there was a marked contrast between the said elitist societies and other kinds of social groups, such as those described by researchers Carmen Victoria Montejo, Lucila Bejerano, and Edita Caveda Román, who speak of a wide range of educational, recreational, and other associations that catered to individuals of any origin or race.

Another scholar, Tomás Fernández Robaina, points out that although Cuban blacks and mestizos made countless demands for equality through their social groups, they were not intended to favor black people over the other racial groups. Furthermore, the state's scant attention cleared the way for racial discrimination. When the state did get involved in racial and ethnic groups—mainly in the employment sphere—it would only fuel dissension and discord among members and offer nothing to bridge the gap. The blacks would leave, or rather escape in secret, from the sugar estate in the countryside and find shelter in the worst urban neighborhoods. Much remains to be studied and put in writing for a true chronicle of black people's social history and role in Cuban society. We saw them arrive in slave ships, in which they traveled in subhuman conditions only to be sold as human merchandise in public squares, treated as farm or domestic slaves, punished in the stocks, worked like horses to earn their freedom or buy it from their owners, become runaways, joined the mambises and fought for freedom, gathered in town councils and other social institutions of the Republic. They were lucky to get a job in the city, and those who had the skills became craftsmen, engaged themselves in trades that the Spaniards deemed unworthy, or were hired as longshoremen on the docks. In short, they would always swell the ranks of the worst-paid laborers.

Some blacks would land themselves a good position in politics and journalism, but there's little information in our knowledge about them, especially when it comes to family history and lineage. And it was much worse in the case of black women, because even if the white husband held an important position, say in the army or in politics, the wife could not attend any event with them—which was the case for the black wives of Batista's army officers.

Racial inequality persisted in Cuba for the entire Republican period and, following the trend in Latin America, extended from the massive sectors of the economy to the most desirable fields of employment. Race continued to be an obstacle to gain access to many professions. Very few blacks made it to the university, and those who did had a hard time finding jobs after graduation. Many of them, mostly women, became teachers, since the training course was short and therefore they could start making money soon. Furthermore, given that education was not forbidden to anyone, there were plenty of students for black teachers. Although salary scales based on skin color were not too different among manual workers, they were quite unbalanced in professional fields, where the number of blacks was considerably smaller and where middle-class whites hogged the jobs. At this juncture, education became a tool in the permanent struggle for racial equality. Still, learning was not enough: other means were needed, such as the connections one could develop only in the high- and middle-class social and political clubs, which were unavailable to the overwhelming majority of blacks. Meritocracy, the chief component of Republican society, would be regularly invoked to keep to a minimum the presence of blacks and poor whites in civil service or the private sector.

Thus prerevolutionary Cuba was profoundly racist, a place where society's hierarchical pyramid rested on the blacks and poor whites— even if the former were usually worse off—and where "black" and "poor" were all but synonymous: not all poor people were black and not all white people were rich, but far and away most blacks were poor. Poverty could certainly be white, but wealth was very seldom black. In this scheme of things, the mulattos were a little bit better off than blacks.

Blacks were almost invariably the poorest among the poor, a status very few managed to evade. Figures have it that white people, almost without exception, would take the higher seats, with mulattos in the middle and blacks mostly at the bottom. And even in today's Cuba, despite so much effort and progress, very little has changed. Not that the non-whites have resigned themselves to the ongoing racial discrimination; it's just that they lack the means to change anything.

During the Republic many studies on race were conducted that shed light on the life and political or military careers of black leaders, mainly those who had fought in the independence war. Most of this research was done by blacks, so criticism of their contemporary place in Cuban society was easily inferred from their works. Others acknowledge black people's role in culture, even if only as part of domestic folklore. After 1920 there was a boom in studies about "black roots" and the African presence in Cuba in an effort to redefine our nationality. The island could be said to have lived through a stage of new awareness, which is why the 1920s have gone down in history as the period when Cuba rediscovered itself as a nation. At the same time, our own modernity was called into question and redesigned as a primarily white nation from a cultural viewpoint. One very important aspect addressed at this time was related to the controversial topic of national identity, and more than once this became the starting point for widespread intellectual discussions, which of course included the racial issue. This process is far from being over, as even now, in the early twenty-first century, there are still sufficient grounds for analysis and debate, and many obstacles yet to be overcome.

With the appearance in the late 1920s of a section called "Ideales de una raza" (Ideals of a race) in the publication *Diario de La Marina*—as a weekly column and a full page in the Sunday edition—the heyday of the polemic about race and racism in Cuba began. This debate took place from 1928 to 1931, exactly when Gerardo Machado's government was most repressive. Promising though he had seemed to Cubans—among other reasons because he had been a general in the war against Spain— his mandate proved to be one of the bloodiest dictatorships in the history of the Republic, earning him the nickname "The Clawed Donkey." Until it ended in 1933, "Ideales de una raza," led by Gustavo Urrutia, played a key role in the struggle of the blacks and mestizos for recognition of their civil rights. This is another cultural project that has not been sufficiently studied, and is likely an inexhaustible source of knowledge for understanding the Cuban racial issue.

Despite the United States' intention to promote a policy of apartheid in Cuba, the independence war, nationalism, the popular struggle during the Republic and José Martí's idea of a republic—"with all and for the good of all"—stopped racial segregation from becoming as firmly entrenched as some people wished. In principle, the Constitution of 1901 and universal male suffrage made Cuba unique among countries with a population of African descent in the early twentieth century. Our non-whites were granted their voting rights thanks to their long-lived revolutionary traditions and the fact, impossible to ignore, that they accounted for 30 percent of the electorate. Every party wanted the blacks and mestizos on its side, which gave these ethnic groups an opportunity to succeed in their demands. However, no sooner had the state of political ferment caused by the elections faded than everything became so much water under the bridge: all promises were forgotten and most blacks were back in the gutter.

Since no racial group was banned from education, the blacks and mestizos made the most of it, and many of them became professionals, and even though it was still difficult for them to find good jobs, their status was a far cry from that of other blacks in Cuba, whose situation remained very precarious. A black person who managed to escape from poverty or inherited an advantageous social level from family felt compelled to move away from both the tenement house and other poor blacks, and would eventually join clubs and societies that barred the latter from membership.

As intellectuals, blacks and mestizos addressed issues that concerned all blacks and mestizos, but they would steadily grow apart, absorbed by the Republic's capitalistic dynamics that subtly forced them to stick to their exclusive clubs, estranged from their non-white countrymen. For this reason, what usually sounded like black discourse was in fact the position of a non-white middle class, the downright expression of the fight waged by these black and mestizo professionals against the systematic exclusion imposed on them by the white elite. That elite kept an imperceptible "cordon sanitaire" around the vast majority of poor non-whites to prevent at all costs the radicalization of the black and mestizo middle class, whose connivance with the status quo was inherent to its very nature as a subordinate stratum.

Accordingly, the Republic never saw a unified movement that brought to fruition the social demands of the most exploited non-whites. From the standpoint of race, what the poorest blacks and mestizos did achieve, if anything, happened as members of workers' organizations and labor unions. Although these clubs kept working hard to make it clear that an openly racist and exclusionary stance was out of the question, the non-white middle class was still the object of endless manipulation and contempt by officialdom. Suffice it to read then-presidential candidate Carlos Prío Socarrás's opportunistic and demagogic speech at Club Atenas on May 5, 1948, in which he came out as a radical in favor of black people's rights. Once elected, however, he did nothing to improve their situation.

Even if racial discrimination had been declared illegal and punishable in both the 1901 and the 1940 constitutions, never in the Republican Period was any individual or official entity convicted of discrimination by a court of law. There was a twofold reason for this: first, racism usually worked in disguise; and second, neither the blacks and mestizos nor their organizations and structures were strong enough to demand justice, let alone see to it that it was done. Although a number of general anti-discrimination principles and even certain promises of equal employment opportunities for blacks and mestizos were included in the 1940 Constitution, all specific actions to be considered for future legislation were postponed due to World War II, and for all the efforts made by communists like Salvador Agüero, all but a few simple declarations by the parliamentary bureaucracy of the moment fell on stony ground.

Finally, with the expulsion of the communists from the Cuban trade unions in 1947, the debilitation of the labor movement, and the ban on the Communist Party in 1952, the cause of racial equality lost its top political allies. This situation was made even worse by Batista's decision to appoint some blacks to high posts in the army to fool them into believing that at long last they had a government behind them. Of course, as in the day of Martín Morúa Delgado and Juan Gualberto Gómez, the white elite took great care not to yield the highest positions in the military hierarchy. Much was achieved under Batista regarding the presence of blacks in the ranks, which was a first, but no progress was made as to their access to the power structure, and black army officers still could not bring their wives to any reception.

Despite the fact that the Republic had been created for all people, it was actually held in place by the great mass of poor blacks, whites, and mestizos, and only a few derived any benefit from the establishment. This validated the coherence of the elite's supposed stance on racial equality and democracy in general, as well as their stated need to build a true republic. The harsh reality was that the forthright, deliberate exclusion of non-whites, and especially of black people, was a regular feature of everyday life.

Equality was a concept defended as one by radical white, black, and mestizo intellectuals as well as by the labor movement, but the reins of power held by a classist domestic oligarchy that kowtowed to U.S. capital and government thwarted any plan for real change. It was thus impossible to design a republic in which the poor had better opportunities, much less if they were blacks and mestizos. Most black people were poor in the Republican Period and had no civil mechanisms to defend their interests as the most discriminated sector. And it was even worse for those of Haitian and Jamaican extraction, who were deemed second-class blacks and discriminated against even by other blacks.

Awareness of racial origins, which so many progressive scholars from every ethnic group fought so hard for, was of paramount importance in overcoming the existing state of affairs. Another factor permanently attached to racial discrimination resulted from a practice with deep roots in the Cuban ruling elite that was reinforced by the U.S. intervention: using racial discrimination as an instrument of power, which it is, after all.

Thus racial stereotyping and prejudice could still be fueled in any social context, no matter how highly educated and cultured. So it happened in our knowledgeable and learned Republic. Racism is not merely a product of ignorance or lack of culture; it comes into being in a social milieu in which racial and particularly sex discrimination and its by-products are used as a means of domination, social control, favoritism, and exploitation of individuals.

In this framework, racism and culture never contradict each other, since from a class perspective those with the highest education are precisely the most racist, above all else for reasons of power rather than culture. And when these learned elites practice racism, they merely intend to take any cultural merit away from their victims on grounds that they are "culturally inferior," rather than it being ethically and culturally reprehensible in a context of class confrontation. Exploitation is structurally designed to achieve such ends.

Exploitation through racism is also caused by our failure to overcome a number of traits bequeathed to us by colonial society that Republican capitalism worked hard to protect and develop in the form of prejudice and stereotyping for the benefit of the ruling classes and groups. Being in power is precisely what turns the ruling classes and groups into racists in the first place, not their lack of culture. These elites can rather be said to be "perversely cultured," because they are fully aware of the importance of using racism to hold on to their power.

Hence the significance of maintaining and strengthening our racial identity within a context of universality and anti-racism. There is airtight evidence that without class consciousness racism can neither be understood nor opposed, and the absence of class differences is not enough to abolish them. We also need race consciousness.

The Europeans arrived in America as part of a colonial expedition, not a scientific mission, and brought with them black slavery, the effects of which have yet to disappear. On the contrary, our society, flawed as it is, sometimes nurtures those effects. Racial discrimination remained unresolved in the neocolonial Republic, because that was a society kept in place by a bipolar development of wealth and poverty. In the Republican Period inequality was essential so that the ruling class could use all forms of discrimination—particularly racial discrimination—as instruments of power to support the social, economic, and cultural structures that would preserve their regime of exploitation. As shown by Cuba's revolutionary experience, putting an end to such a regime was not enough to abolish racism. The task we have ahead will require a lot more time and is much more complicated than that.

# 3—A Model for the Analysis of the Racial Problem in Contemporary Cuba

Fortunately for the nation, scientific approaches are now being used for the study of the racial problem in Cuba and, for a group of Cuban humanists and social scientists, constitute a high-priority concerted intellectual effort. This essay emphasizes the importance of this endeavor, which is aimed to strengthen the national and cultural identity of the country. The essay proposes a theoretical-methodological model for promoting additional considerations and debates that may deepen the understanding of Cuba's racial complexity.

## Some Methodological Considerations

Our analysis and set of variables for the analysis of Cuba's racial problem from a socioeconomic perspective are based on certain theoretical-methodological approaches developed for a recent essay on the United States-Cuba conflict.[1] Synthesizing the concrete historical conditions within which the racial issues have developed, it is possible to consider three fundamental stages, corresponding to three macro-periods that mark Cuban national history. These are:

STAGE I:     Cuban colonial society (from the sixteenth to the end of the nineteenth century).

STAGE II:    Failed independence and the Cuban neocolonial society (1898–1958).

STAGE III:   Cuban socialist revolutionary society (1959–2001).[2]

Indeed, in every macro-period the stage is set with specific concrete situations which should delineate our study. Among them:

- The periods during the struggle for independence (1868–1878 and 1895–1898), including the brief "Guerra Chiquita," framed by the Spanish promise to grant freedom to enslaved blacks and mulattos, who had fought during the first stage of the War of Independence, and the reconciliatory initiatives by the metropolis after the Pact of Zanjón.

- The debate on slavery during these periods, leading to the official proclamation of abolition in 1886. The transition of the so-called emancipated who had to endure the Patronato (indentured to their masters for eight years) meted out by different laws Spain produced to  maneuver the disappearance of slavery.

- The connections between strategies for annexation and the abolition of slavery, whose exploration is of great importance for the understanding of the dynamics of relations between the Creole bourgeoisie and the rising power to the north.

- The particular traits of racism and the racial discrimination in Cuba, after the First North American Intervention (1898–1902).

- The so-named Little War of 1912, one of the most embarrassing series of events in the history of the neocolonial Republic, events that created deep consequences for the racial relations in Cuba.

- Due to its importance in the characterization of the current situation, the revolutionary Cuba stage, special attention will be paid to the periods of 1959–61 and 1989–95. These years encompass points of intensity in the behavior and political treatment of the matter at hand.

## *Fundamental Variables*

Having set the stages for analysis, it is possible to design variables, defined as social phenomena that synthesize the subsystems of the most important contradictions of each stage, or historical moment.

Three categories of types of fundamental variables could be considered:

- Variables of historical-colonial legacy.
- Variables of Republican frustration.
- Variables of contemporary socialist revolutionary society.

The design of the different variables that constitute each category may only be undertaken on the basis of a thorough understanding of the object of study and its integral historical perspective. Such variables must contain the traits of the Cuban racial problem for each concrete historical stage, encompassing the multiple levels of thought, socioeconomic reality, and political practice. Following is our first attempt at composing a list of these variables:

### VARIABLES OF HISTORICAL-COLONIAL LEGACY
- Colonization–Slavery.
- Capitalism–Slavery.
- Slave Trade–Illegal Commerce.
- Racism–Racial Prejudice–Discrimination.
- Fear of Blacks.
- Whitening Policies.
- Ethnicity–Race–Color of Skin.
- Slavery–Abolition.
- Slavery–Annexation.
- Slavery–Independence Movement.

### VARIABLES OF REPUBLICAN FRUSTRATION
- North American Intervention–Frustration of Independence.
- Racism–Discrimination during the Republic.
- Racism–Cuban Capitalism.

VARIABLES OF SOCIALIST REVOLUTIONARY SOCIETY

- •     Points of Departure for Racial Groups.
- •     Inequality–Social Policy.
- •     Cuban Racialism–Revolutionary Idealism.
- •     Economic Crisis–Welfare Model.
- •     Racial Prejudices–Discrimination–Racism.
- •     Race–National Project. [3]

As it is possible to observe, almost all the variables are designed on the basis of a sort of interplay of categories, in which contradictory social reality is reflected; that is, the social reality that produced abolitionism, and the thoughts that surround and promote it, would be inconceivable in a society where slavery did not exist. This does not mean that both sides of the contradiction can only be explained by the relation maintained between them, but rather that it is important to know the poles that face each other in our analysis.

In turn, these variables, at each stage, could be complemented by particular moments in history (not variables in themselves) that may have had a significant yet short-term impact. Variables are the stable social phenomena that characterize the system of contradictions at an essential level for each stage in question. [4]

The model, as designed, contributes to a systemic analysis, as it constitutes the interdependence of a set of determined variables, along with the corresponding particularities of the stages, and integrating a hypothetical complex of interactions. The determination of these variables at the cognitive level has been extracted and formulated from a logical-historical process of abstraction that allows us to determine the set of primary stages in which the object of study (the Cuban racial problem) develops as well as the essential, synthetic expressions of the system of contradictions contained at each stage.

During the previous application of this analytical process, we were able to establish and verify the following about the variables as essential and synthetic expressions:

- The stage in question, to which each variable belongs, reacts quickly to any social phenomenon that affects the determination expressed by the variable.

- A close connection exists between each stage and the variables that compose and connote it at essential levels, proving that they are indeed variables of that stage.

At the same time, however, each stage also operates with relative independence, able to observe that phenomena exist that affect it at first impact. Afterward those effects are translated to the variables, and therefore to the complete system of contradictions that encompasses the stage. The above is clearly evident when institutional changes at the macro-social level begin to affect the structures that determine policies and subsequently affect the variable or variables under consideration at each stage.[5] Then, looking at the whole, the described model constitutes a system, insofar as it is a whole that functions by virtue of the existing interdependence between the parts or stages and the variables that compose it.[6]

Thus we propose to formulate a theoretical model for the understanding and monitoring of the present-day Cuban racial problem. Such understanding will offer a general explanation of certain selective phenomena to promote knowledge of the characteristics of social reality. The model constitutes an intellectual tool that helps to organize knowledge, pose significant questions, guide in the formulation of priorities for research as well as in determining and selecting methods to undertake fruitful future projects. Thus the model will provide the framework to evaluate the theoretical-methodological and political recommendations, explicit or implicit, generated by the scientific analysis.

## Brief Characterization of the Variables

Although variables have been designed for each stage, we should not lose sight of the fact that the subject under analysis has not disappeared from Cuban society. The most important way to characterize the problem in its present state is to determine how and which variables are transposed to the contemporary stage of Cuban social reality. Such transferred phenomena, identifiable as remnants, are forged with the particular phenomena generated by the contemporary scene, and give extremely complex descriptions that aim to understand the Cuban racial problem in the present state.

All of the above can only be realized by means of an analysis that objectively determines to what extent a problem—for example, the dynamic Prejudice–Discrimination–Racism—still survives in a determined mode in Cuban society. This analysis is the only way to be able to make recommendations for the design of policies that may overcome the problem.

In such consideration we start a priori with a Cuban society that in the period 1959–2002 had advanced considerably in the solution of the issues under study, but in which a set of phenomena in the socioeconomic sphere, indicative of the problem and practices of racial prejudices and racial discrimination, had not been overcome. This is indeed the fundamental hypothesis of our research project.

Such are the basic reasons for pursuing the following objectives:

1. To characterize the fundamental set of factors and variables that explain racism and racial discrimination as impediments that weigh on the present Cuban society.
2. To characterize the variables and scenes that explain the feedback of prejudices and racial discrimination in the present Cuban society.
3. To synthetically characterize the dynamics by which racism and racial discrimination threaten to reinsert themselves in the macroconsciousness of the present Cuban society.

Of great importance to consider in the history of the race problem in Cuba is the ever-present issue of the tendency to postpone considering the racial problem as a national reality. It as if to serve national unity the racial question should always be sacrificed or made invisible as a vital problem impeding the progress of the nation.

The impact of the Haitian Revolution of 1791, which brought about the so-called fear of the blacks; José Antonio Saco's thesis of "whitening" and the concessions Carlos Manuel de Céspedes was forced to make after granting freedom to his slaves; the serious contradictions that the racial problem provoke within the struggle for independence, both in 1868 and 1895; and the sadly named Little War of 1912—all of these constitute unresolved stages of our history. Historically, blacks and mulattos have always had to endure hurtful procrastination of their demands, ignorance of their aspirations, or mere silence.

Instead of seeing the racial question as a matter to be confronted and resolved in a process that strengthens the nation, it has almost always been treated as a threat to national existence. Today, the dilemma has not been surmounted, although we have never enjoyed better conditions to face the problem and solve it.[7] The historical situation has been a constant that undercuts the projected model. Obstacles must be removed in order to move from scientific verification of the problematic social facts to finding the political practice that works toward their solution. A revolutionary position of the nation implies we should not reproach it for an imperfection that is a legacy of our grandparents; they, in fact, could not do more than they did.

But it is an emancipatory truth that the most advanced ideas of those who fought for the independence of Cuba, figures of the highest order such as José Martí and Antonio Maceo, did not conceive a republic that would maintain racism or that was not prepared to fight tirelessly for the eradication of its ravages. It is legitimate to think and to defend the self-evident truth that the Cuban nation (that is to say, a nation for all Cubans) will not come to be until racism and racial discrimination have disappeared from the motherland for which so many Cubans fought, for which so many lost their lives. Let us proceed, then, to synthetically characterize the designated variables.[8]

### Racism–Racial Prejudice–Discrimination

In the definition of racism we must consider it an ideological form of social consciousness, one that considers certain men inferiors to others, be it by nationality, social origin, sex, gender, color of skin, et cetera. Racism also becomes an instrument of power, by which some men keep others in a continuous situation of social disadvantage. In turn, racial prejudices belong within social prejudices as racist expressions within the individual consciousness, the family, and social groups that are preserved and transmitted by means of discriminatory ideas. Racial discrimination can be defined as the practice and exercise of racism, whose underpinnings are racial prejudices, overtly expressed in stereotypes. That is, where there are racial prejudices, racism is present, even if it does not exist in an institutionalized way or can be seen as underlying an individual consciousness. If we start from the premise that each individual, group, or family always holds a portion of power in society, no matter how small it may be, racial prejudices will be exerted with that allotted power at some level or region of social reality.

The fact is that men, in the last instance, act as they think, and their actions are determined by the way the phenomena of social reality are reflected in each individual's consciousness.

Racism, racial prejudice, and racial discrimination complement themselves. This subjectivity/objectivity dialectic is limited only by objective and subjective controls, among them the actions that society can exert over social and individual consciousness, by means of laws, social practices, education, culture, politics, and other practices that tend to avoid discriminatory dynamics.[9] It is a matter of levels in continuous feedback, in dialectic between objective and subjective, between praxis and theory, between social and individual. It is a dynamic that tends to be perpetuated through stereotypes, nourished by underlying prejudices that are very difficult to eliminate, and that carry implicitly a discriminatory praxis level, since the objective is to maintain social individuals, groups, or sectors, locked in a low social scale and, if possible, kept completely marginalized, to essentially do without them. This dynamic is clearly evident today in the excluding character of neoliberal economic policies that are applied in the context of globalization.[10] Racism, as an ideology that feeds racial prejudices and the exercise of discrimination, can only survive, and even resurge, in a society where to attain riches and the satisfaction of material and spiritual needs competition and individualism prevail as forms of social behavior. That is, a situation in which personal power and its continuous growth are indispensable conditions for occupying a prominent place in society. In colonial Cuba, slavery (the fundamental base of production) engendered racism that in turn produced the system of values that divided young Cuban society. Such conditions were dominant from the colonial society to the triumph of the Revolution of 1959. It is thus possible to affirm that although capitalism does not engender racism, it can go hand in hand with it and fulfills its needs as an exploitative regime.

## Policies of Whitening

Although we could mention the existence of a policy in colonial Cuba to grant the condition of white by decree, as if it were an indulgence, it is not possible to avoid the socioeconomic and cultural substrate of this phenomenon. "Whitening" was a social necessity, not explained by consideration to the laws, but from the conditioning that generated it as a necessity.

The whitening practice began in Cuba because to be black was a stigma, a disadvantage at all levels of social life based in the institution of slavery. Capitalism, which needed the mass of ex-slaves as workers, applied what can be considered the phenomenon of the "ratification of the working class."[11] Although class discrimination and racial discrimination are not equivalent, the working class is also the object of a discriminatory process, a workforce that must be preserved under that condition and be reproduced by means of the family. Thus appears a discriminatory phenomenon that does not differ substantially from racial discrimination. But the latter carries a double burden because a black worker will be discriminated against for being a worker and for being a non-white. Class discrimination is less difficult to eradicate because racial discrimination resides and is exercised within the working class itself. Racism and racial discrimination transcend the limits of classist structure, becoming a more general phenomenon that does not disappear with the elimination of capitalism.

Thus, the phenomenon of whitening in Cuba was not only a problem derived from policy, but the policy itself was generated and nourished by the economy and culture of Cuban society, surviving from the colony to capitalism until the end of the fifties. José Antonio Saco, in his analyses, saw the process of whitening as a necessity for the social improvement of Cuba, under his well-known motto "To whiten, to whiten, to whiten and soon to demand respect."

One of the specific forms in which whitening operates today is in the underrepresentation of blacks and mulattos in television, cinema, in new businesses or in high positions of state structure and government. This phenomenon of exclusion exists despite the extraordinary educational effort of the Revolution, which places them almost on a par with the white population.[12]

Without a doubt, the importance of this variable resides is that behind it lies a set of subjective phenomena that are only understandable from the culture and psychology that slavery and capitalism generated. The economic crisis at the end of the eighties and the beginning of the nineties brought it to the surface with unusual force.

For this reason, it is still common in Cuba today to meet people who do not take themselves as blacks or mestizos, but as whites, when in fact they are not white. Is this not a manifestation of the individual psychology that generated the phenomenon of so-called whitening? What conditions still underlie our society to cause black or racially mixed people to not find it advantageous to assume themselves as such?

### Ethnicity–Race–Color of Skin

In Cuba the classic scheme of the European nations was not repeated. The origins of the Cuban people, as historian Eduardo Torres-Cuevas states, "seem impossible to reduce to classic concepts and schemes. It was not formed following the linear evolution of one ethnic group and its culture. Against all models, it was not the product of a movement from a certain gene to a tribe, to a people and to the nation. On the contrary, it is the result of the presence in the same territory of ethnic groups and cultures originating in different continents that, by changing their original characteristics here and interacting with each other, are integrated into a new ethno-cultural complex."[13] In this context it is fundamental to understand the phenomenon of "creolization," which was a determining function in the formation of the Cuban nation. It was a process that had at its core the creolization of blacks.[14]

In turn, Jesús Guanche observes: "The Cuban ethnos-nation is the historical-cultural and demographic result of multi-ethnic conglomerates (mainly Hispanic, African, Chinese and Antillean) that fused in a complex and dissimilar way beginning with the sixteenth century, creating a new identity based on the formation of an endogenous population, with its own reproductive capacity, independent of the migratory currents that gave rise to its historical unfolding, with its own set of characteristics."[15]

These variables are extremely important, because they typify Cuba within a set of methodological principles that are essential for the analysis of the racial problem. The formation of the ethnos-nation was not based solely on the peculiarities of the Spanish colonization regarding the racial question, in contrast with ex-English or French colonies, but rather that Cuba formed its ethnos-nation through a complex process of integration, which brought about a uni-ethnic and multiracial society, with great cultural diversity.[16]

Cuba was a nation created by immigrants, but it is not today a society of immigrants. Several ethnic groups convened there, but Cuba is not multi-ethnic. In Cuba there are no minorities.[17] Some groups were kept segregated, but ended up fusing with the rest of the Cuban population. We speak primarily of Chinese, Yucatecans, Haitians, and Jamaicans. The way these groups were integrated to form what is today the fundamental Cuban population provides a basic framework to explain the peculiarities of adapting to the problem of race. It also endows Cuban scientists who specialize on the subject with a set of methodological guidelines and with particular modes of independent analysis in their approach to the Cuban experience. This aspect of the problem, acknowledging the special characteristics of Cuba, is essential in recognizing that, in the primary determinants, the European, North American, or even at times the English- and French-speaking Caribbean experiences are not valid for the study of race in Cuba. As Fernando Ortiz observed, "All the cultural scale for Europe transpired during more than four millennia while it took less than four centuries in Cuba. What arose there step by step, here was taken by leaps and frightening bounds."[18]

In Cuba a nation with characteristics of its own was formed, which places it in a special theoretical-methodological frame for the study of the racial question. Cuba, for more than forty years, passed through a national liberation process that helped it attain the racial integration experience that had manifested itself in the course of Cuban history since the mid-nineteenth century.

This is why the concept of race in Cuba is extremely deceptive from today's point of view. The racial factor does not constitute the main characteristic of the Cuban ethnos, only its physical manifestation.[19] This imposed cultural construction has not dissipated the need for much internal work to be done. That construction was imposed by social structuring under colonial administrative conditions that established internal and external domination and subjugation as the frame within which the Cuban nation structured itself. It was a never-ending process, until the triumph of the Revolution in 1959 opened the historical phase of definitive emergence of the nation. Unlike the case in the United States, where in some states discrimination had been based on having any black blood,[20] in Cuba black blood was not of great importance, because the determinant factor as to whether discrimination took place or not is the color of the skin. Prejudice surges on the basis of appearance and not due to a genetic component. That would seem to make the Cuban case easier to manage but, on the contrary, the density of the subjective component, in an ideological-cultural sense, is highly resistant to elimination. This means that Cuba's dominant and unique form of discrimination is implemented in a different manner.

The so-called Cuban bourgeoisie, at first under the influence of colonial racism and later by North American racism, and feeling insecure under the latter, was the group that always paid the greatest attention to the sophisticated instruments of genetic racism, since it assisted them to exert its power and domination. This led to some rather ironic interpretations of race in Havana. Fulgencio Batista, the president of the Republic, as a mulatto, could not belong to the most aristocratic clubs. Josephine Baker, a most important international performer, suffered discrimination in Havana. The Spanish colonizers, despite close to eight hundred years under the Moors, never adopted their African ancestors, their own racial mixture. This shameful attitude was inherited and transmitted to the Cuban creole bourgeoisie and the white (virtually the only) middle class. This explains, in part, many of the discriminatory attitudes that still exist today in Cuba, mainly within the white racial group. The determinant factor in racial prejudice today, however, entails whether one is black, mulatto, or white on the outside.

Someone with black ancestors, but whose external appearance is light skin, and without other black characteristics like nose, hair, etc., can assume a white identity and go unnoticed, passing as white without a problem except perhaps in front of a sophisticated racist, rare to find today in Cuba. But the deciding factor in Cuba is the color of the skin rather than race. Cuba's race was forged as a polychrome of shades, sometimes with common physical characteristics, and a shared culture and psychology that make the Cuban nation a culturally integrated and almost indefinable multiracial complex. Subtle regional cultural differences do exist that generally are only noticed by Cubans. Deep cultural differences do not exist. Major idiomatic, physical, and behavioral characteristics are not to be found. Perhaps, then, this is the most complex variable to consider, mainly for its importance for shedding light on the present situation in Cuba, an ethno-nation with a complexity of shades and shared characteristics, sometimes even beyond the color of the skin. It is this combinatory state of national culture that Fernando Ortiz denominated as *ajiaco* (stew).[21]

So, how are we to face the underlying racial prejudices in Cuba and their implicit discriminatory practice? It is not at all easy to respond to such a question. What is convincing, however, is that by raising the question as a black, mulatto, or white problem, or directly and exclusively as an issue of race and disregarding underlying historical components, the subject has no solution. The problem is a matter of concern for the whole nation, not parts of the nation, unless we are willing to renounce the entire positive legacy that history has bequeathed to us.

## *Slavery–Independence Movement*

The struggle for independence, from the very beginning, always turns out to be the political current most vigorously in favor of the abolition of slavery in Cuba. When Carlos Manuel de Céspedes granted freedom to his slaves at the Demajagua sugar mill on 10 October 1868, it determined Cuba's fundamental position vis-à-vis slavery, beyond the compromises that were forced upon revolutionary mambises leaders. The socioeconomic context and the principles of independence, equality, and brotherhood under which the War of Independence was undertaken determined clearly that the abolition of the slave trade and slavery were at the very core of the struggle of independence from Spain. The first War of Independence of 1868–78, was the first true battle for the abolition of the slavery in Cuba, although not all who participated agreed on the elimination of so shameful an institution. It was also the moment at which a constant in Cuban history made its first vivid appearance: the subordination of the racial question to the cause of national unity. Although concessions were imposed due to the necessity of falling in line and uniting forces against Spain, the brotherhood that was enjoyed by blacks, whites, and mulattos at the campsites and battles, mainly in the last stage of the war (1895–98), constituted an important milestone for the independence movement with respect to the racial problem. Yet in the end, racism became one of the fundamental factors that seriously damaged the solidarity of the forces that were fighting for the independence of Cuba.

Unfortunately, many unquestionable patriots, whose names would be painful to mention, were racists, and not a small number of their activities reflect it. We must be fair and objective when evaluating their positions, and do so in the context of their difficult times. The problem of racism was exacerbated at the end of the War of 1895, when the most progressive forces of the independence movement did not occupy the main positions of power in the Republic manufactured by the United States. Racial prejudices that were submerged and hidden in the midst of the fight reemerged at the conclusion of the war in their most virulent forms.

For these reasons, history should never be taught to future generations as an interminable succession of heroic acts and perfect heroes.

First, because history is not that; second, because by proceeding in such fashion we would be deriding the efforts of those who preceded us, considering them supermen for whom everything was easy; and third, because when we discover the miseries that are always present in history we can become frustrated, which is extremely dangerous, because it could turn out that along with the miseries we may be throwing overboard everything that is truly worth keeping.[22]

This is why a thorough knowledge of history, filled by the deeds of the heroic and accomplishments by not-quite-perfect men and women, is the fundamental foundation for self-understanding and self-definition of nations. There is nothing to be done for a man or woman without history, without self-understanding and without self-definition, because the first and more important job at hand is to invest that man and woman with the full powers of self-recognition and self-knowledge: Who is she? Where does he come from? Who preceded him? Because we will only know where we are going when we know from whence we come. A beautiful African proverb says it: "When you do not know where you're going, turn back to see where you're coming from."[23]

## Racism–Discrimination during the Republic

The organization of political power in the Republic did not benefit the black and racially mixed population. Having just left slavery, they joined the great uneducated masses; after a war that had impoverished them, they swelled the ranks of the unemployed or toiled in poorly paid jobs. without any hope of social assistance.

The Republic deployed all the prejudices it had inherited from colonial society against the black and racially mixed population. The United States, in turn, did not fail to take full advantage of the moment and displayed its power and control through its perceived sense of hegemonic (also racial) superiority over the island's native bourgeoisie. The North American government was the real power in Cuba; others were mere "also-rans." It was not possible for anything to occur or start in Cuba without the United States manipulating to mediate or tip the scales and always make decisions in favor of its interests. In certain occasions protecting the image took precedent. In 1906, for example, the United States did not consider it advisable to intervene to aid President Estrada Palma until after he requested it.

In particular, the so-called Little War of 1912 gained the attention of the United States, which intervened in support of the administration of José Miguel Gómez and helped him "teach a lesson" to those in the Independent Party of Color. During the Little War many blacks and mulattos were assassinated; even today we have no knowledge of the exact number of victims. Such an event constituted a decimating blow to the formation of a non-white middle class within Cuba.

Following the end of slavery in 1886, blacks and mulattos, after much effort and a long and difficult process, dedicated themselves to various trades that the Spaniards did not consider appropriate for themselves. They worked as dentists, barbers, tailors, hatters, and musicians. Some, very few, managed to attend university and became (primarily) lawyers and journalists. A few others, such as Martin Morúa Delgado and Juan Gualberto Gómez, entered the political field, although surely on different sides.

But though many of these blacks and mulattos were not involved in the events of 1912, they suffered dire consequences, if not absolute repression, and were at a minimum treated as suspects who required persistent monitoring as members of the racist conspiracy. Under this rubric President José Miguel Gómez persecuted and massacred the followers of Evaristo Estenoz and Pedro Ivonnet, the main leaders of the Independent Party of Color.[24]

After such a dramatic event, Cuban blacks and mestizos learned the intended lesson society allotted to them, which did not offer any space for vindication of their demands or recognition of their rights. The few black members of well-to-do groups returned to the fold of the Republican game and founded cultural and brotherly societies or clubs that held no possible hint of political activity.

Some political forces continued their fight, dissenting and showing their disapproval. A good example of this is when, under pressure, the North American government was forced to recognize in Cuba's favor the status of the Isle of Pines, which had been pending since the debate over the Platt Amendment. All those who occupied presidential positions until the 1930s had participated as high officials of the army of liberation during the War of Independence, but the tendency to sell out to foreign interests, to engage in corruption and power struggles, ended up turning them into mere instruments for the implementation of the neocolonial model designed by the United States.[25]

## *Racism–Cuban Capitalism*

Life in the Republic, even after the Platt Amendment was repealed, developed within the syndrome of another possible North American intervention. The native bourgeoisie was devoted to administration and getting rich, but it primarily guaranteed the control of the island by North American monopolies. Whenever they considered the "tranquility of the nation" under any particular threat, they appealed to North America to mediate or, in extreme cases, to intervene.

Faced with the revolutionary outbreak of 1933, the United States immediately located a strongman to control the situation: Fulgencio Batista Zaldívar. An army sergeant stenographer, a mulatto, he was known for being well able to manipulate political situations in his favor, but in addition he brought many blacks and mulattos into the army, even granting them certain rank (for which there was no precedent) and surrounding them with an aura of importance, that made part of the non-white population believe that he was going to solve all their problems.

After the 1952 coup, the United States strongly supported the Batista dictatorship as the last opportunity for maintaining control of the country, which was now facing serious and growing political dissent that had taken form in the revolutionary movement following the 26th of July 1953 assault on the Moncada Barracks. Batista, on cue, being mulatto, tried to gain political advantage and maintain control by promoting his popularity within the black and racially mixed population. As the political situation became more and more tense, the United States tried to prop up the regime, until in 1958 they realized the urgent need to find

a new variant to frustrate the revolutionary triumph. All of which concluded in total failure.[26] The dictatorship finally finished with an ample
record of crimes, torture, much pushing and shoving of the populace,
and social misery. Blacks and mulattos continued in the majority as victims, although their naïveté had led them to think otherwise.

## Points of Departure for Racial Groups
### after the Triumph

Without any doubt, the Cuban Revolution inherited an underdeveloped
economic structure, the fruits of the operations of a neocolonial model
that in many cases had not managed to overcome the social and economic
asymmetries inherited from colonization. The racial groups in Cuban
society at the triumph of the Revolution in 1959 clearly manifested the
corresponding places that had been assigned to them during colonial
times and the Republic. Blacks and mulattos swelled the ranks of poorly
paid workers, the poor, the illiterates, those crowded into tenements and
marginal districts, and those with the worst jobs. They were the smallest minority at universities. Those who managed to complete a second-
ary education followed it with further studies to become teachers or gain
skills in the arts and trades but rarely managed to put their professional
training into gainful employment.

Only after many decades, some labor organizations and brotherly
societies managed some improvement of the black and racially mixed
population. Blacks and mestizos, who composed the poorest and least
privileged sectors of neocolonial society, generally lacked specific organizations and coordinated actions to work for improvements in society.
Cuban society proposed to generate a process of social integration. The
Revolution revealed a mass majority of blacks, whites, and mulattos that
composed the army of the poor and wage workers. But among them,
blacks and mulattos occupied the lowest ranks in the worst state.

*Inequality–Social Policy*

The social policy of the Revolution did not differentiate between racial groups. All benefited, but those whose lives were least privileged still remained in a state of inequality. Having improved their situations noticeably, they still had not attained sufficient stability or were left at a halfway house to dream about a better life. When the crisis at the end of the eighties crisis occurred, all this inequality manifested with special crudity clearly evident to the black and racially mixed population.

The economic crisis seriously affected the developing model of welfare in Cuban society, which was barely consolidated or initiated for those Cubans, generally black and mulatto, who came from the lowest stratum.

As if that was not enough, the economic measures required to face the crisis, which tended to further affect the equality that had been attained, forced the state to negotiate with foreign capital and increase competition for the best-paying jobs in two economic sectors: emergent (tourism and corporations) and non-emergent. Consequently, racial prejudice and discrimination entered the economic sphere, moving slowly but continuously to other spheres of social life. Such dynamics still affect present-day Cuban society.

Competition, until the first half of the 1980s, did not have much importance, but resurged then in the context of unemployment and general shortages. All of this was supported by the underlying remnants of classist structure, very much aware of the surface color of the skin. Skin color became a historical factor, identified with wealth or poverty, the legacy of colonial and Republican society. Despite the extraordinary effort that has been accomplished in education, where only some differences but no major imbalances exist, serious asymmetries ruled in the Cuban labor sector; blacks were denied access to the best remunerated jobs and material rewards in general.[27] It is necessary to ask how such a social phenomenon persists.

## Racism–Racial Prejudice–Discrimination

In present-day Cuban society, racial prejudices and discrimination have arisen in the midst of a situation generated by the economic crisis, with the expected psychological impact of a problem that was considered solved but was far from being solved.

It was idealistic to think that solely on the basis of distributing equality and the great humanitarian work of the Revolution that the racial problem would be settled. It was inevitable that we would have to pay a high price for the social imbalances generated by the crisis.

If economic, social, and cultural measures are not initiated, a (thus far) non-institutionalized racism will move anew into certain sectors of Cuban society.[28]

This social reality tends to be hidden by fear of the inherited divisive racial problem, by having to prioritize a confrontation with an external enemy, and by the unquestionable and magnanimous humanist work of the Cuban Revolution.

Racism, firmly set within the structures of Cuban colonial society, should have received specific attention from the beginning, alerting the masses to form a resistance culture and to face the problem, not to turn it into a dead zone, into a "taboo," as was the case during the first years of the sixties. Until recently and in very discreet ways, we have begun to speak out against the racial problem.

For all that, the challenge becomes difficult to face because it is entrenched in (1) the insufficient consciousness that the problem exists; (2) the lack of acceptance by some sectors, mainly white; (3) the need to accelerate the actions of Cuba's political and administrative structures.

All this corresponds with a limited consciousness about the true priority of the problem, a minimum of confidence about the real potentialities available to face it, and the fear as to how the masses could react during these confrontations. Despite all the efforts invested, the dynamics of racism, racial prejudice, and discrimination are yet to be overcome.

## Validation of the Model for the Current Stage

We start with the hypothesis that discriminatory modes from the past persist in Cuba, only to a lesser degree today. The old generations have advanced and the new ones have gradually been freed of racial prejudice due to the strong influence exerted by the intense Cuban revolutionary process. Although in present Cuba it is much more difficult to exert discrimination, racial prejudice survives, fed mainly by the deep economic crisis that has battered the country since the end of the 1980s. Let us then evaluate and amplify this hypothesis with a concrete analysis of the situation.

Even while Cubans supposedly maintained the perception that blacks and mulattos as well as white folks were being equally impacted by the dire economic conditions of the Special Period, a sort of hypocrisy (unconscious, at times) became pervasive. Many people, whites, blacks, or mulattos, although primarily the former,[29] re-created in their family space or intimate circles different modes of prejudice. It reflected the sort of discriminatory behavior that society kept them from displaying openly.

In addition, regions and phenomena of our present social reality where racial prejudice, discrimination, and racism are continually re-created persist. The lowest socioeconomic status, the majority of whom are blacks and mulattos, cannot contribute to overcoming the situation, for the following reasons:

- They are underrepresented in the tourist sector and in corporations, even less in managerial positions.
- They constitute a meager minority of 2 percent in the private agricultural sector and hardly 5 percent in cooperatives.
- They receive the least amount of remittances from abroad, and 83.5 percent of emigrants are white. They emigrated at a much later date, without external support and ended up at lower-paying jobs.
- They are underrepresented as directors of state companies and in administrative positions.
- Except for the music and sport sectors and the armed forces, they rarely assume leadership positions of national and international projection.

- The presence of blacks and mulattos in mass media is still feeble, especially in television and cinema.
- According to statistics, black and racially mixed people occupy labor and social positions that do not correspond with the educational levels that they have attained.

All these situations seriously affect relations between the racial groups, underlining an inequality among them that cannot easily be justified. This problem must be understood by a set of more specific variables that continue to influence, against the non-white population, the racial component of contemporary Cuban social reality. Such variables are as follows:

- Of all the problems that the Revolution faced from the very beginning, the racial problem was the only one that did not receive specific, systematic, and consistent attention.
- As a result of the above, the social policy of the Revolution never specifically addressed the question with reference to the different points of social departure from which blacks, whites, and mulattos arrived.
- After intervention on the matter in March 1959 by Fidel Castro, Commander in chief of the Revolution, and a few initial attempts to promote the discussion, a zone of silence surrounded the racial question, which did not help at all to an understanding that it required an extensive and specific methodology. No doubt it was thought that including it within the general context of social justice for all would be sufficient.
- The predominant thought that the racial problem would be resolved solely on the basis of a redistributive equity, framed by the great humanist work of the Revolution, generated an idealist error that has yet to be overcome.
- The black and racially mixed population, feeling represented and protected by revolutionary work, plunged into forgetfulness of all the long years of suffering and discrimination. The Revolution had given them clear guarantees that such situations would not return.

How are we to explain why such a position on the racial question was taken and accepted by the immense majority of the people, in particular blacks and mulattos?

## Sources for an Error in Shared Idealism

From the very first year of 1959, the revolutionary leaders adopted measures that produced an almost immediate identification between the masses and the political leadership of the Revolution. In particular, the great work in education considerably elevated the level of instruction of the population, without preferential treatment based on race or social origin. All had equal access to jobs, health care, culture, and recreation.

The standard of living, self-esteem, and the pride of being Cuban grew to a level previously unknown by the population. Generally, the color of your skin did not constitute an obstacle to reach the highest levels of social recognition. The party, Communist Youth, and other organizations were in charge of strengthening the idea, at the consciousness level, that equality existed for all citizens.

An atmosphere was created in which the problem of racial prejudice and discrimination seemed to be resolved. Although citizens admitted that all problems had not been solved, the achievements that had been attained and the rhythm of economic, social, and political life clearly encouraged a hopeful image that Cuba was approaching an optimal operational state at all levels of the internal life of the country.

What happened, then, and how did the racial question begin to be perceived as a problem yet to be solved? Was it a simple matter of perception, or a necessity arising from new conditions? Without a doubt, the internal scene that began to appear in Cuba during the second half of the eighties made many Cubans realize that it had been rather idealistic to consider the social dynamics instituted in 1959 as offering definitive solutions to issues of prejudice and racial discrimination.[30]

The conjunction of a legal attack on all form of discrimination, endorsed and ratified in the Constitution of 1976, and supported by initiatives of extraordinary proportions, aspired to fulfill social demands and to improve conditions of life of the population, especially of the poorest citizens. This indicated that the Revolution was unquestionably moving in the direction of the search for equality.

As a result of this context of equality that prevailed during the first half of the eighties, any appeal based on racial difference to justify or correct any action, regardless of its origin, was (logically) viewed as an attempt at social regression. Another factor that contributed to the avoidance of the racial issue was that during the great revolutionary process that emphasized human dignity, blacks would consider it offensive to receive a benefit for the mere reason of being black.

All of the above took place in the context of a romanticism and idealism that has always characterized the work of the Revolution and its leaders. Of course, without romanticism and idealism it would have been impossible to imagine that a socialist revolution could succeed in Cuba.

A Cuban identity already existed before 1959, but apparently it had been only halfheartedly achieved. In 1959 the demanding and dynamic life within the revolutionary project started mixing blacks, whites, and mulattos, without any of the groups noticing it. Together they met at daycare centers, at schools, at the university, doing voluntary work, and marching with the militias. Together they lived through the dangers the counterrevolution brought, resisting actions such as the attack at Girón, the counterrevolutionaries in the Escambray, the October Missile Crisis, the sabotages, the bombings. Together they suffered the scarcities and hardships of rationing, their needs deferred. Together those who stay in Cuba have been facing the challenges of survival as a nation, except that now it takes place in a less egalitarian context, which brings challenges yet to be faced.[31]

Everything seemed to have been conceived in order to erase race and color of the skin from the Cuban social stage. Such positioning aimed to be positive, but it tended to affect the African component of cultural identity, essentially skewing expressions and manifestations of a culture that is undoubtedly multiracial.

Until 1959, the Hispanic component had been hegemonic and, as far as highlighting the Hispanic components of Cuban culture, Spain enjoyed the means to be more aggressive than any African country could.

It was not simply a matter of subjective intention but also, objectively, a problem of scarcity in economic resources.

In such a situation we find a mix of idealism, ignorance, ingenuousness, and, in some instances, the bad intentions of some people pursuing their yet to be overcome racial prejudices. In the case of women, the racial question added additional contrasts in their treatment. Slowly their reality began to be viewed as being women *and* black or mulatta, which brought to the surface additional social implications beyond gender.

At the same time, a generally dogmatic Leninist Marxism, read the majority of the time without any awareness of the context of Cuban social realities, also brought negative consequences. It introduced models of social and cultural realities that had hardly anything to do, and sometimes absolutely nothing to do, with the reality of the country. In Marxist discourse, the mestizo and black problem was submerged in the general questions of class, diluting it further within the general problems of poverty and marginality. And thus society refused to accept that blacks and mestizos had inherited a particular legacy from colonialism and neo-colonialism, a mark much more difficult to overcome.

Cuba, having advanced considerably throughout the first half of the decade of the eighties in the construction of socialism, as if in a test tube,[32] suddenly saw itself facing racist tendencies and xenophobic attitudes. Without a doubt the impact of the dramatic transformations in socialist Europe on the Cuban economy and society dramatically changed the stage on which the island played out the development of its model of equality and social justice.

During these events, something surprising became known to all, slowly at first and then accelerating quickly: the points of departure for white, black, and racially mixed populations in Cuba were different, and inherited asymmetries began to emerge with special sharpness. At the same time, the return to the most rigid mode of rationing, implemented to guarantee to all a proportional part of the meager available goods, satisfied the needs of some and distributed hunger to others.[33]

Remittances of money from abroad brought a process of relief to the situation. But blacks, whites, and the racially mixed populations did not enjoy the same benefits from this trend. Fewer black and mestizos were abroad, and when they did leave the island they received lower wages, wherever they went, compared to other Cubans in the United States or in other parts of the world.

The black and racially mixed population is the minority in Cuban emigration. In addition, its massive emigration came about not in 1959–60 but in 1980, generally without support from the Cuban community within the United States and wound up in less remunerated economic activities than those of the earlier white upper-class emigration. That is why it is not difficult to conclude that besides undergoing racism, they constitute the group of emigrants whose precarious financial conditions make it more difficult to help their relatives in Cuba.[34]

Certainly, with the triumph of the Cuban Revolution all the inherited contradictions of the neocolonial society were subsumed, subjected to the class conflict and even more to the conflict between imperialism (North American in particular) and the Cuban nation. In that confrontation, the unity of the revolutionary forces was a strategic and unavoidable necessity. It is not possible to forget that it had been precisely the lack of unity of the revolutionary forces and the manipulation of this issue by the North American and colonial government that the independence forces won the war with Spain but lost the revolution.

It was logical, then, that the contradictions between the Cuban nation and imperialism took center stage and received the highest priority because imperialism had always constituted the primary challenge to the existence of Cuba as an independent nation. Nevertheless, it was incorrect to assume that from the perspective of solution of the contradictions with imperialism the racial question would also be resolved.

On the specific subject of racism, this perception, as pointed out above, was buttressed by Fidel Castro, when in March of 1959 he pointed out the divisive issues that threatened to affect national unity in the ongoing confrontation with the United States.

From this point on, several situations in the program of the Revolution did manage to confront the matter of race directly, not elude it, which seemed to be the intention of the political leadership of the country. Such situations were:

- The acute confrontation of classes within the country in the context of many attempts, even armed operations, on the part of the United States with the purpose of destroying the Revolution from its very first moments.
- The continuous calls for national unity, and the implicit appeals to postpone any other internal conflict that could affect that unity.
- The confrontation with the United States and the counterrevolution that demanded the mobilization of all revolutionary people to defend the country from multiple aggressions. During this situation a fighting spirit prevailed and fused the people into a single striking force.

### The Urgent Need for Rectification

Although it is certainly true that the moment of the triumph of the Revolution justified a subordination of the racial problem to unity, for the national project nowadays such policies are not justified. Quite the opposite, and the absence of a debate about the racial problem in Cuba threatens to affect the rhythm of consolidation of the social project of the Revolution. The factors and situations that determined this conclusion are based on the following evidence:

It is evident that racial prejudices, discrimination, and racism have reconstituted themselves again as part of present-day Cuban social reality.

It is evident that poverty, marginality, and criminal disposition, which were exacerbated with the economic crisis at the end of the eighties, are based on the impact the crisis has had in the standard of living of the population. This has especially affected blacks and mulattos.

It is evident that blacks and mulattos fill the ranks of the unemployed, the penal population, and other groups having the greatest difficulty in making a concrete life plan.[35]

It is evident that blacks and mulattos have the least access to the economic activities that constitute viable alternatives for enjoying better conditions of life within the changes generated by the Special Period.

It is evident that blacks and mulattos continue to be underrepresented in the structures of institutional power. This has generated informal alternatives (networks of informal power)—often involving unreliable people—which give rise to delinquency and corruption, and which have a tendency to disrupt and slant administrative activity in such a way that they become a vehicle for the corruption of officials.[36]

To the above we should add, to appreciate the issue from a scientific perspective, the problem of lack of data. The absence of a national census (the last is from 1981), one that considers the category race or color of the skin as part of the data, prevents us from pursuing more fundamental analyses. The 1981 census is totally insufficient to seriously evaluate the situation of the black and racially mixed population in Cuba. It keeps us from making correlations between race or color of the skin and other variables.

In addition, the manner of registering race or color of the skin of the interviewee was decided by a simple observation of the pollster, or by means of a question about those who were not present during the interview. Therefore, the results of the census are not reliable at all. Supposedly 67 percent of the Cuban population is white and 33 percent are black and racially mixed. Nevertheless, the numbers seem false, the data biased by multiple subjectivities and underlying prejudices.[37]

Yet it is not solely a matter of the absence of an up-to-date census, rather that race or color of the skin was eliminated from all the forms and surveys the population was asked to prepare. Consequently the ability to investigate diseases that afflict some racial groups more than others has been diminished. It is not possible to evade the issue that race, color of skin, and classist structures go hand in hand along with the history of Cuba. Thus any negation of this historical reality puts in a critical position all research projects about Cuban society that propose to measure and make projections on the question of race.

The attitude toward the problem has been so absurd that the country has even been deprived of a process of recording how much it has advanced in this field. As far as we can tell, Cuba surpasses any country of the hemisphere in meeting the challenge of racial discrimination. But in the black and racially mixed population of Cuba, despite everything that has been accomplished, there are still to an unacceptable level problems of marginality, poor self-esteem, insecurity, and deprivations of life. These issues are the result of conditions of life that have endured for centuries as the population suffered ruthless exploitation, lived in degrading conditions, and were subjected to racial discrimination.[38] In particular, the presence of mulattos and blacks at certain levels of the structures of power indicates the problem cannot be reduced to simple representativeness by the color of the skin in the institutions of Cuban society. The essential pressing problem refers instead to the consciousness of nation, of an identity to be assumed with all its hues and political, ideological, and cultural implications.

What would be settled for Cuban society if 50 percent of all important societal positions were held by black and mulattos if a significant percentage of them wants to be white? Therefore, it would be the case that they would assume their social functions without ever confronting their low self-esteem. Thus the situation is much more complex than simply to grant blacks and mulattos ample representation in all positions. We cannot be carried away by the mere presence of the mixture, because that has at times led to a false approach.

In essence, it is not a matter of mixing people but of attaining an individual consciousness and a social consciousness, the result of a process of integration at all levels of social life. It means attaining a consciousness where color is absent, whether white, black, or mulatto, to clear the way for Cuban color.


## Power and Discrimination

A fundamental factor that makes the practice of racism possible is the correlation between racial prejudice and the degree of access to power, which is present in any society. It is possible to affirm that institutionalized racism does not exist in Cuba. Nevertheless, such affirmation should not lead us to conclude that we are out of danger from the problem. It is not necessary for a person, group, or class to be in a position of institutional power to wield the power of discrimination. Each citizen possesses a portion of power and, although it may be minimal, it allows him or her to practice discrimination. Thus it is a subjective phenomenon because it depends on the individual consciousness.

In addition, along with the networks of formal power, there are informal networks of power; and although the reach of the latter is possibly
limited, many individuals, groups, or families may reach a level of discriminatory practice whose effects would approach those obtained from
within the institutional structure. It is very difficult to combat this discriminatory practice, due to its dispersion within the social fabric and to
its degree of informality, that is, its capacity of concealment. Otherwise,
how are we to explain that discrimination continues to exist, even sup-
posing the case that our leaders and all those in the flow charts of institutional administration, as the personification of formal power at all levels,
declare they do not practice it?

The answer is that such flow charts do not show formal institutionalization absolutely separated or on the sidelines of the informal networks
of power. The Cuban state power structure does not function like a praetorian guard, but rather is at times part of informal networks of power,
which continuously establish bonds and relations that can inoculate prejudices and discrimination within the formal power structure. As an illus-
tration, what are, among other things, the so-called "socialism," "buddy
system," and "clientism" but an illegal relation between the structures of
formal power and the informal networks of power?

Thus the practice of discrimination is not something related only to
the formal structures of power but to the informal networks of power and
their mutual interrelations with formal power as well. There is no more
intrinsically discriminatory mechanism than the price of basic goods in
conditions of scarcity. But when the informal networks of power, in their
mutual interrelations with institutional power, distribute not only simple merchandise (which disappears after being consumed) but with job
openings in the tourist sector or in corporations, things begin to turn to a
form of racial discrimination with greater social and political impact and
consequences more difficult to eradicate.

Persistent actions of this type are those that end up producing a
conscious and united reaction from those affected, which already even
include implicit political answers.[39] Another direction in which the relationship of power-discrimination operates is as follows. If there is one
single thing the Cuban Revolution has been characterized by, it is as

being a school for the practice of power. The citizenship has learned to wield power, from practice at political organizations and with the masses at all levels of the *poder popular* and state structures. But in terms of the racial groups that integrate society, disadvantages continue to appear[40] expressed in the following way:

- As far as a culture for the practice of power, blacks and mulattos are at a disadvantage in relation to whites because whites in Cuba have always exercised power over all. They learned it in the cradle, a gold power spoon in their mouth, as a family legacy. Now they continue exercising their advantages, increasing their culture at the practice of power.
- Power is not simply a matter of education but a social practice, for which blacks and mulattos need much training. If they suffer from disadvantages at the gate of access to positions, even though they may submit practically identical educational credentials to those of the white candidates, how are they going to traverse the unequal field of decisions? How are blacks and mulattos going to acquire the necessary culture to make it in this land?

It is not difficult to observe that important job responsibilities are left in the hands of whites with little comprehension of the issue instead of in the hands of hardworking and judicious mulattos and blacks. Why? The resultant condition is none other than that blacks and mulattos, in their capacity to practice power, are still discriminated against.[41]

## Racism, Social Policy, and Revolutionary Idealism

At the moment of the triumph of the Revolution, Cuba could already count on a population produced by a long historical process. If we examine that population and categorize it by class, labor sectors, levels of education, income, culture, race or skin color, we'll always find different levels within each category with respect to social capital. Where did these different levels of access to wealth and material goods that the Revolution encountered in 1959 originate?

A society that first experienced an enslaving colonial regime and then a neocolonial republic has structured a reality we cannot forget. It develops from a classist system of differentiation, within which, besides social origin, being a black or mulatto man or woman, constituted an additional burden for those whose place was distant from property, wealth, or the means of production.

Blacks and mulattos never enjoyed, nor do they now enjoy, the privileges of propertied positions in Cuban society. Blacks or mulattos, almost always descended from enslaved ancestors, were granted a legacy of racial discrimination while whites were the heirs to the advantages of their ancestors, people who had generally never been at the lowest levels of the social scale. A popular proverb characterized that reality: "To be white is already a career."

Statistics from before 1959 reflected the situation clearly. In all sectors, but especially in the population groups with more access to wealth and material well-being, blacks and mulattos were extremely underrepresented. As we descend we find that in the lowest levels of access to wealth and material well-being, blacks and mulattos filled the ranks. Then, it is pure and simple idealism, in any type of social evaluation of Cuban society, even today, to forget that reality.

Beyond the fact that the dominant classes aspired to use racial discrimination as an instrument of social control and power, race and its inheritance, the color of skin, have always divided Cuban society socioeconomically, from the very beginning. Whites arrived on the island as colonizers and blacks as slaves, a situation that from the origins of Cuban society delimited who produced the wealth in Cuba and who raked it in and enjoyed its profits. Several centuries were necessary for a meager number of blacks and mulattos to receive some social recognition, a process that racial discrimination would not only restrain continuously but at times do so with cruel shedding of blood. Nationhood was attained, but by means of an integration process that placed blacks and mulattos in the context of white hegemony and supremacy.

Whites on the one hand and blacks and mulattos on the other are the two large sectors, the fundamental ones of our population, with two different points of departure. They delineated the substantial asymmetries in the Cuban population, which were passed on as an inheritance through the centuries and generations, a legacy that had not been erased by January 1, 1959, and cannot be ignored.

The Revolution did not create a project of social policy aiming to balance the existing asymmetries for different racial groups in Cuban society in 1959. Race, or rather color of skin, was not considered a social variable of importance. The racial question was included in the program to which the triumphant Revolution aspired. The issue was raised by Fidel Castro, who stated it clearly.[42] Nevertheless, it was not taken into consideration while delineating social policy, in contrast to gender, which did make it into the program. Indeed, an organization, the Federation of Cuban Women (FMC), was created to drive the policy in relation to women at the early date of August 23, 1960, with a person at the highest level of the Revolution as the director, Vilma Espin. The strategic-political reasons behind this decision to marginalize race have already been explored in this essay. What is now at hand is the need to evaluate the consequences of not having considered directly the variable of race in social policy and a call to rectify such absence. As stated in a 1999 University of Havana economic research report, "In order for development to increase the opportunities of people, every person must enjoy equal access to those opportunities . . . equity must be understood as access to opportunities."[43]

The treatment of racial differences, considered as a producer of social inequities, as is the case of Cuba, necessarily implies the adoption of not very equitable decisions in search of equitable outcomes.[44] That is, it is not possible to equitably treat population sectors composed of blacks, whites, and mulattos merely by considering them as poor people since blacks and mulattos in this category are presumably at greater disadvantage. That is the case even without considering any possible racial discrimination factors, which, of course, would aggravate the situation further in a poor homogenous group. On the other hand, "equality of rights is not sufficient to assure that the opportunities are accessible to those who are in a position of social disadvantage."[45] For this reason, "an unequal distribution would be required in order to move the neediest to a common point of departure."[46]

The problem for blacks and mulattos is not having a common point of departure with the white racial group, even though all Cubans regardless of race have benefitted from the Revolution's redistributive policies. With the greater complexity of the problem at that not common point of departure, we find that many issues of different natures are intermingled, conditioning and complementing, creating a dire social situation for blacks and mulattos.[47] A social policy was proposed to create a program of massive education, to provide equal access to health care for all citizens, and jobs and social welfare for all. But, lamentably, not all the citizens, particularly blacks and mulattos, began from the same starting point when trying to reach all the extraordinary humanistic benefits that the Revolution was making available.

With respect to education, it is now clearly evident that schools in Miramar, Vedado, or Plaza de la Revolución are not quite the same as those in Centro Habana, Párraga, or Pogolotti, districts with a higher concentration of blacks and mulattos. The terms and starting points are not the same. The districts are different, as are the families. Therefore, the challenge to create equal educational opportunity in the schools with a higher concentration of blacks and mulattos is great.[48]

It is not enough that all be born in the same hospital, study in the same school, and go to the same places of recreation. That is, it is not enough to provide an equal starting point at birth because it is not sufficient to balance the historical point of departure, inherited from parents, the racial group, the district, or the family in general. Those about to be born should be provided with a social context that is a continuation of that beautiful work of the Revolution: the right of access to the same health care, education, sports, and culture. And we are not simply referring to material conditions, but rather to recognition and social support for groups with disadvantages. The opposite mode would be giving the disadvantaged up to a life of crime and marginality.

Although all the measures that were adopted did improve the educational level, even the cultural level for all, and improved the quality of life of many people, it was not sufficient to equalize the starting points. Therefore, the uneven irregularities by which different racial groups arrived into society did not disappear with the Revolution. Egalitarian distribution and equal opportunities for people from different starting points end up reproducing inequality in Revolutionary Cuba.

Even though a few blacks and mestizos did reach high levels of social recognition, many others did not manage to overcome inherited conditions and accumulated tensions. That explains, in part, why in present-day Cuba the black and mulatto populations are overrepresented in the jails, that there are almost no black actors in television and cinema, and a dearth of blacks and mulattos in the structures of power. This is taking place especially in the economy of tourism and in the corporations.

The lack of representation in the structures of power of Cuban society is not explained by the educational levels attained, because the black and racially mixed population today is more prepared than it was thirty years ago, but by the fact that racial prejudice still seriously limits the access of the non-white population to leading positions in society.

## The Challenge of Role Models

When human beings, natural and social, are in contradiction to society, when reasons for antisocial behavior arise, the source of that contradiction is not in their biological, neutral qualities with respect to the concepts of good and evil but rather in the structure of the society to which they belong. The ideas and opinions within consciousness have not been produced in isolated solitude but are products of the society in which they live.

In childhood, what we end up thinking during the course of our lives assails us from everywhere. Even biological prejudices, in the form of pride for our ancestors or racial prejudice, lack a foundation based on scientific knowledge and belong to the ideology of our society. All this is valid in a society like Cuba's, because although socialist ideology is dominant, it does not occur in pure form, but instead is contaminated with inherited prejudices. Society displays its own faults when it is still willing and able to reproduce racial prejudice and discrimination, beyond the will of those who lead it, orient it, and control it. Generally, but even more so in Revolutionary Cuba programs that create role models are very necessary; a society cannot survive without them. Negative or positive models may prevail, but they are always present.

Human beings select their role models in a context of similarity and proximity. In Cuba, with a long history of struggle, all the heroes and martyrs, men and women of prestige, serve the function of role models. But mass media and education are generally called to play a role of first order in broadcasting role models and the dynamics of the relation between them and common citizens.

When we say "We will be like Che," it is necessary to complement that idea by searching and spreading what we would call "role models," other ways and means of arriving at being like Che. Otherwise, the call becomes a slogan without real meaning. When we speak of intermediate models, the most concrete references are people that, for diverse reasons, attract our attention for their inherent qualities and social behavior, inviting us to imitate them. It is a fundamental necessity for all the population, in particular young people, and it is vital in the case of children. For example, a teacher in whom a boy or girl sees positive qualities worthy of imitation serves as bridge to lead him or her to approach that seemingly unreachable standard that tends to dazzle us.

Such a situation speaks to the insufficiency of Cuban mass media communication and of television in particular. If a man, woman, young person, or child does not see himself reflected in the television by similar people, it is almost impossible to manage to lead them in the social conduct that is expected of them. Such is the importance of mass media in presenting and emphasizing the best examples, and this can only be accomplished by displaying the multiracial nature of the Cuban population.[49]

## Unity in Diversity

As difficult as it may be to recognize it, the Cuban nation arose from a process of social integration in which blacks and mulattos were incorporated into a society based on white supremacy and hegemony. For that reason, the triumph of the Cuban Revolution in 1959 represented the opportunity to eliminate such bias, which may only be achieved by overcoming the problems of inequality and discrimination that racism bequeathed us, and which the imperfections or errors of the social project of the Revolution have impeded our progress in eradicating racism.

During all of Cuban history, the unity of the forces of progress has been essential to successful action. But true unity must be forged from diversity, and not by force and the simple sum of different elements. It is only on the basis of self-recognition and acceptance of diversity that unity can prevail. Unity may not be an obligation or an acceptance, but it is achieved solely when everything we have in common, irrespective of our differences, is respected and assumed as part of our social project.

In Cuba there is no hatred of blacks or mulattos. Racial hatred does not exist in Cuba. At each step of the way we have experienced the unity of a common history that has been solidified in the years of revolutionary endeavors. All Cubans have lived through a revolution together that has united us, and each day that union is greater. For that reason it is necessary to eliminate—and to exile—prejudices and racial discrimination. Therefore the racial problem in Cuba is not a matter of concern solely for blacks or mulattos but for the entire nation. It is not simply a matter concerning minorities, or of "Afro-Cubans."

A different issue is the problem of equality or inherited inequality, or the inequality that might have been generated due to the exigencies of the process of survival of the Revolution, particularly since the collapse of the socialist bloc. Thinking in 1959 that the racial question would be settled was idealistic. There was confusion between the will to recognize ourselves as equals and to declare the war on inequality, with the objective reality of an inequality imposed by history and thus almost impossible to overcome in so brief a time.[50]

What is most important to maintain unity is to manage to keep equality alive as an aspiration, and that every day, with greater unity, to continue fighting to reach it. We must face the painful reality that until the middle of the eighties we had managed to achieve levels of social equality that made us all proud, but the ensuing economic crisis produced delays and brought serious social consequences that are yet to be settled. And more serious still, the rhythm at which blacks, mulattos, and the poorest population were weaving a new and better life was seriously affected.

In Cuba, those who by the first half of the eighties had still not been able to establish a life project are now living in very disadvantageous conditions for realizing it. The political discourse that may maintain their link to the national project will be one that identifies clearly with the reality these citizens endure, and that urges them to fight, along with the leaders of the country, to overcome it.

## Some Final Considerations

In this essay, our research led us to some considerations that could also be taken as conclusive. However, certain important subjects must be summarized. Cuba is the first country with a long colonial and neocolonial experience that has attempted to end racism and discrimination of all types, although it must reconsider some policies in order to continue advancing. Cuba, which had to endure a colonial and neocolonial experience since the beginning of the sixteenth century until the mid-twentieth century, finds itself in the most complex of conditions in terms of historical inheritance and the attempt to eliminate racism and racial discrimination. Especially because it was colonized by one of the most backward countries of Europe, Spain, such colonial power did not provide Cuba with any paradigms of modernity, or with ethical models for overcoming racism. Since Spain even today does not recognize its African ancestors, it is still no model of integration and unity within diversity.

The situation becomes more difficult if we consider that racial differences in Cuban society had from colonial times a set of causes and consequences, particularly socioeconomic ones, that the nation is still attempting to overcome. Therefore, it is not difficult to understand that forty years of the Revolution, no matter how radical, are not sufficient to have advanced beyond what Cuba actually accomplished. The consequences of historical dynamics like those Cuba experienced do not disappear from social consciousness in so short a time.

To all of this we add, as a delaying factor, an important error of idealism, which was assuming that by eliminating the bases of capitalism and deploying an egalitarian social policy, the racial question would be settled. If, in addition, we consider the geographic proximity to the continental territory of the United States and the aggressive policy of the North American administrations against Cuba, for over two hundred years, it becomes clearer under what conditions the island has had to struggle to make its mission as an independent nation a reality.

To this situation we must add the critical economic difficulties that Cuba has been enduring since the end of the eighties. As a result of the combination of the economic crisis, the needs of internal economic rectification, and the disappearance of allies from the socialist camp, Cuba has been forced to adopt economic reforms that bring challenges to social equality and the survival of its internal political system.

Cuba is no longer today a racist society, nor do racial prejudice, racial discrimination, and racism dominate the Cuban social atmosphere; but this discriminatory trilogy survives and relies on situations that feed upon it. The causes of that situation are to be found in the ring of forces made up of damaging remnants from our neocolonial past, the prolonged absence of a prioritized, specific, and systematic treatment of the problem of race, the economic crisis yet to be overcome and which undermines present economic reforms.

And we must add to all this the insufficient debate on race, which could help to destroy the underlying enclaves of racial discrimination in the family and other groupings, as well as to restrain negative attitudes and activities created by silence and excessive discretion in the treatment of the racial problem.

# 4—Racial Consciousness and the Anti-Racist Struggle

In truth, we should not teach people to give preference to any color, but in a multiracial society such as Cuba's, with the surviving vestiges of colonialism and a racist culture, if we leave color out of education and do not even mention it, then in practice we are teaching that one color retains hegemony: whiteness. This is not a phenomenon exclusive to us, but of all humanity, in which such values remain primary.

Cuba, despite living through a profound process of social transformation, begun more than fifty years ago, has not yet escaped from those values inculcated by the transnational and imperial dominance of the information media, some 90 percent of which are controlled by the United States and Europe. The fashions that are imposed, the patterns of consumption, and the controls of a dominant imperial culture that undertakes to tell us on a daily basis how we should live, with which values we should measure ourselves, and whom we should look like, seek through a continuous assault to maintain national cultures in a subordinate position to the transnational and imperial consumer culture.

In fact, the variable of "skin color," although imperfect, is a variable of social differentiation in Cuba. If we could simply accept this variable in terms of what it offers us and reflect it in our social and economic statistics, we would not be, as we are now, tossing into the wastebasket nearly five hundred years of history. It is true that it is not solely a matter of skin color, but something much more complex; thus we are allowing ourselves to be standardized statistically, turning us into a society whose parameters of characterization do not vary at all, like those societies in which capitalist homogenization dissolves ethnic and cultural differences and multiple distinctive nuances, which end up counting for nothing.

United Nations statistics will never require that we define ourselves as a nation in terms of all of our traits. We are the ones who must impose our true image, avoiding the depiction of our citizens as mere numbers in a statistical display that depersonalizes and denationalizes us. Accomplishing this becomes very difficult, above all if we take into consideration that there are still issues that conspire against a balanced education that accounts for skin color. In this sense, it is necessary to point out, among other things, an excessive Westernism (not, of course, a correct appreciation of Western values, which is something else altogether).

We can easily realize that there is very little, or almost nothing, taught about the racial question in our schools. From this perspective, a few phrases of José Martí are repeated, such as "Man is more than white, more than mulatto, more than black. Cuban is more than white, more than mulatto, more than black," without going deeper into what this means and instead leaving everything as an ethical matter. And we know that ethics is not politics. José Martí thought and fought for a nation "with all and for the good of all," and for this reason the political complement of that immense ethical reserve found in his thinking about race must be sought in his thinking about the nation he imagined.

As a result of that incomplete treatment of José Martí's thought with respect to race, which would assist us greatly in overcoming the problems we still experience, the racist theses of José A. Saco have more presence in our education, with his rejection of blacks and his famous idea of "whiten, whiten, whiten and then make ourselves respected." Thus I lamentably must recognize that Saco's racist thought would find encouragement in our current social context, since the phenomenon of "whitening," his famous thesis of the "advancement of the race," and the strong tendency toward "not identifying as black or denying it" still exist among us.

If we do not attack, with all of our strength, the stereotypes, discrimination, and racism, we are weakening ourselves as a nation. Confronting the need to identify ourselves as we are carries with it implicitly the potential for overcoming the thinking that devalues the black and the mestizo—a way of thinking inherited from the colonial period, enriched and enlarged politically in the Republic, and still not overcome in the revolutionary period. If we still do not take up the issue of educating our younger generations, which will then be the ideas with greatest presence in our reality, with respect to the problems of "race"?

It is clear that in the schools skin color is not mentioned; in our educational system the study of slavery extends barely to the end of the nineteenth century, without much reflection on its consequences. In our teaching we cover very little of the cultures of Africa, Asia, and the Middle East; the study of race barely forms part of our academic university curriculum and, in our scientific work, there is little in the way of research on those themes. Thus, how could it be possible to get to the bottom of our cultural roots, and even more so, eventually overcome the problems of racism and discrimination?

The conclusion is quite clear: not only do we not take up the theme of race in our education, but, even worse, the dominant thinking about race in Cuba today is what the liberals of the nineteenth century took up under the leadership of José A. Saco. This thought coincides with that of some of our contemporaries with regard to the theme of race, and we have allowed it to overtake that nationalist and anti-racist thought that fought against colonialism and racism and struggled for the abolition of slavery and for Cuba's independence in the second half of the nineteenth century. Hence, the consequences of not addressing the theme of race are more unfavorable than we might have imagined. It is a matter of a series of negative impacts that block understanding on the part of the Cuban people of the history of the country and the formation of our national culture.

We must explain, at all levels of our educational system, clearly and with ample historical details, where these differences of color come from that generate stereotypes, discrimination, and racism. We must demystify these differences, explaining in depth that they represent a "social construction" designed specifically by the dominant classes in order to exercise power and exploitation over the mass base of our population—not only blacks and mestizos, but whites and the poor as well, who lamentably adopt as their own this racist thought, undermining the unity that should exist among all Cubans, of all colors, in order to engage in the struggle against the exploiters.

That we Cubans are different with regard to skin color, and even in our position relative to wealth, is not the only problem; the greater difficulty lies in the fact that we allow these differences to be emphasized and used as an instrument to divide us, when we should be united in the struggle against all that divides us and refuse to allow the power elite to exploit us. And that is not only a problem for Cuba, but also for the mass of "Afro-descendants" that continues to be denied representation in the statistics of the United Nations.

Thus we must focus on our need to make racial consciousness an indispensable condition for the struggle against racism and discrimination. Without racial consciousness it is not possible to carry out the tasks of the struggle against racism. The exploiting classes in Cuba have always worked very hard so that simple, superficial physical differences could be projected for the purpose of keeping us divided from a classist and racial point of view, and thus keeping us easily exploitable. Thus achieving racial consciousness does not mean retreating. Quite to the contrary, it means acquiring values without which it will not be possible to liberate ourselves definitively from racism.

# 5—Understanding the Cuban Racial Question

Is there a Cuban racial problem? Is it possible to design social policy for today's Cuban society without taking into consideration the variable of skin color? In a speech at the Presidential Palace on March 22, 1959, Commander in Chief Fidel Castro raised the problem of racism. Fidel stated very strongly that this was a social blight that must be eliminated. Raúl Castro treated the issue in depth in a meeting of the Provincial Bureau of the Cuban Communist Party in Santiago de Cuba in 1959 and later continued addressing it at checkup meetings of the Cadre Policy at the national level. On December 20, 2009, Raúl returned to the issue in the final session of National Assembly of Popular Power.

In 1962, the Second Declaration of Havana established that the issue had been resolved. The theme of race became taboo. The silence that followed the 1960s did not mean that the concern had disappeared. But the issue of race has been viewed and treated as something with a strong divisionist component that threatens the nation's existence. Because of that the theme of race has become the most avoided and ignored of Cuban social reality. There is no topic that has overtaken it in terms of such a prejudicial attitude toward its treatment.

To have proclaimed in 1962 that the problem of racial discrimination and racism in Cuba was resolved was an error of idealism and political will. It was an error to believe that by eliminating the bases of capitalism and deploying an egalitarian social policy the racial question would be solved. In addition, to have not factored skin color into social policy as a historical variable of social differentiation among Cubans, which it in fact is, meant forgetting that the starting points for blacks, mestizos, and whites for making use of the opportunities that the Revolution placed in front of them were not the same.

We argue in this essay that the Cuban nation has yet to overcome the problems of racial discrimination and racism. At the same time, the nation has not moved beyond the starting points inherited from slavery, starting points which during the Republic were reinforced in sophisticated ways. Thus the Cuban racial problem flourishes as one of the fundamental problems in need of debate and resolution. Racial stereotypes, racial prejudice, racial discrimination, and racism—all survive in Cuban society; the inherited and still not surpassed social and economic situation nourishes them, threatening to reinstall themselves in the macro-consciousness of present-day Cuban society. It is still possible to rectify the treatment given to the skin color variable in Cuban social policy, but only through conscious action. In Cuba there is no hatred of blacks, of whites, or of mestizos. Cuba today is not a racist society as it was before 1959. Racial prejudice, racial discrimination, and racism do not dominate the Cuban social context. Institutionalized racism does not exist in Cuba. It is not installed in the sociopolitical system, nor in the structures of power, as it was before 1959. The revolutionary process, with its extraordinarily humanist social policy and struggle against inequality and social injustice, generated a certain anti-discriminatory ethic, which moved into what are now its main niches: the family, the individual consciousness of many people and of certain groups, the so-called emergent economy, and a certain marginal institutionality that resists elimination.

Contacts with the market economy, the reemergence of inequalities and all of the economic and social deterioration resulting from the crisis of the 1990s, brought about the reappearance of racial discrimination.

We might say that until the mid-1980s the country had achieved access to levels of social equality that were the pride of all Cubans, but the economic crisis produced setbacks and brought serious social consequences that have yet to be resolved. That, combined with the weak and nonspecific treatment of the racial question, diluted in the fight against poverty, created a situation favorable for a resurgence of the racial issue with a virulence proper to a problem that was supposedly resolved, but was not.

## Research on the Subject of Race in Cuba and Outside the Island

In Cuba, there is very little in the way of research, degree projects, master's theses or doctoral dissertations on the subject of race. At the University of Havana, like at the oher centers of higher education, the subject is practically absent from curriculums and degree programs, and only occupies a small space in research activity. Many of the studies that had been conducted on the racial problem in the Cuban context generally ended up being shelved, awaiting publication.

It is important to recognize that it is precisely the ignorance of the issue that constitutes one of the most dangerous social mechanisms for the reproduction of racism, racial prejudice, and racial discrimination. If the subject is unknown, seldom debated, and unattended by the educational system or scientific research, how will it be possible to address it and overcome it?[1]

The overwhelming majority of the most extensive studies on the theme of race in Cuba, over the last fifty years, has not been produced by writers or researchers who live on the island. Hence an issue of great importance is not addressed sufficiently by the country's own intellectual community, and we have practically given it over to others, with all the negative consequences that that can bring us. We are not reluctant to share our research topics with people from other latitudes, but what is totally a mistake is our avoidance of the responsibility of dealing with these themes oursleves. Especially because we are aware of the effort made from outside the island, by enemies of the Cuban Revolution, to write our history for us, from the sidelines of our realities and with purposes distinct from our own.

The main periodical publications within Cuba that stand out for dedicating space to issues of race or related themes are *Catauro*, *Temas*, *Caminos*, *Biblioteca Nacional*, *Santiago*, *Estudios del Caribe* and the weekly *La Jiribilla*, the last with an active distribution. The Ministry of Culture and the Union of Writers and Artists of Cuba (UNEAC), and specifically the Cuban Color Project,[2] the Fernando Ortiz Foundation, and the Center for Anthropology of CITMA have worked for many years to ensure that the issue of race does not become an obstacle to the consolidation of the social project of the Cuban Revolution. In the Cuban Color Project of UNEAC the issue was debated systematically, but within a very limited context and almost without media attention. Recently a Commission on the National Library was also established, under the direction of Dr. Eduardo Torres-Cuevas, with the objective of reflecting on racial issues; and on the basis of its research, to design policy proposals to be passed along to governmental and party officials.[3]

The Fernando Ortiz Foundation stands out in the same sense. It was the promoter of the first book to broach the Cuban racial problem in the contemporary context since 1960, *Desafíos de la problemática racial en Cuba* (Challenges of the Racial Problem in Cuba), by the author of this essay.[4] The foundation has also sponsored the excellent *Catauro*, *Revista Nacional de Antropología* (National Review of Anthropology), with nearly twenty issues already published.

Lamentably, the theme of race has no presence, although it should, in the national media, especially in print and on television. On January 20, 2009, race was addressed for the first time on the *Mesa Redonda* (Roundtable) program, and the December 14 issue of the newspaper *Trabajadores* published an interview conducted by the author of this essay, in both cases with broad impact, including internationally. But even the Cuban press, print and television, is pretty timid and avoidant in its treatment of the theme, which only appears with any frequency on the radio.[5]

## Social Blights: Racism and Racial Discrimination

Racism is an ideological form of social consciousness, which considers some people to be inferior to others, whether due to nationality, social origin, sex, gender, race, or skin color. It constitutes a series of attitudes inherent in the dominant culture. Racial discrimination can be defined as the practice and exercise of racism, implicit in racial prejudice, which is expressed in negative stereotypes of the other. In the case of Cuba, racism is the fruit and inheritance of the old cultural hegemony of Spanish colonization, originating in slavery and reinforced by the practices of the neocolonial Cuban Republic, which in some respects sought to emulate the racial discrimination practiced in the United States.[6]

The idea of race is a social invention: a means discovered by dominant elites to legitimize relations of domination and exploitation imposed by the Conquest. The possibility of making racism disappear turns out to be a complex, multidimensional, and multicausal matter, which cannot be produced solely by achieving higher levels of social justice or of culture—nor by eliminating the bases of capitalism. Cuba is a concrete demonstration of this. In Cuba, racism is being reconstructed because of enduring negative racial stereotypes and other economic, social, and ideological conditions favorable to it. Hence the urgency of confronting it forcefully.

## Starting Points for Blacks, Mestizos, and Whites in Cuba

Whites arrived to the island as colonizers and blacks as slaves. That has marked, through to the present day, the fate of the protagonists of Cuban history.

The ancestors of black Cubans had to suffer the genocide of the slave trade. Cuba was the second-to-last country in the hemisphere to abolish slavery. Since 1886, when slavery was officially abolished, only 127 years have passed (just a few generations). This is still very little time for such a tragedy to be forgotten. Blacks always occupied the lowest position in colonial and neocolonial society. Invariably, skin color (as a social inheritance of slavery) divided Cuban society socioeconomically. The so-called white man was always identified with wealth, material well-being, control of the economy, privilege, the dominant culture, and power.[7] Mestizos, but blacks above all, were identified with poverty, abandonment, subjugated and devalued cultures, and the absence of all privilege and power. The starting points for the white, black, and mestizo populations in Cuba were different. In 1959, under the social policies of the Revolution, everyone started as equals, but undoubtedly they did not enjoy the same possibilities and abilities that were so necessary to take maximum advantage of the opportunities presented to them. This is one of the problems underlying why whites, blacks, and mestizos are not equally able to respond to the opportunities they have in front of them. There are in the social  policies of the Revolution the best intentions for social justice to reach everyone equally, yet equal opportunities do not mean equal possibilities of attaining them. I believe that not much effort is required to realize that failing to take "skin color" into account, even in today's Cuba, is like throwing out five hundred years of history.

## Racism and Racial Discrimination in Statistics

A study conducted in 1995 by the Center for Antropology of the Academy of Sciences found that 58 percent of whites believe that blacks are less intelligent; 65 percent believe that blacks do not have the same values and decency; and 68 percent oppose interracial marriage. In the midst of new conditions, generated by the economic crisis of the 1990s, it became evident that blacks and mestizos are the ones who have suffered the most, overall, as part of the most economically vulnerable population.[8]

The new economy that emerged during the Special Period, through an economic policy composed of a combination of measures aimed at overcoming the crisis and grounded in the rise of mixed corporate property, tourism, and a certain approach to the so-called market economy, is still very exclusive with respect to the presence of blacks and mestizos in leadership positions. This is especially true in those economic activities close to tourism and in decision-making positions of authority. With blacks in particular and with mestizos, the so-called emergent economy tends to operate without privileging them much with respect to employment or access to income.

According to the study Dynamics of the Cuban Population by Skin Color (*Dinámica de la población cubana por el color de la piel*), conducted in 2000 by Eduardo San Marful y Sonia Catasús of the Center for Demographic Studies (Centro de Estudios Demográficos, CEDEM) at the University of Havana: "Non-emergent sector: as management, whites, 57.4 percent; blacks, 18.9 percent; mulattos, 23.6 percent. Emergent sector: as management, whites, 75.4 percent; blacks, 5.1 percent; mulattos, 19.5 percent. In the category of technical professionals and administrators, in the non-emergent sector: whites, 39.1 percent; blacks, 27.1 percent; mulattos, 33.8 percent. In the emergent sector, for the same categories: whites 79.3 percent; blacks, 6.1 percent; mulattos, 14.6 percent." As one can see, dramatic asymmetries occur across all categories, above all in the so-called emergent sector. But these differences are in fact even more dramatic if the levels of education of the racial groups are taken into account, and we realize that blacks, whites, and mestizos do not present serious differences with respect to their levels of schooling: whites, in primary, 26.6 percent; middle, 34.1 percent; advanced middle, 30.2 percent; advanced, 8.7 percent. Blacks, in primary, 22.9 percent; middle, 35.1 percent; advanced middle, 34.1 percent; advanced, 7.8 percent. Mulattos, in primary, 26.2 percent; middle, 37.4 percent; advanced middle, 29.9 percent; advanced, 6.5 percent.

It is therefore clear that the principles outlined by the country's leadership since 1985 to achieve a state of racial balance in the cadre policy have still not been fulfilled. The limited presence of black and mestizo leadership cadres in the management structures of the state and of enterprises is worrisome. Blacks and mestizos are also underrepresented in the labor structure, as was made evident by a study conducted in 1999 by the Center for Anthropology of the Academy of Sciences in the two highly representative provinces of Havana and Santiago de Cuba, where serious inequalities of access to jobs was observed.[9]

## Race and Family Remittances

Family groups with a high composition of blacks and mestizos are least likely to benefit from stable family remittances, as they are underrepresented in emigration (83.5 percent of Cuban emigrants are white). In the case of the black and mestizo population, this emigration only became important beginning in the 1980s, which produced the Mariel phenomenon. Many non-whites emigrated then, but without support in the receiving country, and late to leave besides—in other words, when the United States was no longer a country of opportunity, as it had been during the 1970s. These late emigrants did not find themselves with the best jobs or the best salaries, nor with the support they would have had if they had emigrated years earlier. Therefore, as a group, they are not in the best conditions to help their family members on the island. For the same reason, whites are the ones who receive most of the remittances in Cuba.

In addition, blacks and mestizos have much less direct contact with income, given their lower participation in jobs of the so-called emergent economy. They also constitute a tiny minority of the private agricultural sector, barely 2 percent, and they represent a mere 5 percent in the cooperatives.

The presence of blacks and mestizos in the mass media remains weak, mainly in television and in film. Precise data are not available about this, but one needs only to observe the soap operas and other television programming, and Cuban movies. There are practically no black or mestizo actors who play leading roles on television or in film. In addition, the models used for promoting different kinds of activities on television—an anniversary, for example—are generally white. In sum, Cuban television, which shows the Cuban nation in all its multicolor presence during political events, still does not reflect that nation in all its racial groups and individualities.[10]

The absence of a national census on population and housing (the last one was in 1981) that would also examine the category of skin color, has impeded, until recently, well-grounded analysis. The 1981 census was completely insufficient for seriously evaluating the situation of the black and mestizo population in Cuba, and the results are not entirely reliable. It found that approximately 67 percent of the Cuban population is white and that 33 percent is black or mestizo.

Based on the 2002 census, it is believed that the white population is 66 percent, the black population 12 percent, and the mestizo population 22 percent. The data appear to be false. It is still common in Cuba to know people who do not consider themselves black or mestizo but white, when in reality they are not. That may be a result of so-called self-discrimination. The attitude adopted toward this problem has been so absurd that the country has been deprived of the ability to document how much it has advanced in this area. This is the phenomenon generally referred to as "whitening." Another interesting datum: Cuba and the Dominican Republic are the two countries in this hemisphere in which self-identification as white most departs from reality.

The National Census on Population and Housing of 2002 offers greater possibilities for taking skin color into consideration, not only demographically but also in economic statistics. But there is much work to be done to perfect the statistical instruments that provide us more objective measures grounded in the particularities of our population.[11]


## Housing, Crime, and Racism in Cuba

In the city of Havana, the racial issue is linked to the housing issue. There are more blacks and mestizos than whites in the decaying areas, for example, in Old Havana and Central Havana. In 1981, of the residents of those two municipalities of the capital, 44 and 47 percent, respectively, were black and mestizo. Of them, 39 and 52 percent lived in "casas de vecindad" or multifamily dwellings (a higher percentage than in other areas of Havana). In Old Havana and Central Havana 47 percent of housing units have serious structural problems, and it is important to note that 36 percent and 24 percent of their respective housing units have shared toilets. The figure is significant since only 9 percent of housing units in the city of Havana have communal bathrooms. One notes also the fact that in the family dwellings of both municipalities there are fewer house-

hold appliances than the provincial average. These areas are characterized by high densities of non-whites and a deteriorated living environment, and are perceived to be high crime areas.

In 1987, the National Revolutionary Police (PNR) officially identified *focos delictivos,* or centers of crime in Havana, and 31 percent of
these were in areas of higher black and mestizo representation: Old
Havana, Central Havana, and Marianao. These centers include low-income neighborhoods like El Palo, Isla de Simba, Las Yaguas and Isla
del Polvo in Marianao; or multifamily residences like Mercaderes 111
in Old Havana and Romeo y Julieta in Central Havana. These are areas
that were rehabilitated by the state in the early years after the triumph of
the Revolution.

Also in 1987, the research of a commission established by the
Ministry of Justice revealed that 70 percent of the zones identified as
centers of crime did not have higher crime rates than the average for the
city of Havana. From which one can intuit that perceptions anchored
in negative racial stereotypes led the PNR to consider those low-income
neighborhoods to be centers of crime. The crime rate was greater in areas
considered by the police to be better-off neighborhoods. The Ministry of
Justice also found that blacks and mestizos represented 78 percent of the
cases of "social danger" examined by the courts of Havana between May
and December of 1986.

Blacks and mestizos swell the penal population. According to an organization of political prisoners, at the end of the 1980s, in the Combinado
de Este prison 80 percent of the prisoners were black. That is definitive proof that the Cuban Revolution, despite its extraordinary humanist
work, has not been able to achieve social equality among the different
racial groups. In the 1980s, the crime rate turned out to be higher among
the black population.

In the case of housing, despite tremendous constructive effort during
all these years, there are still marginal neighborhoods, and these are
growing. My own personal hypothesis is that this is due in great measure
to the fact that Havana's population is growing as a result of immigration
primarily from the eastern provinces, since it involves people who move
to the capital city seeking better life conditions and who are often willing

to live in whatever conditions are available. There is thus better housing for many, but the number of people living in precarious, marginal, and impoverished conditions in Havana is also growing.[12]

## Some Final Considerations

There is currently a racial problem in Cuba and racism is threatening to reconstitute itself. Racism is becoming a political conflict, incompatible with social justice and the extraordinary humanist work of the Revolution. Cuba finds itself in the most complex conditions for eliminating racism and racial discrimination, since skin color historically has been a factor in social differentiation among the Cuban population. But the black and mestizo populations are today incomparably more prepared than fifty years ago. Despite the racism that still exists in Cuban society, we can state that the black and mestizo population on the island is the healthiest and best educated mass of Afro-descendants in this hemisphere, and that no other country has done as much as Cuba to eliminate racial discrimination and injustice.

Racial discrimination must be definitively banished and eliminated from the Cuban reality, and in that undertaking the entire society and its institutions should participate, actively and jointly, in order to deal with this problem in a prioritized, specific, and systematic manner.

## Recommendations

- Develop racial consciousness in contemporary Cuban society. Without racial consciousness it is not possible to fight against racism and its social vices. The prejudices still exist and many people suffer from them, even though many have no awareness of that fact.
- The struggle for a true, integrated national culture requires more public discussion on the theme of race.
- The Cuban nation needs to understand in depth the place that history reserved for each racial group.

- Society must unleash a definitive battle against racism and racial discrimination
- A prodigious anti-racist and anti-discrimination education program must be developed.
- The state should guarantee social equality, equal access to opportunities, and recognize and continue to support disadvantaged groups.
- The theme of race should occupy space in the media and on the agenda of political and mass organizations.
- The support of academic institutions of higher education and their research programs is essential.
- Researchers need to develop a database that considers skin color and allows for cross-referencing social, economic, and political variables.
- The work of existing national commissions fighting against racism and discrimination must be supported.
- Establish a commission in the National Assembly whose fundamental objective would be to support the work of existing national commissions, thereby institutionalizing, at the highest level, the struggle against racism and racial discrimination.

# 6—The Metaphors of Color

Racism may well be the thorniest, most hidden topic in our present social reality. Some people don't want to hear anything about it. Reactions are unforeseeable and range from denial and cynicism to upset and worried. In Cuba, racism has been approached historically more with the fear of creating social divisions than with a determination to end it. Blacks, mestizos, and many people of conscience have had to wait too long for a discussion. This is now causing contradictions and dysfunction in an extraordinarily humanistic society, which has struggled for social justice, equality, and egalitarianism. Opinions differ. Some people deny that race is a valid topic in Cuba. Unquestionably, there is a lot of ignorance and a false criterion on how this affects national unity, but there's also an attempt to keep the topic from being discussed—as evidenced for a long time in the accusation of "racist," which has nearly always been applied to those who seek to bring the racial question to the fore.[1]

Unfortunately, after many years of silence, in which the topic of race was taboo in Cuba, we are now lagging behind in our treatment of the subject—intellectually, scientifically, and politically. Important intellectuals do not even mention it in their current approaches to the Cuban nation's social and cultural reality. Perhaps, this reflects the fact that they have very different concepts concerning which historical moment of development the Cuban nation is in.

We must accept that all of us Cubans occupy the same place in the process of the nation's formation. Thus it is absolutely necessary to be aware of the various and different historical starting points of all Cubans in order to adopt a more realistic attitude toward racial groups, social inequalities, and the racial question in today's Cuba.

Public discussion is discreet, incomplete, and often unreported. The efforts being made to work with the realities that feed existing inequalities continue to be global, even when aimed at the more vulnerable sectors. However, even in the case of affirmative action, race or skin color still does not appear as a matter to be considered openly in social policy—or at least it is not mentioned openly as something to be taken into account.[2]

Clearly, our Cuban society is multiracial—or rather, multicolored—but this multicolored aspect, which isn't just a simple matter of shades because it includes a long and complex historical background, is far from prevalent in all spheres of our social life. Nor is it a matter of how many whites, blacks, and mestizos there are in the various jobs. Rather, we should take a realistic look at ourselves on an equal footing. The distribution of power is important because not all of the racial groups have equal strength, and an effort must be made to achieve the balances that are so needed in a truly multiracial society. The great scholar and essayist Fernando Ortiz, the third "discoverer" of Cuba, described Cuba as a "stew." I fully subscribe to this idea, but add that the stew is still simmering.

Some people, however, do not feel they are included in the stewpot and even want to turn down the flame. Inside the pot, we have some meat and vegetables—more than we'd have imagined before the economic crisis of the nineties—that haven't become an integral part of the mixture yet. Also, as Isaac Barreal put it in *Retorno a las raíces* (Back to the Roots), the stew should be judged not only by the expected results but also by the cooking process. This is a reality that not everybody wants to accept, but it is of vital importance for the process of consolidating national unity and for forging political alliances with the other colonialized peoples (indigenous and descendants of Africans) of the world—especially those in Latin America.[3]

We Cubans are at a crossroads, even though many fail to understand it or do not accept it. We must either implement measures in all spheres to help all the ingredients of the "stew" blend together or we will lose our only historic opportunity to finish building the society in which the vast majority of we Cubans want to live. If we do not do this, it will adversely affect our alliance with the 150 million descendants of Africans and of the indigenous populations in Latin America who view Cuba as a model of political and social emancipation. We cannot share the idea that a better world is possible with others while avoiding our internal challenges based on color.

I believe that culture and education must be the main protagonists in this battle. It has already been abundantly shown that even though racism is comfortably installed in capitalism, doing away with that social regime does not automatically end racial discrimination nor, not least, the prejudices and stereotypes that nourish it. To do that, paraphrasing Gramsci, we must do away with "popular culture" and the seemingly innocuous "commonsense" things that perpetuate racism and fight to create a truly revolutionary culture. Bourgeois ideology is so strong that it has made many of us believe that all of those residues of racism and discrimination are the most natural things in the world.

An open debate from the cultural and scientific points of view is required if we are to end this hypocrisy, that has nothing to do with the culture of a revolutionary society. Many movies and books, our long historical tradition, and our great cultural heritage in general attest to Africans' participation in the creation and development of our national culture, but some of that laudable work is coming up against our present reality, which still includes negative stereotypes of non-whites, racial prejudice, racial discrimination, and racism. The three most exhaustive research projects of the last forty years about racism in Cuba weren't carried out in Cuba or by intellectuals living on the island. Nationally, very little has been published that tackles the topic as a contemporary problem that must be solved. We have a written history in which blacks and mestizos still aren't given enough space as part of the process of forming the nation and its culture. This has a serious adverse effect on our national identity. We must introduce ethno-racial studies at all levels of learning:

they must be a constant, systematic part of our education and of our mass media—especially television. We must be educated to be Cubans—not whites, as is sometimes the case—and meet the challenges—and reap the benefits—of introducing color.

Our system of education cannot be described as racist, because all Cubans have equal access to it. However, the different roots that contributed to our nationality and culture are not given the same emphasis in our study plans and programs. We do not exclude blacks and mestizos from our schools, but in daily practice they don't receive an education in which all are given equal credit as part of a multiracial society that is objectively ethnically united.

Matters related to the formation of a multiracial or multicolored identity must take their place in Cuban education, because this problem adversely affects everyone, harming the identity of the nation seen as a whole. If this is not done, we will not be educating our children to be Cubans in the fullest sense of the term.

# 7—The Racial Theme and Anti-Cuban Subversion

There are many sides to the conflict between Cuba and the United States, but mainly it involves the American political interest in subverting Cuba's revolutionary society by attempting to subvert social processes on the island or robbing Cuban political leaders in the vanguard of internal changes in order to subvert the socialist regime. Drafted in 2004 and 2006, the U.S. "transition documents" display unlimited criticism of every process under way in the island, seeking to project the worst possible image of Cuba's overall national life. Small surprise, then, that internal political opposition is fostered in order to undermine the progress of the Cuban revolutionary process, engaged as it is in a number of pressing challenges. Among the topics covered by those documents is the race issue, pioneered by alleged scholars who, for all intents and purposes, are nothing but henchmen, subordinated to the U.S. administration's anti-Cuban policy. Some, not all, of the black men from the other side of the Florida Straits try to portray Cuban blacks and people of mixed race as victims in their own land. It goes without saying that the victimizers are none other than the Cuban state, government, and Communist Party, following a distinct trend to tag those living on this side of the political spectrum as little more than sheep or stupid people devoid of any personal will.

Involved in this endeavor to manipulate the race issue in Cuba as a target of political subversion are individuals like Enriqué Patterson, who links this topic either to matters of governance or to an anti-establishment political potential he claims to be boiling among non-white Cubans. Enriqué Patterson was a former professor of philosophy with Havana University's Marxism-Leninism Department before he left the country in 1990, only to appear shortly afterward at the LASA Congress in Washington with two officials from, it seemed, the State Department. Who covered his expenses and the purpose of his presence there may be easily deduced. Settled in Miami, he is now devoted to writing about the race issue in Cuba, and his way of thinking is a perfect match with the aims of the U.S. government. A similar role as manipulator is played by Ramón Colás, leader of a Mississippi-based Race Relations Project, and the journal *Islas*, which until recently was in pursuit of contacts to produce materials on the race issue from inside Cuba. The *Miami Herald*, in turn, continues to be an archive of every article published in the United States on this subject.

It would be foolish and all but anti-scientific to believe that 450 years of colonialism and neocolonial exploitation can be erased in just fifty years of revolution, radical though this process may have been. In line with the social policies enforced by the Revolution, everyone's right to education, health, social security, and employment was recognized. This measure benefited all poor citizens, the vast majority of whom were black or from mixed racial descent. Not that everything is to our complete satisfaction. It is also a fact that, despite being amply addressed by the top leader of the Revolution in 1959, this issue was not fully pursued and instead was hushed up in later years, given the prevailing opinion that an egalitarian social policy that treated all races the same and a far-reaching set of principles conducive to full equality for all Cubans were enough to solve these problems. This premise was totally unaware of the terrible fallout that such assumptions could bring in tow both from the material and subjective points of view.

We must bear in mind that in the early 1960s the U.S. government started a true war of aggression against the Cuban Revolution. The race issue began to draw attention as a potential bone of contention among the revolutionary forces, taking into account the difficult battles they were expected to face. However, without agreeing with the so-called theory of the one-eyed man who is king in the land of the blind, I don't think any country in this hemisphere, including the United States itself, has done as much for justice, egalitarianism, and racial equality as Cuba.

Likewise, I have not heard since before 1959 of any government committed to the interests of people of color or any state or government from which those ethnic groups have received more than just demagogic speeches. Few, if any, concrete actions were made prior to the Cuban Revolution to take them out of their deprived areas and give them free medical care and education, real hopes of decent housing, a good job, and personal dignity, let alone a chance to be on an equal footing when faced with justice. This is a reality still suffered by most African Americans in the United States.

Black people in Cuba struggle everyday in political and social spaces open to them, of which there are many, without letting themselves be deceived by those leaders of the racist Cuban Republic of 1902–1959 who fled to Miami. In reality, Little Havana in Miami was designed to look like the Cuba of the 1950s, complete with its reactionary, racist features. Most of the primarily white exiles are yet to give up the same privileged place they had back in Cuba's neo-Republican days, even fifty years later. And forget about black people's progress regarding access to power, only available to the wealthy whites, much like it was in Cuba before the Revolution. Yet, other forms of discrimination still hang over Cuban-American whites who, regardless of their wealth, stopped being "white" to become "Hispanics" when they arrived in the United States.

Therefore, just like researcher and writer Carlos Moore, many non-white Cuban-Americans admit to the presence of racism and discrimination within the Cuban population in the United States. On the other hand, Cuban non-whites work from a vantage point in which they're aware of their status. That is why we can say with absolute certainty that the number of black people in Cuba who make it to the power structures increases by the day, as does the number of white people willing to share such power. After all, that was one of the Cuban Revolution's goals. That's the true platform for assuring equality, and the rest will be solved in good time, helped by the existing political dynamics and the will of both Cuban black people and the vast majority of whites. Not that black Cubans are living in a dream world, thinking everything will come as a godsend: they know that rain and snow are the only things they can expect from heaven, and that everything else calls for a lot of wrestling.

The main battle facing Cubans of black and mixed racial ancestry, then, is to keep building the society that opened so many doors to them, and also why not share the power with the non-whites in a milieu marked by unique realities and opportunities. This is unquestionably more feasible in today's Cuba than anywhere else, at least in our hemisphere. And again, I am including the United States where, despite its civil rights movement and matchless wealth, more than one quarter of African Americans still live below the poverty level.

What's the plan of those in the United States, and particularly in Miami, who sell the victims' speech to Cubans on the island? Plainly and simply, to burden non-white Cubans with forms of struggle that never worked for blacks in the United States to establish organizations, factions, and sects of discontentment backed with USAID money. In the end these USAID projects only serve the heralds of racism in Washington and Miami, a sorrowful mission undertaken by some U.S.-based black Cubans.

I do not think the non-white Cubans on the island who participate in USAID–funded programs do so without knowing they are betraying their fellow human beings; it is just that lining their pockets is more important. Like it or not, they have thus become pawns of the same Miami mafia whose only aim is to recover whatever properties and privileges they left on the island. The paradox is that those privileges included discriminating against black people in Cuba. Actually, there in the background of their  victim's role lies the intention that these non-white Cubans work for counterrevolutionary subversion, that is, to undo the political, social, and economic process that has made it possible for those ethnic groups to attain a social status in their country that very few of them could only dream of, its existing problems notwithstanding.

The bottom line is that Cuban blacks and people of mixed race have no use for such "victim speech," nor do they need it. Therefore, those in the United States could better use their time and effort to come up with a narrative of their own so they can help themselves survive in the midst of the racism so characteristic of American society and especially of Miami. In Cuba we know exactly who's a friend and who's an enemy.

# 8—Skin Color, Nation, Identity, and Culture: A Contemporary Challenge

Not only are we dealing with a number of problems that are essential to understand what we could describe as the "ghost" of the alleged disagreement between "skin color" and "nation" in today's Cuba, we are also facing challenges imposed by the linkages between color, identity, and culture in a nation hitherto unable to overcome racism.[1]

Cuba had to fight for many years on end and against many "demons" before it could rise as a nation. This long process has been the glue that keeps the vast majority of Cubans together, regardless of their skin color. The greatest outcome of a revolutionary work started more than fifty years ago, as a continuation of multiple wars for national independence and sovereignty, is the real unity of the Cuban people around our socialist project.

Our island was discovered and colonized by one of Europe's most backward powers, Spain, which Cuba considered neither a model of modernity nor an example of unity in a setting of diversity. To cap it all off, Spain left us nothing in terms of ethical values to fight racism and discrimination, as it had always refused to accept its own African roots.[2]

In the early sixteenth century, Spain established a colonial regime in Cuba that included an airtight monopoly on our foreign trade and relations, the brutal subjection of black people to slavery, racism and discrimination, barefaced administrative corruption, immorality and, in many cases, a stubborn diplomatic behavior, to say nothing of political wrongdoing.[3]

Spain's greatest ambition had been to exploit the island's riches to the point of exhaustion in order to defray its expansionist ventures. Only when Cuba had lost its political value and Spain had neither the time nor the strength to maintain it as a colony did the mother country give it the right of self-government. Granted, Spain's headstrong refusal to sell the island to the United States was honorable and worthy of certain praise. But as befits a consistently colonialist country under a lot of pressure from the emerging nation and its own domestic situation, Spain finally decided to hand Cuba over to the Americans rather than give it to the mambises, who had fought to get it for over thirty years.

## Skin Color and Nation

The aim of the First Independence War was the abolition of slavery. However, in the first years of the war, and despite the symbolic gesture made by Carlos Manuel de Céspedes and some other patriots who decided to release their slaves, the pro-independence movement was forced to design political tactics that combined the abolitionist attitude of the many and the attitude of the few who had joined the struggle for independence and were in favor of slavery but whose money and resources were essential to carry on with the war. So from a practical viewpoint, the Ten Years' War's well-defined abolitionist goals failed to gain a foothold from the very beginning. It was the first time that nation and abolition— or rather, race and nation—countered one another and paved the way for concessions regarding the first real step toward the future existence of a nation for all Cubans regardless of skin color.[4] Undeniable at the time, and since, is the fact that our struggle for independence has always included the fight against the legacy of slavery we know as racism.[5]

At any rate, slavery came to an end not only as a result of the ideas defended by the leaders of the abolition movement—headed by Carlos Manuel de Céspedes—but as required by the war itself. But racism often took center stage, mainly in the attitudes toward General Antonio Maceo, his brother José, and the top black and mestizo brass, who more than a few pro-independence supporters always accused of being "non-whites fighting for a republic of blacks,"[6] which suited Spain's propaganda very well in its efforts to make the white population feel afraid. This was not a difficult task if we bear in mind that "fear of the black" had hung in the air since the Haitian Revolution (1791–1804). The dread of seeing Haiti's "disaster" replicate in Cuba "loomed large throughout Cuban society and somewhat, somehow, has been until today a regular feature of national life."[7]

Racism remained constant within the Liberation Army during the 1895 war despite the outstanding role played by the black and mestizo Cubans, the increasingly popular and revolutionary nature of the war, and the stance taken by many white Cubans who never put up with such attitudes. And let's not forget to mention that after—and as a result of—the 1868 war, Spain had no choice but to free all slaves regardless of on whose side they had fought. Furthermore, in 1886—nine years before—slavery had been officially abolished in Cuba,[8] as if the whole idea was to draw a lasting line between a formal declaration of abolition and the continuity of racism and racial discrimination.

What is certain is that racism blossomed not only out of slavery but also—and especially—out of a culture that this scourge developed in Cuba. It must be said that ever since Cuban culture began to take shape and push aside the Spanish way after centuries of almost total dominance, it started to feel—and to suffer from—the impact of the resulting melting pot of different cultures, albeit without losing its control over them.

Between the late eighteenth century and the mid-1850s, slavery stood out as the most important social issue of its time. As staunch support-ers of such a disgraceful institution, most Cuban landowners demanded both that it be maintained, along with the unhindered entry of African blacks, to preserve the so-called slave trade. Three of the figures who played a key part within this global coalition by proposing changes of reformist persuasion in their respective fields of action were Francisco de Arango y Parreño, José Agustín Caballero, and Tomas Romay, with the first as the ideological leader of the bunch at the time and the latst as an advocate of slavery.[9] In other words, the project to modernize Cuba put forward by these thinkers was of a reformist nature and was unfeasible without slave labor.

By then, "Haiti's economic devastation, caused by a lengthy war against a coalition of capitalist powers, the sanctions they imposed following national independence, and an assortment of domestic problems led to the rise of capitalist Cuba, its conversion into a thriving source of profit, and the establishment of a permanent destination of New World–bound African slaves."[10]

Later on, from 1830 to 1837, reformism came to the fore again, although with slight differences and with José Antonio Saco (1797–1879) as its greatest exponent. Most of these liberals, all of them racist, pioneered reform from the late eighteenth century until well into the second half of the nineteenth—long after the end of the First Independence War in 1878—with José A. Saco at the front of the pack. They were also in favor of getting rid of the blacks by either sending them back to Africa or submitting them to a "socio-demographic wash" or "whitening." As far as they were concerned, there was no room for black people in Cuban society except as slaves, or in any event, secondhand labor, but always at a disadvantage when compared to white people.[11] Simply put, if they couldn't be physically eliminated or taken back to Africa, at least their color would be washed off the fabric of our society.[12]

However, since the very first quarter of the nineteenth century these positions conflicted sharply with the sugar industry's need to grow at a time when Cuba was taking over a market left vacant by Haiti. The "fear of the black" instilled by the increasing import of slaves, together with the existing racial and demographic imbalance and the failure to comply with the agreements that England systematically imposed on Spain (as in 1817 and 1835, for instance), brought about an unlawful traffic in slaves that obviously lined the pockets of British and Spanish officials alike. Throw in the fact that in the second half of the nineteenth century many rich landowners in western Cuba who pushed for the island's annexation to the South of the United States put their plans into action, eager to keep slavery in place.[13]

Even if slaves had to keep coming at any cost to maximize profits, the blacks had to disappear through a swift and deliberate "whitening" process that gave European immigrants the right of way until well into the Republican period. Who better than white Catholic Europeans to meet the requirements of the desired type of population?[14] From this wide spectrum of attitudes toward slavery and the place assigned to black people—slaves or otherwise—in Cuban society sprung the political forces who fed the independence movement. These were made up of names ranging from Salvador Cisneros Betancourt, a racist who deemed blacks unworthy of a slot in our society lest they be whitened, to Carlos M. de Céspedes, who freed his slaves and turned them into citizens so they would fight alongside him for Cuba's liberty.

It is also safe to say that the *criollo* reformists, the racists, the well-equipped and battle-hardened Spanish troops, and the mother country's principled reluctance to grant Cuba its independence were not the only strong, dangerous obstacles to the pro-independence movement's goals. In the end, other problems got in the way of the struggle, both in the 1868 and the 1895 wars.

Early in 1898, the Liberation Army and the organizations of the Republic-in-Arms were getting the better of Spain on the battlefield but losing ground to infighting. They were riddled with racism, voluntary or "involuntary" annexationist positions, and pro-reform attitudes. These eventually combined with all sorts of tactics deployed by the U.S. government to tip the balance in favor of its intentions to take over the final stage of the fight for Cuban independence.[15] Presidents Cleveland and McKinley were both bitter enemies of Cuban independence, and as such they pretended to be neutral while actually taking Spain's side as they waited for the right time to intervene. Finally, and all their setbacks notwithstanding, the pro-independence fighters were close to winning. Spain was coming to terms with the fact that the war was lost. Given the prospect of a U.S. military intervention, and the problems they had at home at that time, the Spanish Crown chose to deliver the island to the United States rather than surrender it to the Liberation Army.[16] That's how our nation fell into the Yankee imperial eagle's clutches in spite of all the blood that Cuban whites, blacks, and mestizos alike had shed for our independence.

From a dialectical viewpoint, racism is to be blamed three times over for the unsuccessful attempt to found our nation. It became a reason to fear unity, a source of divisiviness in our ranks and, as if that weren't enough, an excuse to exclude non-whites from joining the nation. And even if we have no reason to be afraid of these issues anymore, when it comes to racism we still seem to be essentially frightened by the division that acknowledging its existence may create in our midst rather than determined to fight back and get rid of it once and for all.

All this manifested itself through a widespread aversion to recognizing its existence and tackling the subject as part of the reality of our life. This, of course, not only fuels popular ignorance but also comes in handy for many racists-in-disguise who let this cat out of their bag at the earliest opportunity. Some nineteenth-century liberals are still wandering around in our own backyard. Others skip over the fact that racism has always been part and parcel of our culture. They keep saying instead that it was imported from the United States. That's the rough edge we must once and for all remove from our culture.

### Skin Color and Identity

While our independence wars were only possible when Cuba's most illustrious minds acknowledged that whites, blacks, and mestizos must all rise as one against Spain, such realization was also pivotal to clear the way for the birth of our nation. Unfortunately, there's still a huge bump on the road: the emergence of the Cuban nation is usually depicted in most of our recorded history as a nice-looking blend of patriotism, social consolidation, and mixture of different races that eventually delivered a mixed culture. Nowhere are the "labor pains" taken into account.[17] To some it was an unfinished process that failed to fulfill black people's most cherished aspirations. It could not be otherwise, because that is how Cuban society had been designed to function and, as we all know, those who supported Martí's idea of a republic "with all and for the good of all" were not exactly the same ones who assumed power at the end of our independence wars.[18]

Much as it was met with resistance, this terrible legacy of previous centuries, reinforced by the U.S. intervention and a period of neocolonial policy up to 1958, took racism, discrimination, and social exclusion to unfathomable depths, to the detriment not only of Cuban blacks and mestizos but also to the vast mass of poor people. Therefore, if, as a result of all of the above, we come to the conclusion that the nation inherited by the victorious 1959 Revolution in Cuba was still "flawed," how can we expect it to be otherwise for the blacks and mestizos whose identity had always been under fierce attack both in colonial and Republican times?[19]

Non-whites in general and blacks in particular have always seen their identity under attack and been forced to make their way through a mine-field of non-recognition, non-acceptance, racial stereotyping, along with race-based hegemonic values permanently scornful of any sign of other-ness. All of this has been seasoned with hypocrisy, cynicism, and subtle hints of racism concealed in phrases like "He's black, but decent," "He's black, but not stupid," "He's black, but honest" etc.[20]

These highly complex issues can only be addressed through scien-tific knowledge, honesty, and a concerted effort of various sciences work-ing in unison, not on the basis of the empirical, ignorant, or strong-willed attempts that we so often bump into when it comes to the race problem. For anyone to feel part of a nation or a social group it is essential to live in a context of sameness, as you cannot be part of anything if you cannot be yourself in the first place. Therefore, that someone tries to strengthen himself is nothing to be afraid of, since only then will he be able to be part of anything else, even if only in theory. Black people should be aware of their racial identity and the certainty that it cannot possibly just dissolve into national identity. Rather, the two must go hand in hand, because rac-ism, like machismo, will be around for a long time, and both must be fought from the bastion of our own individual identities. It is because "being Cuban also involves being fully aware of our ethnic roots and the racial heterogeneity of our people and coming to terms with the historical plinth underlying discrimination and racial prejudice."[21]

Therefore, blacks and mestizos must preserve and increase their awareness of what they are lest they never find sufficient ethical, moral, and ideological strength to resist the racist attitudes that still weigh heav-ily on them, both individually and collectively, and on the purposes of our revolutionary social project. The bottom line is, we don't live in a perfect world. Not by a long shot, but in a country like ours—and this goes for gender as much as race—we cannot let national consciousness pinch-hit for "racial" consciousness. If we do this, we will lack the socio-political and cultural consciousness we need to prevent the danger of a socially dysfunctional Cuban Revolution. Our current project must come to fruition on the basis of unity in a framework of diversity, acceptance, inclusion, and respect for "race" and cultural variety, not the other way around. Unity is part of our project and utopia, whereas diversity is an objective notion.

Look at it from another angle: since poverty was never just any poverty for "non-white" and, especially, black (and black female) Cubans, it can't be considered from a general perspective. Poverty always came together with racial discrimination against black people, which is not just another kind of discrimination either, as it is something that we in Cuba wear on the outside, or simply put, it is skin color.[22] We even have whites who may have lived their lives in far worse material and spiritual conditions than many blacks and mestizos. But the latter are not as able to escape such situations as the former. Many of them are non-whites who could get a better education and improve their material and cultural status, not to mention that the shade of their skin may also make it easier for them to "blend into the landscape" and evade discrimination, an impossible task for black people. If not, what color can they mingle with to avoid being discriminated against?

That is why the reality of life has it that a white person, by himself or with a little help, can come out of poverty, but a black person has to be res-cued from it and put in a social milieu where racism is less effective. Our conventional wisdom has put it quite well in the sentence, "Being white is already a university course."[23] We're not trying to build new identities here—ours are very objective and were long established, with all their challenges and complexities. Rather we see that they are expressed in a positive way with a view toward a full-fledged social balance among the different racial  groups (white, black, and mestizo) that still constitute Cuban society.

The socioeconomic differences we still have stem from the various places and degrees of power these groups have been assigned by history, all infected by the negative stereotyping, racial prejudice, discrimination, and racism still hanging over blacks and mestizos and getting in the way of society's consolidation in a project built on equality and social justice for all Cubans. Any attitude opposed to this vision is nothing short of idealistic and even paternalistic. It is out of line with the efforts of a country striving to overcome colonialism's many-faced, reproducible heritage. Otherwise, how could our national identity develop in form if it is shackled in content by stopping our blacks and mestizos from being an element of such an identity?

Hence the need to protect the place of individual racial or gender identity in the context of our national identity. Ours is a complex, diverse collection of identities that must be recognized as a whole to make it possible. Indeed, it is a matter of making unity work in a context of diversity. Unity may be an aspiration, but diversity is always objective, and the latter must be reckoned with as the catalyst for the former. Without acknowledging diversity we can have no identity and, consequently, no unity.

If we ever expect to boast of a national identity, whoever calls himself Cuban must welcome every individual trait and attribute, be it related to race or color, sex, place of birth, cultural level, or social origin, to name a few. Otherwise we will not be fully Cuban, because national identity in itself is nothing without the people who forged and shaped the nation. A piece of land or sky and a flag are merely tangible attributes created by a people who turned them into symbols of their history. Therefore, a national identity without the particular identity of its individuals and their attributes would be just an empty concept useless to understand or explain anything.

That is why the Cuban Revolution's greatest achievement is that it gave us a nation that gradually started to be for all when Fidel Castro called racism "a scourge to be extirpated from society's body."[24] However, other "ghosts" got in the way of a more coherent bond between "color" and "identity," when, in the early 1960s, we saw a revival of the age-old fear that a debate on race would seriously jeopardize Cuban unity[25] given the real menace posed by those in the United States who always, but especially in those days, wished for the demise of our nation.[26]

Forty-five years later, many people still associate this bond between "color and nation" and "color and identity" with the risk that addressing the race issue may pose to our unity and the preservation of national identity.[27] They do not realize that failure to do so now is precisely the real danger to these values, that we still face long-postponed and largely unfulfilled cultural and political needs.[28]

We are paying a higher price now for not dealing with the race issue than we would for facing its challenges. This is, first of all, because any topic involving today's Cuban society that we fail to analyze in depth—given our current ideological confrontation with imperialism—will always backfire on us.[29] And we cannot give anyone our national topics as a gift or a loan, let alone put them up for sale.

## Skin Color and Culture

In 1959, when Fidel Castro stood face to face with racial discrimination, he was coping with a question that could not possibly be boiled down to the place of blacks or mestizos in the Cuban economy or how much social space they could share with so-called whites. He was actually talking about a problem closely related to national culture and its process of consolidation.[30] On the other hand, in as radical a revolution as Cuba's, how much could we have harmed the development of our national culture by failing to study the race issue openly and in depth?[31] Maybe there were very good reasons for not doing so from the outset. What is certain is that this debate remains an unresolved matter and probably the most complex and difficult problem in our society today.

Whatever we hope to learn or understand regarding our national culture and life in general would, without a thorough study of the race issue, be useless. There would always be a "black zone" that many would choose to stay away from, get around, underplay or simply deny.[32] It is interesting to see how often our writers, and particularly the poets, addressed the race issue in all these "years of silence." To them we owe the fact that the subject survived even after it was declared over and done with or silenced in the early 1960s. No one can deny that the "race issue" was a risky topic to write about from a scientific point of view, hence the reason that literature and poetry became its lifeline. Cuban cinema, theater, dance, art and (mostly popular) music are worthy of mention in this respect. They made—and still make—a great effort to rescue Cuban culture's African component and have frequently depicted the "race issue" in their contemporary works.

However, a scientific approach was thought to be very dangerous in that it supposedly cast doubt on the "official silence" about the issue and undermined revolutionary unity. That's how it became a political issue, which meant we had to run the risk of being called "racist" and "divisive," the worst piece of adverse criticism a revolutionary could get at the time.[33] Then came the economic crisis and the Special Period, which set in relief what many people already knew: that racial prejudice, racism, and racial discrimination were anything but gone. Unfortunately, those who were somewhat aware that avoiding the topic did not do much good hesitated to act during the first years, between the mid-1960s and the mid-1980s, when the period of silence and even repression was at its height in Cuba's social, cultural, and political life.

Obviously, in each of America's former colonies—including Cuba— national culture was born under and molded by the cultural patterns that always prevailed in the mother country and among its subordinate classes.[34] Ours took shape through an intricate cross-cultural process of assimilation. It merged with elements of other conquered cultures, but never have these cultures, either in Latin America or the Caribbean, been able to come together in a wholesome, well-balanced system with the formerly hegemonic part of our national culture. Ours is a synthesis but still a home for the hegemony of Cuba's formerly leading culture. This is in turn a cultural deficiency, since the island has not been spared by this process despite the remarkable and matchless accomplishments of our radical and far-reaching revolution. It's a very complicated matter with room for neither subjectivism nor oversimplification.

It is true that we cannot rate Cuban culture by colors, but we cannot forget colors when we try to understand its origins and current status. If we want such an understanding we cannot start from culture itself, especially if we disregard the intricate classist dynamics of our culture, where race, skin color, class, and power are inseparable.[35] We cannot possibly speak of a white and a black culture in Cuba, where such dichotomy is totally absurd. But in order to grasp how our national culture was formed and developed until today, it is necessary, if not essential, to consider the dynamics of our nation and the role of its citizens in that process—and not as the formation of a particular entity that is separate from the overall nation, but quite the opposite. Nation and culture were born from two inseparable processes, even if eventually, and for a long time, we paid more attention to our national rather than our cultural identity as a result of the difficult political struggle we were forced to wage in order to survive.[36] Nation and culture came into being within a context imposed, first of all, by the existence of an economic model, a state, and a systemic set of economic, political, and ideological relations. These were dictated, in the case of Cuba, by its colonial status, not to mention that at the same time we were in the crosshairs of the policies the United States had at the ready to either get hold of this island, bound as it was to be free one day, or in due course snatch it out of Spain's hands.

Cuba had no other space outside this context[37] and would remain a Spanish possession as long as it did not fall into U.S. hands. Such was its fate and the setting in which its culture began to take shape, marked by hegemonic relations established by the ruling class. In a word, Cuban culture developed in colonial circumstances, governed by a classist environment and under U.S. geopolitical threats. Still, there should be no doubt that the formation of Cuban culture was more complex, independent, and spontaneous than the inception of its economic and political regime, much as both processes are indivisible.

What happened is that a subjugated class in a colonial situation had more opportunities to make itself felt from a cultural than from an economic and political viewpoint. When it came to its formation, any culture, be it submitted or not to a given economic and political regime, can be said to enjoy possibilities and a certain degree of "democracy." This was typical of the Spanish colonization—in that its members couldn't possibly become as one, because Spain was more lenient than Britain with the cultures of African origin but far more inflexible with its economic and political relations.

Then, if we only take into account the possibility of slaves and non-whites in general (even if they could buy their freedom at a very early stage) to participate in Cuba's economic and political power, they would have never been able to make the same impact on the formation of national culture as the blacks and mestizos, free or otherwise.[38] Suffice it to see how that happened in the United States.[39]

How was it that the process of cultural formation in Cuba offered this chance to the most subjugated and exploited classes? In the context of Cuba's slavery-based colonial regime, this had to do with culture's inherently emancipating and liberating character and its potential to stand up to other cultures, including that of the ruling class. Culture affects our spirit, habits, fascination with the unknown, the way we look at life, the enjoyment of visual images, sexuality, music, dance, religious beliefs, etc. People from the same geographical region receive this influence without even realizing it.

One major complexity in the formation of our national culture is that even the African cultures that supposedly submitted to white domination were and still are capable of making a great impact on the cultural outcome of the basic bond between economic and political hegemony. Cuban culture is a mixture that reacted to the ruling class's power by absorbing its culture, which—the masters' reluctance notwithstanding—melted into others and ended up embodied in a particular type of individual with specific customs and cultural leanings. Otherwise, it would have been impossible for Cuba to have a national culture derived from the one that prevailed in the island until the mid-nineteenth century. At some point it was compelled to "beat a retreat" and make room for a new mixture in the making that eventually became a mainstay of our pro-independence ideas.

Whatever from the outside is grafted to the trunk of the emerging national culture can go either of two ways: either it helps undermine the existing hegemony or it nails it on the spot and even breeds other forms. This process never ends with the disappearance of the socioeconomic and political regime that gave it life in the first place. No culture goes away together with the slavery-based colonial regime or the capitalistic system from which it took nourishment. What takes place instead is a long period of ideological struggle such as the one still going on in Cuba.

This struggle is not only against the burdens bequeathed to us by past regimes, but also our own flaws, the attempts to penetrate our culture, and the errors made along the process of emergence of the social regime we want to build nowadays.

The truth is, culture also tends to be a means to reproduce the authority exerted by the current ruling class or the one no longer in power but still intent on perpetuating its ideology. This is the source of the great difficulties we have in finding a proper solution for this problem and achieving the right syncretism. For instance, that all African religions have been long discriminated against in Cuban culture and portrayed merely as pieces of folklore is plain to see.[40] We have often overlooked the fact that they're actually an endless source of knowledge, rules of conduct and ethical principles, as well as an inestimable cultural treasure for any nation, as in the case of the so-called "Ochá Rule."[41]

Leaving other considerations aside, it is more than sufficient to say that Cuban blacks, whites, and mestizos are yet to share in a systematic and well-balanced way the spaces provided by our national culture.[42] This is so even if many of them practice the same African creeds that laid the foundations of popular religion in the island, regardless of the believer's skin color and despite their strong presence in our culture. If we throw in the fact that the "race" issue is hardly ever touched upon in Cuban academic circles, syllabi, or scientific research and that there is still a huge gap between the schoolroom and social reality in this connection, how can we expect blacks, whites, and mestizos to be on a level with each other in Cuban culture? What's left out of our the educational system never makes any cultural grade, and the color issue remains largely unknown, avoided, and even denied in our schools at every level. Ask the rector of any Cuban university about the "racial" composition of the student body or the faculty and you will be lucky if you get an answer from any of them.

Only when all racial groups in our country are in a socioeconomic and cultural position to demand their share of power will Cuba be a true multiracial—that is, a multicolored—society. And as long as blacks and mestizos are denied the leading role they deserve alongside white people in our economy, society, and power structure, our national culture will be unable to develop. The danger of taking backward steps will always haunt us, and we will never get over the effects of colonialism. We have gained a lot of ground, but much more remains to be done. Don Fernando Ortiz, our renowned ethnologist, historian, and third discoverer, said, "Cuba is a melting pot," except that we believe it's still in the oven.[43] Nevertheless, most of the meat and vegetables therein are not done to a turn yet—much less than we would have expected to have accomplished before the Special Period.

Indeed, building a culture unaffected by the old cultural hegemony imposed by the mother country—and reinforced during the Republic with elements of "Gringo racism"—as befits a free, sovereign nation where all social groups or sectors participate and share the benefits thereof on equal terms and one in which "Cuban color" prevails, will take much time and effort, as well as measures to cope with the risk of going backward. Cuban culture has secured a strong foothold, even if it is still riddled with a good deal of racism handed down to us by the Spanish colonization and the Yankee presence in Republican times.

### Racism Still Exists

Cuba is no longer the racist society that it was until the end of the Republic, but non-whites are still made into stereotypes (blacks in particular) and racial prejudice and discrimination still breathe in our social environment.[44] Our national culture cannot be said to be racism-free by a long shot. This is despite the extraordinarily humane work developed by the Revolution in every field and the fact that nearly fifty years of economic, political, social, and cultural change have managed to bolster anti-discrimination ethics throughout society. These ethics are so strong that now we can describe the fight against all forms of discrimination as an unshakable mainstay of the Revolution's domestic and foreign policy.[45] The huge, far-reaching social and cultural work achieved, and the internationalism practiced by Cuba, prove to be two great living examples of this assertion and true models of the Revolution's endeavor to abolish discrimination and social injustice.

The racism that still dwells in Cuba comes from neither the state's institutions nor the government. On the contrary, these structures of our society work hard, as no one ever did in our recorded history, to design policies in favor of social equality that in more than a few cases have bordered on egalitarianism.[46] In Cuba today we are all ruled by a government, a state and a political leadership, that make our needs their own—particularly for the good of the poorest and formerly discriminated against strata. They strive to take social assistance, welfare, and every conceivable benefit to the four corners of our geography. However, racism and discrimination have survived with the help of racial profiling and prejudice, still lurking in some institutions, individual consciousness, our economy, family, and society at large. This has been fueled since the 1990s by the profound effects of an economic crisis—which shows glimpses of social crisis—that we are merely starting to overcome. This is nothing but a colossal slap in the face to those idealists who stubbornly held in 1962 that racism had been banished from Cuba.[47]

Cuba is perhaps one of the few countries worldwide where whites, blacks, and mestizos geographically share more common social, economic, cultural, and political spaces in which mixture is the rule thanks to a radical and extraordinarily humanist revolution. This revolution declared war on discrimination, exclusion, poverty, and inequality, and more has been done, and is still being done, to eliminate these evils and improve social justice.[48]

It would be absurd, then, not to make the most of the fact that for the first time in Cuban history blacks and mestizos can get rid of all forms of discrimination and share Cuba's fate with the so-called whites on equal terms from their rightful place in a multiracial/multicolored society.

Some problems, however, remain as yet unsolved, such as the failure to tackle the race issue from within. This only makes it harder to banish racism and discrimination from society's macrocosm, especially in Cuba at mid-crisis, and impairs the development of our culture, national identity, and social project. The most serious problems in this regard are:

- Cuban recorded history is still insufficient in attending to the role played by blacks and mestizos—and particularly by black women—in the construction of our nation, which affects our national and cultural identity as a whole.

- The expressions of racism as a means to exclude blacks and mestizos—mostly the former—seen in some socioeconomic spaces, which we must fight more openly, systematically and collectively.[49]
- Poor cultural education and knowledge about race, an issue many people choose to stay away from, get around, underplay, or simply hold as unworthy of mention.[50]
- The new economy, which emerged during the Special Period as a result of measures to cope with the economic crisis and that was supported by joint ventures, tourism, and a rapprochement to the market economy, still gives blacks and mestizos a very low level of participation, mainly in the field of tourism and advancement to managerial positions.
- The goals that the Cuban government set itself in 1985, with a view toward seeking a racial balance in the top leadership, are yet to be reached. The limited number of black and mestizo officials in Cuba's hierarchical structure, to say nothing of our corporations and tourist organizations, is cause for concern, which is inconsistent with the high educational level achieved by members of those racial groups.[51]
- Our educational system, in turn, has yet to address the skin color issue in its scientific, cultural, historical, and political study programs. These were designed for students who at some point in their social life will come face to face with the negative racial stereotyping of blacks and "non-whites" in general, as well as with racial prejudice, discrimination, and racism. Cuba remains marked by a deep-seated dichotomy between school and social reality, to the detriment of our youth's cultural and political development.[52]
- In school, blacks, whites, and mestizos learn nothing useful regarding their acceptance, in a coherent, well-balanced way, as equal members of a single, multicolored ethnic group.[53]
- Skin color is openly and directly disregarded as a variable in our social policies, currently focused on poverty, social injustice, and inequality, and although they toy "discreetly" with so-called affirmative action, they fail to get to the bottom of the existing differences among the racial groups that make up our population today.[54]
- Our social sciences and humanities, particularly at our higher education level, fail to consider the race issue as worthy of study and

research with a view to a better understanding of today's Cuban society and its indispensable improvement.

- Our public discourse against discrimination is still shallow and poorly disseminated despite the fact that its ethical content is of itself important in fueling debate on the race issue.[55]
- Many Cuban intellectuals do not even mention the race issue, let alone see it as a problem to be solved. Therefore, it's safe to say that there's a great deal of disagreement within our intelligentsia as to when to take timely action to consolidate the Cuban nation and its culture.[56]
- Our socioeconomic statistical information all but skips over "skin color," thus paving the way for doubts about its scientific rationale by leaving out of any analysis a fundamental variable of the Cuban identity. Another opportunity to display one of the Revolution's true social accomplishments is thus missed.[57]

## Some Final Considerations

All of the above makes it quite plain that, socially speaking, there is widespread ignorance about the race issue in Cuba today. This is shown by both avoidance of the topic and the efforts to hush it up by restricting discussion to just a few concerned individuals, groups, and institutions. This is clearly noticeable in the scant attention this issue receives from our statisticians, scientists and writers, as well as from our media in general and, especially, our history books. To make things worse, the responsibility for a contemporary scientific approach to the race issue has been laid at the door of a number of authors who disagree with us non-whites about our day-to-day experience in today's Cuban society. Virtually every relevant research work on the race issue published in the last forty years that describes our contemporary problems has been done by people who live abroad.[58] This means we are giving up our primacy in this field to others not nearly as linked with our real of lives as we are, with the resulting inconvenience that this entails.[59]

At every turn we have a feeling that many people who are fully aware of this problem and seem to be in favor of a solution choose to avoid it, let alone discuss it. As far as debate is concerned, it was not until a few years ago that we started to take the first steps, if modestly and hesitantly.[60] That's why any form of discussion about the race issue in contemporary Cuba has merely survived in a sort of underworld shared by a few interested individuals and institutions. This is a tendency that favors ignorance, a very dangerous social condition that breeds racism, prejudice, and discrimination in any society and, worse yet, helps these to remain rooted in society's collective consciousness.

The lack of an open—or at least discreet—wide-ranging debate on the race issue puts Cuban unity at risk in more ways than we might imagine. Dodging or hindering discussion about the subject is far and away the wrong approach we should try.[61]

It looks as if the link between skin color, nation, identity, and culture, a problem dating back to the independence wars of the nineteenth century, has yet to be solved in our country.[62] Finally, we emphasize the need to keep in mind that Cuba is an example to many African peoples and 150 million of their descendants, the indigenous peoples, many African Americans, and, in general, white and non-white individuals who consider the island a model of economic, political, social, and cultural emancipation.

# 9—Statistics and the Color of Skin

Race does not exist. It is a social construction, an invention, a useful dynamic for the purpose of concentrating and manipulating power on the part of the exploiting elites within the frameworks of the unavoidable class confrontation. However, *racism* is realized at each step; it haunts us and it will continue to haunt us for a long time. As social invention, it is something that should be deconstructed, but we will not achieve that if we turn our backs to the issue. Avoiding racism is similar to the ostrich that buries its head in the ground, exposing the most vulnerable parts of its body.

In today's Cuba, that invention is expressed by the "color of the skin," no matter how absurd it may seem to us. Skin color exists and it is not, in our case, simply a bigger or smaller quantity of melanin in our skin, nor is it a question of shades of skin color.

In today's Cuba, skin color hides five hundred years of history, so when we do not consider color, we are throwing those five centuries of history in the trash bin.

## A Color and Nation

The nation is, in the first place, the people that compose it; so knowing how the population was formed gives us the key to learn what the nation is today. The Cuban nation emerged from the decomposition of the pro-slavery colonial regime that Spain implanted in Cuba in the sixteenth century. It emerged as a nation of immigrants: black and Iberian (mainly Spaniards), certain indigenous descendants, and later the Chinese. The Spanish people who arrived on the island had credentials of whiteness, but did not remain as such after their blood was mixed with the indigenous who inhabited the island. Some people were brought by force, but the immense majority came looking for fortunes, which many of them found.

In contrast, blacks, hunted on the coasts of West Africa, occasionally sold by their own tribes, brought here against their will, came in the slave ships, separated from their cultures, languages, and families. Without fortunes and lacking any means of achieving it, they were sold as merchandise in public squares, the same way animals are sold, and then sent to plantations to work as slaves or, for the lucky ones, as domestic slaves, as settlers' servants. Later on, Chinese also arrived, virtually as slaves.

That is the origin of the population inhabiting the island today. Later, people came from the Antilles, Yucatan, other European countries, and even North America, Lebanon, etc., crossbreeding in the population. Although some crossbreeding took place with the indigenous peoples, as a result of men arriving alone on the island, the indigenous quite quickly disappeared when inserted into a system of brutal work. They were not only exterminated by physical stress and lack of food but by illnesses brought by the settlers. The Cuban mestizo emerged mainly from the crossbreeding of black female slaves with the white Spaniards. Thus, the shades that today underscore our skin and certain features come from a centuries-old history. The wise man Don Fernando Ortiz called the mix of people in Cuba *ajiaco*, a stew, which we sometimes say has not finished simmering

## Color and Population

In Cuba today we have the "racial" classification collected in our census: white, mestizos, and black, three racial groups. They are one nation, united by common history, forming one people, but with different starting points. That explains, in part, the social differences we still carry with us, and which the Revolution, despite its magnificent work, has not been able to eliminate. This is how the population was created, and today it forms the core of the Cuban nation. Therefore, it is very important to understand and to take this composition into account, thoroughly and integrally, when analyzing any phenomenon in today's Cuban society.

Our composition was transmitted from one generation to the other, from the colony to the Republic, and from it to the socialist society in which we live today. Our composition forms the social and cultural fabric of the nation, and it is the foundation of its complexity, in theory and in practice—politics. The population that inherited the Cuban Revolution in 1959 was not homogeneous: all were Cuban, but each person had different historical starting points, based on the racial group to which he or she belonged. Different historical starting points, in one nation, are manifested at all levels of social and economic life. Overall, a highly cultured society but affected by the racist component, inherited and fed, inhibits all racial groups from participating in society in a balanced way.

In the inherited statistics of the Republic, we moved from a station of wealth to that of poverty: the so-called whites always appeared to enjoy a better situation; mestizos were at an intermediate level; and the black ones were, in general, at the bottom rung of society. Cuba today has achieved much to advance the quest to reach social equality, but there is still a long road ahead. Five hundred years of colonialism are not overcome in fifty years of revolution, no matter how radical it has been able to be.

Although poverty can also be white, the wealthy are hardly ever mestizo, much less black. All white folks are not rich, but the vast majority of blacks and mestizos are poor indeed. This is a reality that in spite of everything the Cuban nation has done to advance, still persists. Blacks, mestizos, and whites shared poverty in the midst of Republican capitalism from 1902 to 1959. This poverty was strongly attacked after 1959 by a new social politics, but it has still not been resolved to any extent.

Although the non-white population in Cuba never had it better than now, with a government that looks after their interests, our social policies have had difficulties.[1] Our social policies committed an error in considering "poor"as homogeneous in the whole population, and not taking into account that the color of the skin is a solid variable of social differentiation.[2] Whether we like it or not, the color of the skin differentiates us socially. All Cubans are not the same. So a poor group composed of whites, mestizos, and blacks, from better to worse conditions, provides a scale to measure poverty. And the larger the sample, the more behavior can be measured. Yet it is not possible to attain an objective scientific analysis of the Cuban population if one disregards the reality of skin color as it affects poverty. Thus, social policies cannot treat the different racial groups as equals. Nor even inside each group is it feasible to treat everybody in a homogeneous way.

To solve a problem like that, it is necessary to know what differences, or variables, are manifested, firstly regarding the racial groups. For reasons of different starting points not all people can realize the opportunities that the social policies try to place within their reach.

Differences are  expressed in the different racial groups, though in a special way for blacks and mestizos, regardless of whether or not we recognize the existence of the negative racial stereotypes, racial prejudice, discrimination, and racism. We speak of differences as "inherited structural objectives," and the only thing racial discrimination does is to worsen them. Because it is about differences that existed, epistemologically speaking, prior to the exercise of racial discrimination.

Non-whites present an unfavorable position in society, and the existence of negative racial stereotypes, racial prejudice, and racism makes it more pronounced. The phenomenon requires another kind of analysis that we cannot approach in the short space of this essay. This phenomenon is implied when the "*compañero*" Fidel says: "Objective discrimination, by its nature, historically affects the population's poorer and excluded sectors."[3]

It is not possible to gather statistics on Cuban social activity without taking into account the color of the skin. It is not possible to scientifically change today's Cuban society without taking into consideration the color of the skin. It is not possible to design the social policies of today's Cuban society without taking into consideration the variable of skin color. If we do not do it, the specificity of Cuban social policies, and therefore their effectiveness, are compromised.

For Cuba, the matter is even more complicated because race does not exist, but the color of skin does: skin color is objective. And the matter of discrimination based on the color of skin, a typical form under which discrimination is exercised in Cuba, is not a simple cultural fact but an entire social mechanism, a system, built over centuries, that is still reproducible in the current Cuban society we are forced to deconstruct. We lack much of the statistical data to contribute in a more effective way to that task.[4]

This is a problem—albeit with an important difference in terms of the political will to solve it—that we, along with the United Nations Statistical System and the Economic Commission for Latin America and the Caribbean (ECLAC), share in the hemisphere, where about thirty million indigenous and one hundred and fifty million Afro-descendants are waiting to be differentiated in statistics.[5] Such an absence allows the neoliberal governments to hide the real poverty and, paradoxically, does not let Cuba show the true work of the Revolution. Of course, the matter of skin color analyzed in this essay is merely one of the many challenges that have to be approached in the context of the racial problem of contemporary Cuba, which without a doubt exceeds, by far, a simple treatment based on social statistics.

# 10—Shooting without a Scope: An Interview

by Hilario Rosete Silva

## Inside the Malecon

"Even though it was already a thorny matter before we began the independence struggles, little has been written about the issue. Few historians paid any attention to it and studies that deal with it in the present are rare. I lament the fact that the subject is taken up by people living outside the country who do not always share our circumstances." University professor Esteban Morales began talking. When he directed what is now the Center of Hemispheric and United States Studies (CEHSEU) at the University of Havana, Morales believed that the racial issue could become an Achilles' heel and a target for the darts of those who make U.S. policy against Cuba.

EM:     "How valuable it would be if attitudes coming from us would set the pattern," he added. "The problems in our reality should not be dictated to us—we should be the first to take them up. The racial issue could be another one of the arguments the United

States uses to attack us. It is an issue 'from inside the Malecon' that concerns Cubans."

A two-term member of the Academy of Sciences, Doctor of Economic Sciences and Doctor of Sciences, Esteban has served as visiting professor in some twenty institutions of higher learning in ten countries in the Americas, Asia, and Europe. Every time he goes to the United States, he is asked—just because he is black—how black people are treated in contemporary Cuba.

### Cuban Ostrich

EM:   "They are interested in the racial issue in Cuba. Since any black person from Cuba who appears before the public in the United States, no matter what the subject, will be asked about racial discrimination in Cuba, they should study the issue in depth. Because ours is one of the countries that has worked the hardest for equality and opportunity for all, and we must not remain silent on the subject. We face a complex problem that has to do with how Cubans have been treated historically and in contemporary times. It influences the context of relations between Cuba and the United States and the island's political alliances, and it is related to our capacity to learn from errors committed in connection with other issues."

HRS:   *As a black person, do you run the risk of becoming obsessed with such research?*

EM:   "I waited fifteen years before getting my feet wet," he said, "preferring to let the matter mature inside me. Picking topics for research is one thing and starting work on them is another. I began work on it in 1986. I found that the literature had several flaws. There was a social reality that was not being addressed.

"I was sixteen years old in 1959, black and poor. I had suffered discrimination but could not write from the position of the sufferer, whose focus is never objective. It would also have been hypocritical. Because of the social and political organizations I belonged to, my academic and professional résumé, my frequent appearances in the media, it could be said that I was one of those blacks who made the best use of the rights that the Revolution guaranteed to all Cubans.

"Resisting subjectivity is one of my goals when I sit down to write, but I am not obsessed with the issue. I have a scientific approach to the subject, although emotion cannot be absent either. So, I try for a balance between the two poles with the understanding that the problem is a burden for my country and that, as a revolutionary intellectual, I have the duty and the right to add my grain of sand to its study, understanding, and resolution. In historical analysis, we have to be honest and avoid behaving like the ostrich that hides its head while leaving its vulnerable parts exposed."

### Shooting Blanks

Esteban was a student assistant in the School of Economics at the University of Havana, where he received his degree in 1969, then worked there as a professor and at various times directed the School of Political Sciences and the School of Humanities, both at the University of Havana. He said that the most recent chapter in the investigation of the subject was opened by Fidel in March 1959, but that after 1962 there was a long period of silence that, fortunately, has now ended.

EM:    "Yes, the racial problem has been a complicated one throughout our history. It was always a source of contention. Since the late nineteenth century, the U.S. and Spanish colonial justification was that the blacks who fought for the independence of the country were eager to establish a republic in the Haitian style and criticized the authority of Maceo and other black leaders. One hundred years later, the racial problem did not appear in the Moncada Program, though it was a concern for the July 26 Movement and would be included in its plans to establish civil liberties and political democracy. It is no accident that at the end of March 1959, Fidel Castro began to raise the issue in several of his speeches."

*Alma Mater* looked at the March 22, 1959, speech. The Comandante called for a campaign to end the inferior treatment of blacks in Cuba. "There has been in our country," said Fidel,

"the shameful practice of excluding blacks from work. . . . There are two types of racial discrimination: one in cultural or recreational centers, and the other in the workplace. . . . If the first one defines the possibilities of access to certain circles, the other—a thousand times more cruel—limits access to the places where one can earn a living . . . and so we commit the crime of denying to the poorest sector, more than to any other, the possibility of working. . . . There must be a ban and a public commendation against those . . . who have so few scruples as to discriminate against some Cubans . . . because of lighter or darker skin. . . . Let us end racial discrimination . . . and work for an end to that odious and repugnant system."[1]

### Set Afloat

EM:     "However, in 1959, the conflict between Cuba and the United States began to intensify. In January 1961, Washington broke diplomatic relations with Cuba; in April came the mercenary attack at the Bay of Pigs; imperialism continued to support counterrevolutionary bands. So once again there was an environment unfavorable for the study of the problem. The specter of racial difference, seen as a source of social division or an element of divisions within the revolutionary forces, things that the enemy could take advantage of, spread in this period. In 1962, on the threshold of the October Crisis, after sectarianism had been denounced, after the Second Declaration of Havana and the exclusion of Cuba from the OAS, and after the U.S. presidential order establishing the total blockade of commerce between the two countries, the issue 'flew' from the public arena and became taboo. When anyone talked about it, it had to do with an earlier time. The silence lasted until the late 1980s and early 1990s. The crisis that hit us from outside and provoked an internal crisis extended into all areas and set the issue afloat. Despite the great social and human achievements of the Revolution, the issue had not been definitively resolved."

HRS:    *By what signs did it become more or less clear, at the height of the Special Period, that the issue needed resolution?*

EM:     "There were obstacles to employment opportunities—a painful form of discrimination—which, as Fidel said, limits the possibility that a person can make a living, as well as limiting access to higher education and important roles in certain areas. There is another fact: 85 percent of Cubans living abroad are white. Blacks and mestizos make up only 15 percent of the total and they emigrated late, almost without any support in the receiving countries, which was usually the United States. Consequently, they are least able to help their relatives in Cuba. Those in Cuba who receive remittances are essentially white. Among them are intellectuals and people who traditionally had purchasing power."

## *Lack of Conscience*

Esteban wrote several works on the subject and a masterful book, *Challenges of the Racial in Cuba*,[2] presented at the 17th International Book Fair in Cuba, 2008. Its premise was based on an essay on the challenges of color, which received third prize from the jury in the third

International Essay Competition on Countercurrent Thinking, which met in Havana in 2006. In its decision, the jury said the essay offered a critical view of a current issue in our America—the racial and cultural question—and addressed the complex process of lifting the burdens of racism in a revolutionary country.

EM:    "The essay argues that the race problem is perhaps the most complex, 'unknown,' and the most difficult one in our social reality. No other problem causes more anxiety, concern, and distrust. It is easy to find people who do not want to hear anything about it, and if they do hear of it, they decline to comment. Are they unaware that this issue is linked to others such as the economy, equity, human rights, inequality, social justice, marginalization, and religious discrimination?

"The potential outcomes from this problem will depend on who manipulates it and for what purpose. On the negative side, as we have seen, is its potential to create social division; on its positive side, it is linked to the pursuit of social and cultural integration and the struggle for national unity.

"But returning to the matter of ignorance, I mean ignorance in a dual sense: it is true that many people know little about the issue, but there are also many with a weak conscience who coldly prefer to remain ignorant."

### Felicitations from the Cradle?

HRS:    *In our efforts to understand the origins of this problem, might we forget that the burden of discrimination still exists in Cuba?*

EM:    "We might forget that there are some who wish to practice racism. We might even avoid the question of whether Cuban culture is capable of reproducing segregationist attitudes per se. All we need to do is review our history again. Whites, blacks, and mestizos start from the same place. The colonizer with white credentials—and that does not mean they were white—arrived as such, while the blacks were brought as slaves and the mestizos arose out of the mixture. The labels were passed down from one generation to another.

"When it comes to wealth in Cuba, statistics from the bourgeois Republic show that blacks and mestizos had little of it, but after 1959, the fact that the starting places continued to reflect traces of colonialism and neocolonialism shows that five centuries of racism cannot be erased in five decades.

"We talk about the innate prejudicial character of our culture. The Hispanic element has played a dominant role ever since the Discovery. The Cuban scholar Fernando Ortiz concluded that class, race, and culture were all part of the sixteenth-century invasion. Do we understand that?

"Perhaps it is not very difficult today for many Cubans to admit that they are macho, but it is rare to find anyone who admits to being racist. Asked if they are racist, people take offense. Nevertheless, racial discrimination is also a remnant of that birth and development."

### I Hate You, My Love

It is paradoxical, said *Alma Mater*, that despite the discriminatory context of the  hegemonic spirit, from the first color scheme of contrasting black and white tones and the later coding system based on  the differences, that in the end, it all would be cooked up into a "Cuban stew."

EM:     "The levels of race mixture in the Caribbean and Cuba are greater in the English-speaking, French-speaking, and Dutch-speaking Caribbean. There, the processes of social mixing were based on the physical distance between the white masters and the black slaves. Today, all Cubans sing and dance the same. We are not really a Catholic people nor are we seriously religious, but we are syncretic believers combining Christian beliefs with

African religious elements without ceasing to be one people. We have no ethnicities or minorities; we are a multicolored people. I remember the photographic exhibition of the faces of thousands of Cuban artists, athletes, and women that a French photographer presented in the late 1990s in Havana.[3] In them, you can appreciate that we have a spectrum of tones and gradations of black and white, a catalogue of the shapes of lips, mouths, noses, hair, and so on.

"As for Fernando Ortiz's 'Cuban stew,' watch out, the stew is still not boiling and we must continue stirring it and making sure the cooks do not lower the heat. Some people are not interested in being part of the broth where more ingredients are cooked than we could have imagined."

## Only by Exception

Fidel publicly addressed the subject of race again on February 7, 2003. The leader of the Revolution said that, despite the rights and guarantees achieved for all citizens, "the same success in the fight to eradicate differences in the social and economic status of black people had not been achieved."[4] The Comandante took up the subject again on December 5, 2004, at the close of the Eighth Congress of the UJC (Young Communist League). *Alma Mater* checked the text:

"I spoke the words in this paragraph," said the then Cuban president, "without hesitation at the close of the International Pedagogy Congress in 2003. . . . It was something that I carried inside that I wanted to express, the sad legacy of slavery, a society of classes, capitalism, and imperialism. There never was real equality of opportunity anywhere. The possibility of studying, of getting ahead and obtaining a university degree was always the exclusive preserve of the sectors that had more knowledge and economic resources. The poor who escaped this fate were the exception."[5]

EM:     "It took forty-four years, from March 1959 to February 2003. Fidel again encouraged us to continue our study, proclaiming that the progress achieved through socialism had created the foundation, but what was missing was the leap forward. He was right to say that, thanks to the 'Battle of Ideas,' the lives of children, adolescents, the young, and today's Cuban families are no longer what they were in the late 1990s. Racism in Cuba is not institutional. The government, the party, the institutions are not racist. Never before did blacks and mestizos have a government that would defend their interests, but discriminatory burdens remain within the individual conscience, in the attitudes of groups and specific individuals. From this dichotomy comes the force that tries to suppress the subject and, through that conflict, contributes to a resurgence of segregationist ideologies and raises the danger that racism could be reconstructed in the social conscience of the nation."

# 11—Cuba: Science and Race Fifty Years Later

In this three-part article I will try to summarize the research on the race issue done by Cuban intellectuals during the last fifty years, with particular emphasis on race-related scientific essays about negative racial profiling and prejudice in today's Cuba. I will make reference to the output of Cuban authors who live on the island and elsewhere and other articles written by foreign scholars. Some topics related to the history of the race issue are hardly ever addressed or properly understood, a problem we will solve insofar as our need to grasp the full extent of its current signs and dynamics would allow.

## Scientific Research on the Race Issue by the Cuban Academia

In order to go deeper into this subject we should take the following into account:

- The extent of domestic intellectual works on the race issue in Cuba and their connection with other studies done outside Cuba.

- Research works that failed to either approach this topic as a histori-cal issue or appraise its fallout on today's Cuban society and instead made a cursory analysis of slavery or its anthropological nature.
- Intellectual work that takes an in-depth look into this issue from a latter-day perspective and the scientific and institutional obstacles it had to overcome.

We should also bear in mind the difficulties we still face whenever attempts are made to address the race issue in Cuba, especially from a contemporary scientific viewpoint. The main problems are:

1) Lack of sufficient support by our higher education institutions and their research apparatus in general. Most universities and research centers are still reluctant to include this issue in their syllabi or to allow willing students focus their PhD or doctoral thesis on this topic.
2) Lack of an elaborate statistical base that allows cross-referencing social, economic, and political variables, including skin color.
3) The trend to try to dictate a researcher's view on reality and the social sciences as if their research is political in nature and not supposed to serve education, culture, our people, and even their own purposes.
4) The media, mainly the press and TV, which are all but totally unwill-ing and averse, out of ignorance, to address the race issue.
5) Exclusion of the race issue, which is hardly ever mentioned, in our national education system, which fails to provide the required sup-port in terms of human resources, literature, and expertise.
6) The remaining social prejudice against the race issue, seen in general as something likely to cause social division.
7) The discussion agenda of our political, mass media, social, and cul-tural organizations never includes the race issue.

All of the above problems pave the way for a social atmosphere where the race issue is nearly a taboo subject confined to a small number of interested circles. To be fair, however, I have to acknowledge that it has been increasingly addressed since the late '80s and early '90s.

### Research on the Race Issue at Domestic Level

Research on the issue at domestic level has gone through plenty of ups and downs. It was idealistically said to have been dealt with for good back in 1960s, but it was not entirely consigned to oblivion, as it found shelter in literature, dance, theater and the arts, where it thrived on efforts to rescue and ensure the recognition of the Cuban cultural identity and its African roots. And even if political circumstances led us to give our national identity right of way for a long time, many scholars kept paying attention to these cultural concerns.

It is worth mentioning that the race issue was the subject of extensive press coverage in early twentieth-century Cuba by, among others, the black journalists Rafael Serra and Serafín Portuondo Linares. A major project at the time was Gustavo Urrutia's *Ideales de una Raza*, a follow-up to Cuban publications headed by intellectuals, both black and of mixed race, to assert their civil rights publicly. Started in the nineteenth century, this effort was brought to the fore by Juan Gualberto Gómez in magazines like *La Fraternidad, La Igualdad, Minerva,* and others.

Black Cubans made the most of a wide public debate that took place from 1910 to 1930 and stretched to the day of the 1940 Constitution to press for their social rights, but their demands fell on stony ground despite countless reassurances given by parliamentary bureaucracy. After fighting in three wars of independence and lending a hand in the creation of the Cuban nation and its culture, black people's foremost demand was to have their nationality recognized in the Constitution, their point being that the Republic was made up of citizens of all races. Juan Marinello, an outstanding revolutionary intellectual, stated: "A Cuban state cannot claim straightfacedly to be a democracy and go on living a grotesque lie by standing for us as if we were a country of white people when we are not such a thing."

And yet, by 1959 blacks and mestizos were organized in hundreds of societies nationwide to cope with racism—institutional or otherwise—ready for the anti-racist battle that their future promised to be. These societies never came up with any significant academic work on the race issue, but fought nonstop for recognition of their rights in ways that were somehow or other the subject of many newspaper articles. In and around 1940, ideologists like Juan Rene Betancourt and Alberto Arredondo supported black people through important articles against discrimination. In 1959, Sixto Gastón Agüero published *Racismo y mestizaje en Cuba*, and Juan René Betancourt and Alberto Arredondo also wrote articles on race from a theoretical and sociological viewpoint. In that same year, and following up on Fidel Castro's statements about discrimination in the workplace, Ramón Cabrera Torres gave us *Hacia la rehabilitación económica del cubano negro*.

Yet, inasmuch as the revolutionary government itself took on the defense of the subject, all debate-promoting intellectual production faded out, soon followed by the "colored societies," albeit not without resistance in some cases. Thus the topic stopped being related to the political fight waged by blacks and mestizos to become a matter of widespread struggle for equality and social justice.

Why did the blacks and mestizos lose their societies in the early years of the Revolution while the Galicians, Asturians, etc., kept theirs until today? Where was the prejudice that for so long weighed down on the religions of African extraction? These associations of blacks and mestizos were the only casualties of the Revolution's early deinstitutionalization period; they never saw the light of day again because they were considered a blight of times past that we had no use for in the middle of a process that deemed all Cubans equal. Quite a breakthrough if we look back at the old Republic, but also a trap that prevented people from grasping the very essence of inequality concepts inherited by our nation.

All the indications are that the changes that came in the wake of the revolutionary victory took place so quickly that they brought confusion and led many to believe that centuries-long discrimination could be done away with in just a few months. Although it was quite without intention, Comrade Fidel Castro's anti-discrimination speeches added fuel to the flames of the idealistic view that everything was already—or would soon be—completely over.

Since the blacks and mestizos seemed no longer to need to stand up for their rights or have someone else do it in their stead—the Revolution's own institutional nature would do the trick—they welcomed the new circumstances, convinced that they would see all their high aspirations fulfilled in the near future. It turned out, however, that they still had a long way to go to reach their rightful place in our society, as the revolutionary process stripped them of their ammunition when the discriminatory mechanisms on the other side were anything but dismantled.

Therefore, it would not be preposterous at all to try to recover a part of that institutionalization we think we still have use for, especially when it comes to the role the media used to play in the Republic with regard to discussing the race issue. That is how the topic was put aside in favor of efforts to rescue our African roots, mostly by those who would eventually establish the Ethnology and Folklore Institute of the then newly formed Academy of Sciences, including founding director Argeliers León, Rogelio Martínez Furé, Alberto Pedro, Rafael López Valdés, and the then-young scholar Miguel Barnet. This group brought back to life, for instance, the works of Rómulo Lachatañere, who in the 1930s was quite ahead of his time. In 1961, twelve issues of the journal *Actasdel Folklore* were published, which made room for writers like Isaac Barreal, Rogelio Martínez Furé, Alberto Pedro, and Rafael Valdés, among others.

The official proclamation in 1962 that the race issue had been settled was followed by a long period of silence that stretched until the late 1980s, when it was taken up again in a number of publications, though rather confined to slavery-related matters—by José Luciano Franco, Julio Carreras, Carmen Barcia, and Eduardo Torres, to name a few—and not going deeper into the impact of that silence on contemporary Cuba. Based on historic facts, their research contributed greatly to the rescue of our culture's African component, but by overlooking the significant and complicated effects of slavery, they failed to dissect the real race issues facing us in Cuba today.

Our African heritage is vindicated by hundreds of works in every field of the arts, organized as a result of Pedro de la Hoz's praiseworthy endeavor, but they are not focused on the race issue proper, sometimes not even on the very reasons why we are still compelled to defend our culture's African origins. Unfortunately, only here and there do these brilliantly designed works refer to racism and discrimination in Cuba today, if at all. They certainly foster the fight against these evils, but in ways that people often find very difficult to understand.

For all the emblematic films we have made in Cuba—such as *La Ultima Cena* by Tomás Gutiérrez Alea; *Rancheador, Maluala*, etc.— others made in 1960 like *La Decisión* and *Playas del Pueblo* or Sara Gómez's *Guanabacoa, crónica de mi familia*, are virtually the only ones leveling some criticism at the existing racism and class barriers. In most other Cuban movies about slavery or the colonial period there is a gap between the matters related to our African heritage and the treatment of racial stereotyping, prejudice, and racism—in other words, the very issues we are still dealing with in our society nowadays.

## Some Research Works in Cuba after 1959

Some important books were published in the early years, to wit, José Luciano Franco's *Biografía de Antonio Maceo, Afro América* (1961), *La Conspiración de Aponte* (1963), *Plácido* (1964), *La presencia negra en el nuevo mundo* (1968), *Esclavitud, comercio y tráfico de negros* (1972), *Los palenques de los Negros Cimarrones* (1973), *La Diáspora Africana en el Nuevo Mundo* (1975), *Comercio Clandestino de Esclavos* (1980), and *Ensayos sobre el Caribe* (1989).

The first volume of Manuel Moreno Fraginals's *El Ingenio* came out in the mid-1960s, and it has been required reading since. This three-volume book about slavery was finally published in 1978.

There's also Pedro Deschamp Chapeaux, winner of the 1970 UNEAC Award for *El Negro en la Economía Cubana del Siglo XIX*. Others were *La protesta de los Negros Lucumíes* (1966), *Los Batallones de Pardos y Morenos* (1976), and *Los Cimarrones Urbanos* (1983). An early book by this historian was *El Negro en el Periodismo Cubano del Siglo XIX* (1963).

Another remarkable researcher, Juan Pérez de La Riva, added unique notes to this issue through *Contribución a la Historia de la gente sin historia* (1974), *El Barracón y Otros Ensayos* (1975), and *¿Cuántos Africanos fueron traídos a Cuba?* (1976). There's also Julio Carreras with *Esclavitud, abolición y racismo* (1989) and *Los recursos humanos en Cuba* *al comenzar el siglo: inmigración, economía y nacionalidad 1889-1906*, published in *Cuban Studies Yearbook No. 1* (Havana: Editorial Ciencias Sociales, 1975). An honorable mention goes to the work of our national poet Nicolás Guillén, who wrote not only poetry but also plenty of essays and newspaper articles about the race issue.

Walterio Carbonell, a revolutionary closely connected to the student struggle before 1959, worked at the National Library throughout this period, but he did his research at a time when nothing was published about racial discrimination in Cuba. Only in 2005 did the second edition of his book *Como surgió la cultura cubana* come out as part of the library's Escribanía Collection, and it proved to be highly valuable for subsequent discussions. All this research is a key contribution to Cuban historiography, as it is one way or another basically related to the race issue in contemporary Cuba. But as I stress, very few of these works address slavery's obvious impact on Cuban society's ongoing racial problems.

## From the 1980s to Today

Several historiographic contributions made since 1980 are worthy of mention: *Componentes africanos del etnocubano* (1985) by Rafael L. López Valdés; *Esclavitud y sociedad: Notas y documentos para la historia de la esclavitud negra en Cuba* (1986) by Eduardo Torres Cuevas and Eusebio Reyes; *Los que volvieron a África* (1988) by Rodolfo Sarracino; *Burguesía esclavista y abolición* (2004) by Maria del Carmen Barcia, winner of the Casa Award; *Los cimarrones en Cuba* (1988) and *Los palenques en Oriente* (1991) by Gabino de La Rosa; *El negro en Cuba: 1902-1958: Apunte spara la historia de la lucha contra la discriminación racial en Cuba* (1990) by Tomás Fernández Robaina; *La esclavitud desde la esclavitud* (2003) by Gloria García; and *Yoruba: un acercamiento a las raíces* and *De la africanía en Cuba* (1993 and 2007) by Rigoberto Feraudy.

Also important were Jesús Guanche, *Componente sétnicos de la nación-cubana* (1996) and *Etnicidad y racialidad en la Cuba actual* (1998); Argeliers León, *Tras la huella de las civilizaciones negras en América* (2001); Olga Portuondo Zúñiga, *Entre esclavos libres de la Cuba colonial*

(2003); Silvio Castro, *La masacre de los independientes de color* (2002); Elvira Cervera, *El arte paramífue un reto* (2004); Ana Vera, *La familia y las ciencias sociales* (2003); Maria E. Benitez, *La familia cubana* (2003); Juan Pérez de La Riva, *La conquista del espacio cubano* (2004); Fernando Martínez, Rebecca Scott, and Orlando F. García, *Espacios, silencios y los sentidos de la libertad: Cuba entre 1878 y 1912* (2002); Sandra Morales Fundora, *El negro y surepresentación social* (2001); and Francisco Pérez Guzmán, *Radiografía del Ejército Libertador* (2005).

Other works includeTato Quiñones, *A pie de obra* (1990); Nancy Morejón, *Nación y mestizaje en Guillén* (1982); Gema Valdés Acosta, *Los remanentes de las lenguas bantúes en Cuba* (2002); Jesús Guanche, *Transculturación y africanía* (2002); Isaac Barreal, *Retorno a las Raíces* (2001); Gabino La Rosa and Mirtha T. González, *Cazadores de esclavos* (2004); Alessandra Basso Ortiz, *Los Ganga en Cuba* (2005); Lázara Menéndez, *Rodando el coco* (2005); Gloria Garcia, *Conspiraciones y Revueltas* (2003); Rafael Duharte Jiménez, *Nacionalidad e historia* (1991); Aisnara Perea Diaz and Maria de los Angeles Meriño Fuentes, *Esclavitud, familia y parroquia en Cuba* (2006).

Finally, some major works of reference are Carlos Venegas Fornias, *Cuba y sus pueblos: censos y mapas de los siglos XVIII y XIX*, (2002); Esteban Morales, *Desafíos de la problemática racial en Cuba* (2007); Tomás Fernández Robaina, *Cuba: personalidades en el debate racial* (2008); Graciela Chailloux, editor, *De dónde son los cubanos* (2006); and the interviews given to Gisela Aranda between 1990 and 2002 by Pedro Serviat, Eliseo Altunaga, Ignacio Ramonet, Enrique Sosa, Carlos Rafael Rodríguez, Francisco Pissani, Eusebio Leal, Regina Duarte, Eduardo Subirats, Nizia Aguero, and Pedro Deschamp Chapeaux.

Although they do not cover the race issue as such, these works on the topic of social inequality prove very valuable: *Politicas de Atención a la Pobreza y la Desigualdad* (CIPS); *Efectos Sociales del reajuste económico: desigualdad y procesos de complejización de la sociedad cubana* (Luisa Iñiguez); *Territorio y espacio en las desigualdades sociales de la provincia Ciudad de La Habana* (Mariana Ravenet); *Investigación sobre desarrollo humano y equidad en Cuba* (Osvaldo Martínez, 1999); *La erradicación de la pobreza en Cuba* (José L. Rodríguez and George Carriazo); *¿Pobreza,* *marginalidad o exclusión?* (Pablo Rodríguez); *Cuba: efectos sociales de la crisis y el ajuste económico de los 90* (Viviana Togores); *Familia y pobreza en Cuba* (Maria del Carmen Zabala); *Acercamiento al estudio de la pobreza en Cuba: Ingresos y Desigualdad en la Sociedad Cubana* and *Reforma Económica y Población en Condiciones de Riesgo en Ciudad de La Habana* (Angela Ferriol), to name just a few.

I apologize if I forgot to cite some contributions, but I must say—for the sake of the names left unmentioned—that the number of articles and books on slavery, poverty, inequality, marginalization, the formation of our nationality, and other similar subjects that can be classified as studies on race in Cuba is really overwhelming. But the works on race from the standpoint of the survival of racism and racial discrimination in today's Cuba are still very few. Elvira Cervera's research deserves to be particularly highlighted, given the extraordinary experiences she recounts and its stress on family, even if black and mestizo families are regrettably absent from the latter. How can we leave the skin color variable out of our approach to the Cuban family?

With the exception of a few, the research mentioned here fails to properly address the race issue, which is mentioned only indirectly and implicitly. Still and all, it is very important, worthy of consideration, and a useful tool if we keep in mind that the research was done by scholars whose superb scientific skills could come in handy to study race in Cuba today, even if many of them prefer avoiding the subject because of the risk it entails, while others believe the race issue is not worth the trouble.

It would be safe to say that much of this research was done in a period marked by the difficulty of raising an issue officially deemed settled, which no doubt restrained the scope of the work. It was a very serious situation in a sociopolitical context in which those who said there was still racism and discrimination in Cuba were morally and politically chastised.

Some institutions and personalities played an important role in dealing with the race issue and the studies to support research. Pablo Rodríguez, Rodrigo Espina, and Ana Julia García (deceased), among others at the Anthropology Institute of the Ministry of Science, Technology, and the Environment (CITMA), have extensive scientific research under their belt that is yet to be published and therefore impossible to disseminate. Rodríguez and Espina managed to publish some of their best works on race in Cuba as articles in magazines like *Temas* and *Catauro*. Research on racial prejudice, discrimination in the workplace, leadership policy, etc., has been done at CITMA, but much as its findings bring to the fore elements of the race issue in Cuba they can only be consulted by other researchers or a few interested readers. I have personally used many of their results in my book, *Desafíos de la problemática racial en Cuba* (Challenges of the Racial Problem in Cuba).

From the Cuba History Institute I must mention Ohilda Hevia Lanier's work *Directorio Central de Sociedades Negras en Cuba: 1886–1894* (Havana: Editorial Ciencias Sociales, 1996). Ohilda has also been published by *Revista Ciencias Sociales* and other journals and is considered an expert on this subject, just like Olga García, who has devoted a lot of time to studying slavery and recently published *La esclavitud desde la esclavitud*.

At the University of Havana, Dr. Lazara Menéndez is notable for her excellent award-winning research *Rodando el coco* and other articles and studies. As a professor, most of her teaching is confined to the School of Arts, as if to leave no room for doubt that there is a gulf between scientific education and humanistic formation. This knowledge, so helpful to understand Cuban history better, is not even available to historians, let alone our economists or sociologists. I must also mention her monographs on Cuban culture, originally published as *Cuadernos H.*, Publication of the Humanities, University of Havana.

At FLACSO (Latin American School of Social Sciences), María del Carmen Zabala, a professor and researcher who in 1999 got her doctorate, not before overcoming many obstacles, with *Aproximación al estudio de la relación entre familia y pobreza*. She's the only one in our university to have pulled off a dissertation with a race-related topic. Truth be told, the race issue is absent from most syllabi in the Cuban higher education system, and is hardly ever addressed by researchers.

Excelling at this topic in the university's Demographic Studies Center are professors Sonia Catasús, Carlos Albizu, and Eduardo San Marful with their research works on skin color–based demographic dynamics of the population, mortality, fertility, etc., in close connection with ONE (National Bureau of Statistics) with a view to improving our databases.

Finally, the teachings and research works of professors Dr. Digna Castañeda and Dr. María del Carmen Maseda, from the School of Philosophy and History, are worthy of mention. The former has worked extensively in the field of Caribbean studies, and the latter has done plenty of research on Africa. Their results have been a mainstay of this topic for over forty years.

No other school of social sciences or humanities of the University of Havana pays any attention to the race issue. And it is even worse in the rest of our universities. In general, there is too much prejudice in higher education schools and institutions across Cuba for this topic to get the attention it deserves within social research. It was only recently that race as a subject appeared in CITMA's research projects, if in a very individualized and hierarchical manner that separates it from other gender- and inequality-related topics. The reason is that except for a few Cuban academic circles this subject has never received its rightful attention in a society otherwise bent on avoiding it for such a long time.

The main Cuban periodicals devoting space to race issues are *Temas, Catauro, Caminos, Biblioteca Nacional, Santiago, Estudios del Caribe,* and the weekly *La Jiribilla* which, together with the website *Cubarte,* has taken an active part in disseminating the subject in recent years. It's been on the Web where most related articles have been published. But other journals like *Universidad de La Habana, Ciencias Sociales, Casa de las Américas,* etc., have barely printed an article. Others never have.

As a rule, the topic has not been covered by the daily press and magazines. *Bohemia,* for instance, has always stayed away from race issues, and the newspaper *Granma* has only allocated space to recall Comrade Fidel's speeches on the subject in March 1959. *Alma Mater* magazine, in turn, recently published the work of a group of journalism students and an interview, and *Revista Cuba Socialista* also made its debut with an article.

The magazine *Santiago* and the Caribbean Studies Center contain the great historical essays of the late Joel James. Important research and cultural works are done in this center to strengthen Cuba's role in the Caribbean and vice versa. Valuable contributions have been made by

Olga Zúñiga, Rafael Duharte, and Olga Portuondo, mainly through studies on slavery, as well as by Casa de las Américas, especially the work of
Professor Yolanda Wood and National Literature Award winner Nancy
Morejón, whose efforts to develop and promote this topic from a cultural
viewpoint are praiseworthy.

The Juan Marinello Center for Cuban Culture Studies is actively and
effectively involved in research and publication of subjects that increase
our cultural wealth. I am pleased to mention *Catauro de seresmíticos y
legendarios en Cuba* (Manuel Rivero Glean and Gerardo Chávez Spinola,
2005) as a great cultural and practical work. There's also *Socieda des
negras en Cuba: 1878–1960*, by Carmen V. Montejo Arrechea (who
unfortunately has passed away), an excellent research work and essential
reading for those willing to work on these topics, as well as the book
*Estudios sobre Ideales de una Raza*, by young researcher Pedro Cubas. It
was not my intention to list here everything published by the above-mentioned authors, but just a few of the most representative of their works
published mainly as books.

Other centers stand out, like the Fernando Ortiz Foundation and
its anthropological, cultural, sociological, and ethnological studies, the
studies on contemporary racial problems published by its excellent
magazine *Catauro*, and its efforts to promote books and articles that
help understand them, such as Isaac Barreal's *Retorno a lasraíces* and
Carmen Barcia's *Capas populares y modernidad*. The Fernando Ortiz
Foundation promoted the first book since 1960 about the race issue in
contemporary Cuba, *Challenge of the Racial Problem in Cuba*, by the
author of this essay.

The late Leyda Oquendo, an excellent researcher, worked closely
with Casa de África by promoting events, publishing articles, and doing
research on the runaway slaves. In a recent book, renowned historian
Oscar Zanetti says: "The race issue and, particularly, black people's
social status throughout Cuban history, have not been without followers
in the past few decades, even if their stress falls on the anthropological
side of it all. Good examples are the works of Enrique Sosa and Rafael
López Valdés. I could mention many others, but these two suffice to
illustrate my point." I totally agree. With those who fail to address the

race issue from a contemporary viewpoint, those who only do it from an anthropological perspective, and those who stayed in the nineteenth century, we still have very little research about this subject as a current problem of Cuban society.

## Some Research Work on Race in Cuba
## Done Abroad

Though many in-depth studies are carried out in other countries directly related to or critical about the race issue in today's Cuba—as defined in the introduction to this essay—there are still very few of us here on the island who delve into this topic. Moreover, what has been published is very rarely the work of Cuban scholars and intellectuals who live here.

Among the first to write about race was Lourdes Casals, a Cuban who lives in the United States and gave us *Race Relation in Contemporary Cuba* (Minority Rights Group, report No. 7, 1979, 11–27). Then came Miami-based Isabel Castellanos and Jorge Castellanos with their four-volume work *Cultura Afrocubana* (Editorial Universal, 1990–94), and a Haitian intellectual long settled in Cuba, René Depestre, with *Lettre de Cuba* (the magazine *Présence Africaine* 5: 42–105).

More recently we have seen Carlos Moore's *Castro, the Blacks and Africa* and *Pichón*; Jorge de La Fuente's book *Una nación para todos*; and Mark. Q. Sawyer's *Racial Politics in Post-Revolutionary Cuba*. Other books cover different periods, such as those by Rebecca Scott, Aline Helg, Ada Ferrer, and Laurence Glasco. Some of them are of a historical nature, but they are all focused on trying to interpret the situation in modern-day Cuba. These works in general are no different from what we have done in Cuba, except that we have been unable to publish ours, limited and sporadic though they may be, because of practical difficulties.

Those of us who live in Cuba ought to be leading the way in writing about the reality of our life, especially when most of the above scholars draw to a large extent on our own literature and sources. What has enjoyed the privilege of publication is but a pale reflection of the abundant research done by Cuban academia, hardly an advantage for its members, many of whom share their work with colleagues from overseas but without ever acknowledging the need to address our own issues.

Actually, we should be forced not to waive our findings about domestic issues, which must be attended to by no one else, nor let anyone tell our own story or explain our own reality to us. Someone said that "whoever controls our past rules our present," and I would add, ". . . and can design our future behind our back." Therefore, no part of our reality of life should be out of reach of the Cuban intelligentsia's expertise.

Much as the race issue had never ranked high on the list of U.S. centers involved in Cuban studies, the topic has aroused a great deal of interest lately, especially when there seem to be no short supply of funds for that purpose. Besides, many barely academic, scientifically and intellectually poor articles are published, mainly in Miami, by virtually unknown authors motivated to vilify Cuba by political ambitions and economic survival rather than an intention to make a contribution to the subject. Useless to both sides, their treatment of the race issue adds absolutely nothing new, further proved by the fact that no serious scholar who deals with this topic ever refers to them.

To cap it all off, and in line with the above, there is a notably huge difference between the dissemination of race-related art works, books, films, etc., and the efforts to highlight the race issue in today's society. Prejudice—a factor that is gradually, if slowly, passing out of sight—and the holdup of research after long years of silence, ostracism, and repression are important reasons for this. That is why we cannot really flaunt a scientific, alternative discourse of our own, either to learn from or useful to counteract the wrong interpretations, ill-natured or otherwise, made in Cuba or elsewhere.

### Some Final Considerations

If we take stock of the ways the race issue has been approached in the last fifty years, it is easy to see that it was not deemed a specific topic of modern-day Cuba until very recently. And even those of us who do research nowadays still risk misunderstanding and being tagged as divisive and/

or racist by people at any level of society, even if in the last few years the debate has spread and the issue has been a little more popularized.

However, we are extremely behind schedule: not only was the issue hushed up for almost forty years, it is insufficiently addressed today. There is still a gap between the studies on slavery and the realization of its impact on contemporary Cuba. The prejudiced view that it can only feed social division and the failure to consider skin color as a variable of social distinction in today's Cuba have put obstacles before research from methodological, theoretical, and political standpoints that we are just starting, albeit slowly, to overcome.

Above all else, the lack of an articulate academic and political debate and the all but nonexistent media and editorial coverage of this topic have brought forth a phenomenon of cultural dysfunction that we must solve at any cost if we expect to achieve a general, all-embracing cultural dynamics, full social justice, and true democracy. Science must find the proper ways to analyze our race issue from a contemporary viewpoint, which has eluded us for so long.

A fundamental and inescapable element for dealing with our racial problem is the need to do a thorough study about the colonization and slavery in Cuba and its consequences. We have come a long way in this regard, but we are yet to discern a link with the race issue in our society, since as a rule these studies only go as far as the nineteenth century or the early twentieth century.

First Arango y Parreño and then José A. Saco tried to exclude black people from the Cuban society, but they both failed. Nor could they make them disappear by sending them back to Africa or "whitening" our population. In general, the greatest difficulty facing blacks and non-whites in today's Cuba is how to live in a society that for centuries built the cultural mechanisms for their exclusion. What is certain is that there is a racist component underlying our culture that stems from mechanisms generated not only by slavery but also by the biased mentality of Cuban-born whites of European descent who kept seeing black people, slaves or otherwise, as inferior beings, a state of mind they passed on from one generation to the next.

This means, for instance, that a black "whitened" with a title bought by his father was allowed to wear tails, ankle boots, white-collar shirts, a tie, a derby hat, and a watch chain. But if he happened to be stripped of such clothes one day he would be just another black and perhaps even sent to the stocks while things were being settled. All over America, and particularly in Cuba, slavery had one color, and that's a fact that mimicry can do nothing about. As a self-adjusting mechanism, racism is a system, and it operates accordingly. If we only take away a small cog, the other parts will take over the role of the missing one, which means that all levers of the system must be set in motion to keep blacks and non-whites from being discriminated against.

We must educate people and work on their racial awareness, because discrimination springs from ways of thinking with deep roots in, and used as power instruments by, the ruling social elite, and negative racial stereotyping can thus gain a strong foothold in a social context of higher educational and cultural levels. Consequently, education alone is not enough, since we could be creating "cultured racists," who are the worst kind. That is why racial stereotyping, prejudice, and racism grew stronger in the Republic—more educated and cultured than colonial Cuba— because these problems are not just the result of ignorance or lack of knowledge. Instead, they are bred by a social context where racial discrimination in its every form is used as a tool of social control and domination, elitism and exploitation against individuals permanently kept at the lowest strata of society, because classist interests are always the power behind the throne.

That is the reason why education is paramount to put an end to racism even if it's not the sole solution. We must make people fully aware that we do have racial problems, so the key is to provide an anti-racist and anti-discrimination education.

We have made progress and keep striving to foster a debate that is gradually making its way in our country. However, only when our whole society can see the race issue as a major problem that should be discussed by everyone will we be able to find a solution. Racism in today's Cuba is not a matter of color or social groups, but a problem that involves all Cubans. No effort should be spared to fight a dysfunctional trait in our midst and make it go away. It may very well take a long time, but the important thing is that we take the first steps toward that end. The existence of the Grupo de Reflexión Sobre la Racialidad en Cuba, established by the top leaders of the Communist Party of Cuba and headed by our National Library and the Race Commission of the Union of Cuban Writers and Artists (UNEAC), will no doubt smooth the way toward a solution.

# 12—Racism in Cuba
# —An Unresolved Issue: An Interview

by Patricia Grogg

"No issue has been more avoided and disregarded or treated with more prejudice in today's Cuba than the racial problem," warns Esteban Morales, whose countless research works, articles, and essays make of him an authority on a subject highly sensitive in this socialist country. To the author of the book *Challenges of the Racial Problem in Cuba*, it's a topic to be studied and discussed in depth and even included on the political agenda of the Sixth Congress of the Communist Party (PCC) at a date yet to be set.

Morales also knows a thing or two about the United States, where around sixty intellectuals, some of whom enjoy great prestige, have accused Raúl Castro's government of persecuting and harassing people based on their skin color. He believes those accusations "ignore" the reality of his country and fall within the same campaigns that various U.S. administrations have launched for years against the Cuban Revolution.

"We speak of racism and say we must keep improving our civil and democratic rights, not only of blacks, but of the entire society. In that struggle we have allies at the highest levels of the country's political lead-

ership," he affirmed, not without admitting, however, that "the main difficulty" today is to make many people understand that "this is a real problem that must be attacked at its roots."

PG:     *Late in 2009, when U.S. intellectuals accused Cuba of being rac-*
        *ist, a young Cuban professional said they seemed to be talking*
        *about a country very different from hers, even if she was quite*
        *critical of the racial discrimination problems that, in her view,*
        *subsist in Cuban society. What's your opinion? Is there any differ-*
        *ence between the United States and Cuba when it comes to racism?*

EM:     Well, it's a reasonable perception. First of all, it's true that there's
        racism, racial profiling, and discrimination in Cuba nowadays,
        and it's not just a burden, but a phenomenon that Cuban society,
        flawed as it is, has made great strides in effectively addressing.
        But racism in Cuba today is not like racism in the United States
        or elsewhere in this hemisphere.

PG:     *Why the difference?*

EM:     We have to go back in time. The Spanish and the British colo-
        nization were not the same. What they had then in the United
        States was an apartheid-like system where the slaves could not
        sing their songs, speak their language, or practice and develop
        the culture and religious beliefs they had brought from Africa.
        They had to speak in English, even if they could not mix with
        the whites, the only ones who were seen as real persons. British
        slavery strongly discriminated against the blacks, with whom
        relations on either side were very limited at best. That was
        because the British settlers brought their families along, while
        those who came to Cuba were mostly lone men and very few
        women, so naturally the colonists mated first with the native
        women and then with black women.
            As to trade, banking and participation in political decision-
        making, the Spanish colonization was quite inflexible, but not

so much with the cultural and social links with the blacks, I dare saying. Another important fact was that as of 1526 blacks in Cuba could buy their freedom and thus mixed more with whites. There were slaves working on plantations, and not only in the fields but also in the main house, where things were not so strained and the landowner's family was usually friendlier to their slaves and often taught them to read and write, good manners, etc., without forgetting their condition. Of course, these house slaves lived under threat of being sent to the fields or straight to the stocks as punishment for the smallest slip-up.

At any rate, slavery was firmly aimed at leaving blacks culturally impoverished, only with those elements of their culture that would allow whites to make the most of black labor. In the end, the plantation was just a prison secluded from urban life where the blacks received everything they needed to survive, so their only chance to integrate into mainstream Cuban society and culture, if they ever succeeded in buying their freedom or otherwise get it from their master, depended on their age. If they were old, all that remained was for them to lay down and die by the side of the road. After leaving the plantation, many suffered the effects of so-called institutionalization: until then they had everything they needed to live as workers, but once outside they didn't know what to do. Some were luckier and managed to learn a trade or find a job in the city, but the vast majority would just lead a life of social exclusion in slums, where many came to be known as urban runaways.

PG:     *Is that how the blacks eventually began to mix with the whites?*

EM:     Not only that. Cuba went through the so-called whitening process, that is, white landowners would sometimes buy a white-person title for the children they had with slave women, which meant they had to be treated as white and even granted the right to inherit. In some cases, a landowner who expected to die soon would free a favorite slave who had kept him company for many years. Ironic, if we keep in mind that usually the said slave was very old himself and hardly able to enjoy his freedom. This is called *manumission*, something that slaveholders used to their advantage, taking into account that blacks could buy their freedom.

Thus the crossbreeding began. Slavery was not as tough for the mulattos here as it was in the British colonies; still, it was a harsh regime that lasted so long because first of all it brought a great deal of wealth to Spain. In 1886, slavery was officially abolished in Cuba, the last country, but for one other, to do so in our hemisphere. That's why racism here has special traits bequeathed to us by the colonial regime we endured until 1959. A tool of exploitation in Republican times, racism loomed up out of capitalism no more than it ended with it. There's no better example in this hemisphere than Cuba to prove that the end of capitalism by no means entails the end of racism.

The Spanish colonization was somewhat different from the British in that here we had a strong nationalistic and abolitionist current in the second half of the nineteenth century. Then came the sociopolitical process in 1959 that changed Cuba and had a major impact on our human and racial interrelationships, as it gave rise to a certain anti-racist culture and anti-discrimination ethics that has made considerable headway in the last fifty years, even if it's yet to be fulfilled to the gills, as part of our struggle for equality and social justice.

PG:     *All right, but what happened with the racial issue in Republican times?*

EM:     Racism in the island before 1959 was a remnant of a colonial, slave-trading Cuba. Such combination was a key factor in the emergence of a social phenomenon that boomed at the turn of the nineteenth century with the U.S. intervention in Cuba and the control that ensued over a newly formed Republic soon to become a protectorate. In the early twentieth century there were plenty of whites-only signs across Cuba, and even earnest, if fruitless, attempts to found our own Ku Klux Klan in 1910. There was also talk among some people of returning to Africa, a sort of emulation of what was happening in the U.S. those days that never caught on here, where the Cuban blacks had a strong sense of their homeland. They had fought in our wars for independence, on which they had pinned all their hopes for freedom and a better life without ever thinking of going back to Africa, barring very few of them who actually went back. What those blacks did feel was great frustration because most of them came out of the war landless, illiterate, and unable to find a decent job.

Be that as it may, racism in Cuba was never as violent, exclusive, or predatory as in the United States. Here the so-called Little Race War of 1912 led to the creation of the Independent Party of Color and then to the aggravation of already existing racist feelings. We still do not know how many people died then as a result of the attacks against its members and the party's disagreement with the Morúa Amendment,[1] but all indications are that more than 3,000 or 4,000 ended up dead. Those events were really shocking and very upsetting for the Cuban black population, but they are hardly known and mostly ignored by our national education system.

PG:    *Where did the Cuban Revolution's social project go wrong that it failed to eliminate the disadvantages of its black population?*

EM:    With the triumph of the Revolution, social policies treated all poor people equally, and no distinction was made with respect to blacks. However, this was something that should have been done, because the color of one's skin is a strong variable of social differentiation in Cuba. Whites came here of their own free will, with life goals that were often realized, whereas blacks were shipped in by force and turned into slaves, and that's a wound impossible to heal in fifty years of revolution. That's how diverse the origins of the races that make up the Cuban population are and the reason why their impact is still felt today.

But then again, mistakes were made within the revolutionary process. For starters, no social policy made distinctions as to skin color. The goal was to fight a status of poverty that was deemed equal at all social layers. Accordingly, all poor people saw their standard of living improve but the blacks ended up better off, something we only figured out when we were faced with the so-called Special Period. We could establish that the blacks and mulattos were the hardest hit by the recession, as well as the fact that it was more difficult for them to forge a way for themselves in life than it was for whites. That's what we're seeing in Cuba now, described by Fidel Castro as "objective discrimination."[2]

Our second mistake was caused precisely by the situation facing Cuba since the very first days of the Revolution: the confrontation with imperialism, particularly with the United States and its economic war through counterrevolutionary bandits in almost every province, sabotage, assassination attempts, the 1961 mercenary invasion in the Bay of Pigs, Operation Mongoose, and a clash in 1962 that put Cuba on the brink of being caught up in a nuclear war. In that same year, and taking into account that Fidel had leveled fierce criticism at racism—especially in March 1959, when he called it a social scourge that we had to cure—the problem was said to have been solved for good. The idea was to prevent any sign of division underlying the racial issue from coming to the fore right when we Cubans were supposed to be closely united to stand up to the serious problem of the counterrevolution.

There came a long period of silence around the issue, justified with certain views about the need to preserve unity and avoid playing into the enemy's hands with talk of differences. Therefore, given the social pressure of that time, whoever insisted on the subject was labeled as racist and divisive. In those days Cuba was going in quest of equality and social justice for everybody, but also for a kind of egalitarianism capable of smoothing out at least some of the differences, even if it all led to an atmosphere of social and political repression against any attempt at again bringing up the issues of racism and discrimination. There were some, mostly intellectual people, who kept talking about it, for instance, Walterio Carbonell, who were displeased at the silence, but those were rather isolated voices, and right though they were, they had neither impact nor success. We think they were right in that the issue should have never gone unheeded, but the climate then was anything but suitable for such arguments.

Even today some people either react badly to or raise their eyebrows at comments that there's racism and discrimination in Cuba today; you can only imagine how it was like back in the 1960s and '70s, when we had a whole different kind of worries and most people were unwilling to talk about something they considered as settled lest the issue should cause deep divisions in our midst. That's why the main hurdle in front of us these days is how to make people come to terms with the fact that the problem exists and must be tackled with great energy.

PG: *Let's go back to the statement made by U.S. intellectuals, including some of international renown. Do you maintain they're totally wrong?*

EM: Absolutely! Not a few of them have always supported the Cuban Revolution, but now they have been manipulated into signing a document that is way off the mark regarding racial issues in Cuba. Some of them eventually requested their names to be withdrawn from it. Unfortunately, the spirit behind this action is Carlos Moore, whose mercenary activity in Africa is beyond question, as he was a translator for NLFA leader Holden Roberto, with whom he traveled to Washington more than once during his exile in the United States. Besides, the Afro-Cuban Alliance, the Cuban Culture Encounter Association and the "Independent" Libraries for Cuba, all headed by Moore, have been steadily funded by NED, a device created by the U.S. government to channel CIA money into Cuba-oriented subversion.

That is why this document has its little quirks, as it's not solely intended to present an opinion on race relations in contemporary Cuba. It is part of a campaign run by some people in the United States who use some of our problems to dissect racism in Cuba and paint a very bleak picture of things. They lash out at discrimination and racism, but not the way we do it when we fight for black people's civil rights. This is about stereotyping and other long-neglected issues we have to solve here in Cuba. Secondly, they say this gentleman[3] is not in prison for committing a crime but because he's a black man who fights for his people's civil rights, and that's not true. This gentleman is no fighter for any black people's rights, but rather an unknown individual who participates in the internal fight going on in Cuba today against issues that our society must overcome once and for all.

However, they blame our political leaders for what racism and discrimination exist in Cuba and base their criticism on the same arguments usually articulated by various U.S. administrations to accuse Cuba, saying that black Cubans have no human or civil rights and liberties, which means they're up to the same standards as both our home-grown mercenaries and the counterrevolutionary attacks launched from Miami or Washington and by political factions of the so-called internal dissidents. Here we base our criticism on different parameters and never use terms such as totalitarian dictatorship, lack of democracy, or violation of black people's civil rights. Instead, we speak of a fight to be waged by the whole Cuban people to improve a social project aimed at equality and social justice for all Cubans.

Those who signed the statement are also trying to get involved in this kind of criticism to give it a "dissident," counterrevolutionary bias, although I'm sure that many of them would be astonished at the scope and strength of our stance should they become familiar with our situation. We criticize as revolutionaries who take these things almost as self-criticism, aware that, no matter how many problems we have, we blacks would have never come such a long way without a revolution in Cuba. That's what makes our situation so different from any other.

So those of us who fight racism and discrimination in Cuba would be very foolish to let ourselves be swept along by siren songs that promise something better than what we have here nowadays outside the Cuban Revolution and under another political regime. Those who criticize from abroad had better focus their energy on fighting racism and discrimination in the United States and see if they have as much freedom and support there as we do here, because here we have no use for the kind of defense they want to put up, supposedly for our sake.

In an interview with the weekly paper *Trabajadores* on December 14, 2009, I said that we must improve democracy and civil rights, not only for black people but for the whole society. Racism in Cuba is not institutional, nor a sectoral problem. Even if it should look like it in some cases, it is not consciously practiced by our institutions or following a guideline laid down by the Communist Party or the government. It is a multifaceted phenomenon that concerns society as a whole, opposed first of all by the joint forces of the said party and government. And at the forefront of the fight is Fidel Castro, the first who raised this subject in 1959 and then took it up again in conferences of teachers, the Congress of the Union of Cuban Artists and Writers (UNEAC), and other meetings held during the years of the Special Period.

EM:     *You have said more than once that racism in Cuba is not insti-*
        *tutional, but also that people in this country are raised "to be*
        *white." Can you explain this contradiction, and do you believe*
        *it's fair to consider such contradictions as forms of "institution-*
        *alized" racism?*

EM:     Yes, it's a certain form of institutionalization, not based on a con-
        scious political provision but because of flaws and errors in the

educational process, the teaching of history—Africa, Asia, and the Middle East are far from being sufficiently studied—and the lack of racial representativeness in our books. And we can blame it on our education authorities no more than on some aspects and problems of social life and dysfunctions and imperfections of our society. It is not because there's a given institution that practices racism based on any superstructural consciousness or by means of any organized ideology.

PG:     *To be precise, how does this education to be white become apparent?*

EM:     We must get rid of some pro-Western traits of our education that have been hanging over us for years; we must teach history in greater depth and make our literature more diverse from the point of view of our racial diversity. We must discuss racial discrimination in our schools, so that our students can react properly in defense of our multicolored culture whenever they are the target of, or otherwise witness to, a racist attitude in our streets. Owing to inadequacies of our education about Africa, Asia, and the Middle East, our students graduate without really knowing the origins of our culture. What general, comprehensive knowledge about Cuban culture can we flaunt when all studies on slavery stop at the nineteenth century without addressing its effects on our present society?

Actually, education should be biased toward no specific color. But if we leave the color issue out of the equation in a multiracial, multicolored society still ruled by whites, we would be teaching people to be white for all intents and purposes, and more so if there are other barriers to a balanced role of color in our education. It's easy to see that our schools teach very little about race. Some of José Martí's phrases are repeated to no end, for instance, "A Cuban is more than white, more than mulatto, more than black," going no further than their ethical content without studying their meaning in greater depth.[4] As a result, José Martí's thoughts about race are less taught in Cuban schools than José Antonio Saco's theses with his disapproval of blacks and his famous appeal to "whiten, whiten, whiten and then gain everyone's respect." What's more, Saco would feel encouraged in Cuba today by our "whitening" practices, the argument of the "advance of the race," and the trend you still see out there among black people toward not coming to terms with, or refusing flat out, their blackness. Truth is, we don't fight stereotyping, discrimination, and racism as fiercely as we should.

We should ask ourselves whether these ideas about race can really put down roots here if our schools fail to instill them in the new generations, never mention color, take the study of slavery no further than the nineteenth century, and hardly cover Africa, Asia, and the Middle East, and if our scientists seldom delve into the race issue. Only in the last twenty years has the subject been covered again, and timidly at that. This being said, the conclusion is self-evident. It's not that we have a problem for not internalizing the race issue: to make things worse, the concepts about race that prevail in Cuba nowadays seem to be those championed by nineteenth-century liberals like José Antonio Saco, whose views are now more of a factor than the nationalistic and anti-racist positions that others adopted then against discrimination, slavery, and colonization in favor of our independence. That is why by leaving the race issue untouched we cause a far graver problem than we can imagine.

PG:     *From a cultural standpoint, sometimes it seems that blackness becomes all but a thing of folklore.*

EM:     Not only that. There's also discrimination against African religions that people often tag obscurantist without taking into account the ethical, cultural, and philosophical patrimony they endow our life with, as in the case of *la regla de Palo Monte, Ocha y otras.* My grandmothers had concepts of education, diet, health, ethics and good manners that they learned from neither a pro-Western education nor many years of schooling, but from a deep-seated family tradition to appraise certain ethical values sprung from their own religious beliefs and principles which sometimes originated with slavery itself. Yet, too many people still call those religions obscurantist, even if to the shame of quite a few of them, but they managed to prevail and become the key to the religiosity of the Cuban people, be they white, mulatto, or black.

However, things were different in times of capitalism, when black Cubans were not allowed in companies, banks, industries, or department stores in Havana. But even if the Revolution put an end to all that and made it illegal and wrong, there may still be isolated cases that we must counteract through society's cultural, economic, and political life. A personnel manager may fire a black worker or be more demanding with them, but that manager will never say it is because the worker is black, so we stress the importance of making it impossible for any manager to get away with something like that in violation of the laws promulgated by our state. We must come up with solutions against discrimination in everyday life instead of leaving it to people's conscience, to subjectivity, or to spontaneity.

PG:    *Do you think black people don't know how to make their rights count?*

EM:    Yes, I do. The lack of a race consciousness is such a serious problem that you would think we are trying to go back in time. It is no big deal to the so-called whites because they have always been on top, but the blacks and mulattos must be aware of the need to fight for their rights, act on their conscience to eradicate racism, and find their own place in Cuban society, and understand that they must fight as well for their identity as blacks and mulattos, and be clever enough to realize when they are being discriminated against for being black, since blackness fits into their identity by their own right and historical background.

Black people in the United States have little protection what-
soever from the institutional, legal, or any other point of view.
Here in Cuba we try to enhance that protection both at the individual and at the collective level through our revolutionary institutions. We still have some racism, but without race consciousness there's nothing we can do about it. I must be aware of the
fact that I don't live in a perfect society where everyone is willing
to respect my rights. And I must be aware as an individual that
I have to strive to assert my rights regardless of the protection I
can get from the state, the government, and our institutions.

There are two learning channels on Cuban TV where until
very recently you would see no black or mulatto faces. Some cast-
ing directors choose only white actors and actresses and, with a
few rare exceptions, our black performers seldom land a leading role in a soap opera. I've even heard some cameramen assure
that "black doesn't televise" well. Until quite recently we had TV
programs for children where not just a few but almost all children
were blond-haired and blue-eyed. We're just starting to make
some progress in this regard, but very little has been achieved.

PG:     *Would you say then that racism is a matter yet to be resolved in
        Cuba?*

EM:     Yes, because it still lives in people's conscience and in our family,
        and also in some institutions, even if it's morally and socially pun-
        ishable. It's something impossible to eradicate in fifty years; we
        need to work hard on every generation's educational and cultural
        level and sniff out racism from its administrative hideouts, with-
        out forgetting the part about equal economic opportunities for
        all, because there are many places where blacks are nowhere to
        be seen in leading positions, namely—and especially—in tourist
        facilities, foreign firms, etc., where the dollar economy prevails.

PG:     *If racism shows up in so many ways in your society despite institu-
        tional Cuba's rejection, what failed or what remains to be done?*

EM:     Much remains to be done to make up for our failure to pay due attention to this issue when we pronounced it settled in 1962, and since. Only in the last twenty years have we put it on the table again, but without really definite results in practice, as we still have to knock on some "private" doors and penetrate some "exclusive groups" whose ranks are tightly closed to keep 'outsiders' away.

PG:     *So the problem was pronounced settled when it still existed?*

EM:     Yes, out of sheer stubbornness and idealism and for political considerations, since it was believed to be potentially dangerous to our unity then. I agree that the '60s and the '70s were critical to the survival of the Revolution, and also that you have to be very careful when debating a thorny issue lest it should cause a rift in the fabric of society. But I think people need to know, in light of what we've been through, that the problem is real so they can identify its symptoms and how harmful they are not only to the blacks and mulattos but to the revolutionary project itself. People should understand that not all Cubans are alike. We're all equal in the eyes of the law, but social equality is a more complicated matter that goes beyond economics, politics, or ideology to become a many-sided phenomenon linked to our culture and identity.

        We must start from the premise that there's inequality. Equality is our ultimate goal and greatest wish, but every day we come up against inequality and disparity. We must be well aware of that fact if we ever expect to eliminate inequality. Only then will true, long-lasting equality be possible. It's a big mistake to believe that we're all cast in the same mold. We must become aware that there's inequality, and despite a long-drawn-out struggle that took us to the very edge of egalitarianism we have serious problems in that respect, not only the ones we have inherited but also others that we have left to grow and spread out as a result of imperfections in our social model, which has to be improved and cleared of malfunctioning traits that won't disappear by themselves. Much as we aspire to have full equality, we still run up against all sorts of snags. In some respects we will have to make do with some balance, say, the fact that some people get remittances and others don't—that's not in our power. Over 80 percent of the Cubans who left for the United States are white, while only 15 percent are blacks and mulattos. The former send more money because the latter arrived in that country too late and in general had less support to find the best jobs.

I've traveled through Miami about forty times, and rare is the day when you see at the airport more than two or three black families standing in line to fly to Cuba. That is a sign that most of the money comes from white Cubans, who are in a better position to help their family in Cuba because they started to arrive in the United States in 1959 and received help from their relatives there, whereas the blacks first started to leave en masse through the Mariel boat lift in 1980, only to find that the big party was already over and there was nothing but leftovers from the big feast laid on precisely for those who most discriminated against blacks and mulattos in Cuba. That is why the blacks have the worst jobs and fewer opportunities to send packages and dollars to their families, a fact particularly noticeable during the Special Period. It is the whites and the intellectuals, not the blacks, the mulattos, or the workers, who get most of those remittances.

PG: *Why are poverty and marginalization more common among black Cubans when your policies on education, just to mention a major stepping stone to the top of the social scale, make it free and equal for everyone?*

EM: That is because the whites have always had a significant lead over the blacks in several respects, including culture. Blacks have a lower cultural level and less self-esteem; they lagged behind in the race for the best places in the big picture and are less prepared to get by in society. Culture is about knowing how to live, so the blacks are at a disadvantage and are the ones who more often than not choose to excel in negative areas when they realize that the best options have been denied them.

As a social group, the blacks have usually had less access to wealth and general culture and not much chance of playing an important role in the scientific-technical revolution of a pre-dominantly white society. Throw in the fact that, historically, they have been given the worst jobs, are discriminated against on account of the color of their skin, forced to live in the poorest neighborhoods, and left to make their life contingent on whether they have a computer at home, a family that urges them to study, and the consumer goods they need to live. Hence Fidel's words, when he talked about 'objective discrimination' in connection with the allotment of knowledge and the chances to enjoy decent standards of living.

There was a time when I argued about these things at length. For instance, every year a report on poverty in Havana was pre-sented that I would oppose without fail, telling the authors that their work would be incomplete and they would never really find poverty if the variable of skin color was not measured; for it's the blacks with whom poverty really resides. And when they did, they reached another, far more accurate conclusion: being poor and white is quite different from being poor and black or mulatto. If on top of that you're a black woman, then you have a third cross to bear.

PG:     *Whatever happened to all the social projects of revolution?*

EM:     For years those social projects failed to take skin color into account. They do now, because the Special Period made us see that despite our many achievements in education, culture, and technology, black people are still on the bottom. If you visit the Genetic Engineering Center today you will see plenty of black doctors, experts and researchers, but if you drop by certain neighborhoods you will see mostly black people playing dominos, drinking, or otherwise killing time, ignored by society. It's the reason that our prison population is mostly black, because society has put them at a disadvantage and therefore turned them into the most prone to commit crimes. Not because of the color of their skin, but for having suffered like no one else from the scourge of slavery, racism, and discrimination that the Republic bred and the Revolution has been unable to pluck out even after half a century.

PG:    *When were those problems brought to light for the first time?*

EM:    Since the onset of the Special Period, Fidel personally gave directions to that effect. We had in Havana 80,000 youths, most of them blacks and mulattos, who neither worked nor went to school. That's what set in motion the Social Workers Program and other useful plans to channel our efforts into the search for solutions to a number of problems. Back then I had 70 students in my class, 14 of them blacks and mulattos. It was then that the university began to "go whiter." Of those 14, only 6 remained at the end of the semester, all of them Ethiopians who had come to study here. The black Cubans had dropped out as they rushed off to find a way to survive and support their families. It's a situation you could drag on for generations on end if you don't attack the problem at its roots.

I'm the only intellectual in my family. My children followed in their parents' steps and went to the university, but in my time I was the only one who could do so. My father was a carpenter, my mother a housewife, and both my grandmothers were domestic servants. None of my brothers ever graduated from the university. My father was a wonderful man who loved me very much, but there were five of us living in one bedroom and we had to turn off the lights at ten p.m. sharp because he had to get up at four in the morning. When I needed to study I had to sit under the only light bulb there was in the courtyard of the tenement house, or else do it by candlelight.

PG:     *What's your personal experience in these matters? Have you felt*
        *excluded or discriminated against at some point because of the*
        *color of your skin?*

EM:     I must admit that from 1959 until the present day I have felt
        discriminated on the odd occasion. However, I had a terrible
        experience in my hometown before 1959. I had sat a competi-
        tive examination in 1953 to apply for a student grant offered by
        the local Catholic school, and I was required to write an essay on
        José Martí. The application form demanded no photographs,
        but when they notified me that I had won and I appeared before
        the examining board, there was a buzz in the room. At first they
        asked me to wait outside, but one of the board members was a
        Catholic gentleman who was married to the lady of the house
        where my grandmother was hired as a maid and it seems that he
        put in a good word for me, because in the end they took me. Being
        from a poor family, that scholarship was my ticket to college, so
        I went to the school of the Trinitarians in the town of Cardenas,
        where the priests treated me like dirt and discriminated against
        me. One of them, however, who was Italian, treated me well.
        Then came the Revolution, my enrollment in the Young Rebels
        Association, a five-year stint as a voluntary teacher in the Sierra
        Maestra and then in the province of Holguin, and my deploy-
        ment as an artilleryman during the Missile Crisis. I went to the
        university together with many children of workers and peasants,
        so I did not feel any discrimination then, nor have I felt it since,
        thanks to my education as an intellectual, which I use as a fire-
        wall of sorts against whoever pretends to make me feel bad.

        I know some who spoke out against racism and were either
        fired or demoted as a result. Another member of my family who
        could have made it to the university was an uncle whose father
        was a moneylender and a rip-off artist who could have paid for
        the trips from Cardenas to Havana, not to mention the price of
        clothing and lodging and the tuition fees, a luxury no poor peo-
        ple were able to afford. In general, no blacks or poor whites could

study at the University of Havana before 1959. We're discussing race, but let's never forget the class issue. Thing is, a poor black person is discriminated twice over. Take the case of the United States, where the difficulties to raise the money for the tuition fees have become a standing issue that even American films have covered. Why were so many blacks of both sexes working as teachers? Because it was one of the few decent jobs available to them after a short time in a training college. That also explains why very few blacks were doctor, or lawyers.

PG:    *According to the latest census in the island, 10 percent of the Cubans are black and about 25 percent of them are mulattos, while others hold that black people are in the majority and place the figure above 62 percent. What can you say about it?*

EM:    Our statistics on race are quite contradictory. Not long ago I published a paper titled "Skin color and Statistics." Let's take the case of the United States as an example. I have studied U.S. economics in depth, and I can tell at a glance that the federal rate of unemployment—currently at 10.2 percent—is different in every state, but then the demographic data on unemployment show that the figure is 20 percent among Hispanics and 30 percent among African Americans (and up to 40 to 50 percent in the 25-to-35 age group). I believe we must review our figures and take not only skin color but also other social parameters into account. That is why some say that 35 percent of Cubans are black and mulattos or that only 10 percent are black. There's a certain trend toward crossbreeding that accounts for the higher number of mulattos and vice versa, but I honestly think that more than 60 percent of the Cuban population is made up of non-whites. Cuba has proved to be one of the countries in this hemisphere where the presumption of whiteness doesn't tally with the facts about how many people really are white or black, so much so if we bear in mind that many non-whites fail to see themselves as blacks or mulattos. No newborn child's skin color is registered. In the pictures they took of me when I was born I look white, even if both my parents were black.

PG:    *Do the mulattos admit to their skin color or do they see themselves as white?*

EM:    There's a whitening phenomenon going on here that gained special momentum in the eighteenth century under José Antonio Saco, for whom black people had no place in our nationality. There are many black people who have yet to come to grips with their skin color, and other influencing phenomena like the so-called advance of the race. No survey application form registered the subject's race. We did in the 1970 census, but the data were never processed. Needless to say, a truly inconceivable mistake. After 1981 we made an offprint classifying the Cubans according to skin color, but it's hardly of any help to make comparisons. My eldest son is your typical mulatto; he once lost his ID, and when he applied for a new one he had to declare what his race was. He wrote down "black," but they told him that it couldn't be, so he said, "Well, mulatto," and again they said, "That doesn't exist," and finally they wrote down "white" on his ID. Incredible, the degree of prejudice underlying these cases, as our census revealed.

       "We have always had qualms about color-based figures. Suffice it to check the social data we send to the United Nations every year, which we publish in statistical yearbooks and which I cite in my essay "Skin Color: Nation, Identity and Culture." I don't want to hear anymore that Cuba has this or that rate of unemployment; what I want to know is what color are those people who have no jobs and where do they live, for I assume that if we have a social project we must measure its progress starting from the lower strata, where we find the most backward and destitute. We don't seem to realize, and this also goes for our statisticians, how deceitful the analysis of a social problem can be that neglects skin color.[5]

All studies on any specific issue, be they on housing, job-lessness, family income, who receives remittances, education, domestic violence, or even death, bring to light this problem. It's a fact that we are different on the basis of skin color, and for a very simple reason: barring a few honorable exceptions, our research work is bogged down in the nineteenth century even though slavery still has social fallout, despite fifty years of revo-lution. Before 1959 there were around 800 tenement buildings in Havana, and now there are more than 2,000. Why? Because in Havana we have seen a massive influx of people from the countryside, mostly blacks and mulattos from eastern Cuba bent on making a living in the capital city no matter how. What can be gathered from this fact is that a dissection of the problem in other provinces seems to be in order, as long as it allows for the variable of skin color in the fields that I mentioned above. Color must be present in each and every study we carry out, keeping in mind that since crossbreeding is fairly commonplace among us we tend to disregard it, and then the more comprehensive your survey the easier it is to see that the blacks are at the bottom and the whites at the top, with the mulattos in between, which leaves us with a socio-demographic structure that we have been unable to modify.

PG:     *Do you propose a specific policy for black people?*

EM:     In Cuba we have implemented a certain "affirmative action" policy—although we do not use that name—based on in-depth studies about family, children, the disabled, and other social groups that lead to practical affirmative action for the benefit of the least favored, most of whom are blacks and mulattos. We're still keeping an eye on poverty, but devoting special attention to these race groups, who are the worst off.

PG:     *Do you believe then that the black population in Cuba is vulnerable?*

EM:   The blacks are the most vulnerable, so when a black and a white is competing on the same terms to fill a vacancy, the former should have right of way. Raúl Castro said that it was a mistake to rely on a quota system to secure equality. Universities in the United States allot specific quotas to blacks and other minorities—what some call reverse racism—but that is as wrong as it is discriminatory, and therefore the object of widespread debate in that country. This is not a matter of telling someone, "Hey, you can come and study in this university because you are black." Our affirmative action formula, spearheaded by social workers, involves training these people for a future job. A quota system cannot possibly be the solution.

PG:   *If the Cuban president himself has touched upon this issue, why isn't there more debate?*

EM:   Discussion is gaining ground in intellectual circles and cultural community centers. I gave an interview in October 2007 that was published in the magazine *Alma Mater*, which few people ever read, but another one has just appeared in the newspaper *Trabajadores*, which most people read, a sign that the topic is getting more and more attention with every passing day. Cuban society must be aware that we all have to pull together to solve the race issue, starting with education to instill anti-discrimination principles in everyone from an early age. What stays out of school stays out of our culture. We must talk about it at home and in the workplace, as well as within our social and political mass organizations. That's what we call for. I have black friends, party members to boot, who say, "No way my daughter will marry a white man"—and vice versa—because racism among blacks has become part of their culture as a reaction to white people's racism. Our media, especially our television, must pay special attention to that problem.

PG:     *What if what happened before happens again and some people decide that such discussions might fuel division and be used against the Revolution?*

EM:     On the contrary, failure to put the subject on the table, which is at the root of every anti-Cuban campaign, is what can really divide us and torpedo our sociopolitical unity beyond repair. A discourse totally divorced from our reality, as when we make foolish statements along the lines that there's no such thing as racism in Cuba, is what really harms us from the political standpoint. Many of my friends in the United States translate and distribute my articles and books so as to let it be known that this issue has long been debated in Cuba and to prevent others from twisting our ideas about racism into a dissenting speech or putting it into the context of the Cuba-U.S. dispute to use it as still another instrument of subversion and hostility. Mark my words, if it were not for the Revolution, we black people would have had to sweat blood to accomplish what some of us have, so we won't just let anyone link this issue to our social conflict and hand it to the opposition on a platter. It is a feature of our reality that we can even chat about among friends, but one we must tackle and overcome by ourselves. We just cannot let others be in charge of our own history, because he who controls your past also controls your present and future life.

PG:     *Are you against the participation of the internal opposition in this debate?*

EM:     There is no room in this debate for the so-called dissidents because they always give it a touch of counterrevolution. If we have made it this far with the race issue it is only because we have a revolution, and we would have accomplished more if we had taken up the subject earlier. What may certainly divide Cuba in these times is any attempt at brushing aside a problem that brings so much suffering to black and white people alike, because in the final analysis the Revolution has managed to inculcate in us sound anti-discrimination principles. It's absurd to talk about wholesome culture in a society where people are not yet color-blind. What true democracy can we claim to have if there's racism? The finish line in the race for equality may never be reached, but all runners in society must be able to compete on an equal footing. The Cuban Revolution has given blacks and mulattos plenty of opportunities, but the fact that these race groups started from different historic premises, the combination of past mistakes and present flaws and our neglect of the race issue have often prevented it from reaching that goal.

PG:     *Do you think then that race should be an item on the political agenda?*

EM:     Of course it should, and to that effect some studies on race are now under way in a party commission that Esteban Lazo headed for many months before it was placed within the National Library's jurisdiction. Furthermore, a standing commission on racism and discrimination was established by UNEAC whose foremost objective is to undertake actions and organize discussions conducive to a political agenda. These are multi-race commissions whose members must be experts on the subject or otherwise be involved with it. And the fact that President Raúl Castro raised the issue in his speech to the Parliament on December 20, 2008, makes me think that it will be on the agenda for the next congress of the party. Maybe not, but at any rate I believe it should be.

More dissemination will of necessity turn it into a political issue, so we keep calling for the establishment of an ad hoc parliamentary commission. There's still a lot of prejudice, but not as much as in previous years. I've published several essays and a book that many people have bought, and a second book will soon come out in the United States and Venezuela. However, there is very little TV coverage yet. This is actually a domestic discussion, one to be held on this side of the Malecon,[6] as we say, and in response to no one, and it's getting stronger by the day. So if hurting us and launching a political attack on the Revolution out of the whole thing—definitely no laughing matter—is what those critics had in mind, their plans have surely backfired on them: never before has this battle aroused so much enthusiasm in Cuba.

A community project called *Cofradfa de fa Negritud* [Brotherhood of Blackness] is also playing an active role on account of their sound approach to the subject, as I witnessed days ago when I gave a talk at their General Assembly. Its membership comprises not only intellectuals, but also many ordinary citizens who engage these topics with a fresher, more straightforward style and work very hard to raise people's awareness through public debate in our neighborhoods about the documentary film *Raza*, made by the young Cuban filmmaker Eric Corvalan, shown already in the United States and other countries. Another interesting detail is that what we write is being published. A collection of articles on race and racism compiled by Esther Perez and Marcel Lueiro, from the Martin Luther King Center, was put on sale recently, and in February the Havana International Book Fair hosted a number of presentations and a very successful panel discussion. As I said, the race issue is breaking new ground.

# 13—Cuba Is the Only Country where Blacks and Mestizos Have Government as Their Ally: An Interview in Trabajadores

by Ana Margarita Gonzalez and Rafael Hojas Martinez

This interview with Esteban Morales appeared in the December 14, 2009, edition of the Cuban newspaper *Trabajadores*. In this interview Morales responds to a slander campaign organized by Carlos Moore, a decades-long opponent of the Cuban Revolution that charges the Cuban government with sanctioning racial discrimination.

EM:    It would be absurd to think that in Cuba there are no racial problems, negative stereotypes, discrimination, or racism that exist as deadweight, but not only as deadweight but also as something that an imperfect society is still able to reproduce. The recent declaration by some Afro-Americans supposedly supporting the struggle for civil rights in our country manipulates and magnifies these problems, trying to make it seem that the racial problem in Cuba is similar to any other country in the hemisphere, which is not true.

The above is the point of view of Dr. Esteban Morales, political scientist and essayist, signer of the message sent by Cuban intellectuals to their Afro-American colleagues, in which they reflect on the truth of this controversial subject.

EM:      The fundamental weakness of their declaration is that their criticism is based on the same pillars that, historically, the U.S. government has used, arguing that there is a totalitarian dictatorship here, that we are a country without human rights, no democracy for blacks, and blaming the problems on the government and political leadership. The humanitarian policies of the Revolution have helped overcome this obstacle. Institutional racism does not exist. It is a phenomenon that was dragged along and reproduced during a relatively long period, during which we were not paying attention. In 1962 we idealistically proclaimed that racism was resolved, but what it did was hide itself, and it reemerged in the midst of the economic crisis. As opposed to what critics of Cuba suggest, it is Fidel Castro himself who, in March 1959, in a number of speeches, recognized the existence of racism and discrimination and the necessity of doing away with it and seeing it as a social defect. He himself returned to this theme during the Special Period at Union of Artists and Writers of Cuba congresses and at meetings on teaching. And his arguments are still valid.

AMG/RHM: *Why do these symptoms persist?*

EM:      We have made mistakes. The first: the idealist conception that the Revolution's policies would cause racism to slowly disappear like other scourges from the past that we inherited. Cuba may be the country that has advanced the most in its eradication, especially in the inequality and injustice that goes hand in hand with it, but fifty years of revolution, as radical as it may have been, are not enough to end a problem of 450 years of colonialism. All of us Cubans must continue struggling against this deformation, in education, in culture, in the media, to make people conscious that the problem exists and must be solved. It is not possible to speak of a general, unified culture if this is not resolved, but the Cuban reality is quite far from, for example, that of the United States, which is the most racist society the world has ever known, despite having elected a black president.

In our country we have many shortcomings in the teaching of history. The multicoloredness does not get into the books the way it should, the racial question is not mentioned or explained, and the near-complete absence of Africa, Asia, and the Mideast makes it difficult for kids to leave school with a deep sense of the roots of Cuban culture. The difficulties are being discussed in national commissions created to deal with this.

The second error was to not take into account variations in skin color, which is an index of social differentiation, and is the starting point for the racial groups that shaped our country. The Spanish came here of their own volition, the blacks were brought over in slave ships, caught on the west coast of Africa or sold by their own tribes. They became the slaves, which in this part of the world was based on color. In classical slavery, the slave could be blond or blue-eyed. Here it was the Indian or the black. From the mixing of these and others came the Cuban color.

Walk the streets of Havana today and you'll see what I am talking about. Despite the fact that there are many young blacks working at the Center for Genetic Engineering and Biotechnology, in our barrios you'll find many marginalized people who don't succeed in taking advantage of, or reaching, all the benefits the Revolution has provided. And they do not because their starting points were different. You can see this in many parameters of daily life: housing, quality of employment, institutional support, access to jobs in the public and private sectors, above all in the so-called new economy. The level of democracy and civil rights we have achieved is the same for all racial groups. The extent to which we have to improve is the same for everyone. Some will take better advantage than others because they are in a better position to do so. The racial question in our country is not simply economic. It has to do with everything, and, politically, the topic should be on the agenda of all the organizations and discussed.

AMG/RHM: *So, another attack on the Revolution?*

EM:     These people, the African Americans who have issued this declaration, grab onto our difficulties to attack the Revolution. However, Cuba is the only country in the world in which blacks and mestizos have the state and government as their ally. If there had not been a revolution, the blacks would have had to make one in order to reach the level that more than a few of us have achieved.

   I am convinced that some of the signers did not know what they were signing. They were manipulated, and one person asked to have her name taken off because she realized that there were distortions, that they were trying to twist reality, to inject themselves into an internal debate and turn it into something to do with "dissidents."

AMG/RHM: *Cuban aid to African nations: proof that the Cuban Revolution is not racist?*

EM:     It is a piece of evidence. The fact that Cuban doctors, teachers, and medical technicians—white and black—go to the most remote places in the world to help those who need help, is evidence, but it is "practical" evidence. We need theory, because at the same time we are doing that, we are not dealing with the racial problem openly, completely, and profoundly, as we must do internally.

This is a contradiction; it would appear to be demagogy. We dealt very well with it on the outside, we're friends of the blacks, the Indians, and the wretched of the earth, but here there was a certain atmosphere of social repression, where to speak of racism could get you called racist and divisive. We used to think that it was not necessary to talk about it, that it was going to be resolved simply through the unfolding of profoundly humanistic policies. It is proven that even after capitalism ends, racism remains in the consciousness, in the institutions, in people's way of life.

AMG/RHM: *There are experts who say that this declaration could affect the Obama government. What do you think?*

EM:     We cannot know exactly what effects it will cause. Obama has always tried to keep away from the racial question, including not being able to present himself as a black candidate. He tried to sidestep it, and he did. But Obama has once again revived the restrictions and charges against Cuba and this declaration goes in the same direction. The document these people signed is being discredited as witnessed by the fact that ours is gaining signers and theirs is losing them.

In the United States there is a great deal of sensitivity to this problem. At times there have been quotas for blacks in our organizations in order to guarantee representation. Is this an example of racism? It was a failed attempt, a mistake as to the form which we believed could solve the problem of representation. But the problem is more complex. We have a lot of people who, although they are black, don't think of themselves that way.

There is a phenomenon of whitening, and if you as a black do not come out and say what you are, it is a demagogic posture, it's not ethical. In Cuban culture it is absolutely necessary that people come to terms with and be what they are. The challenge is to create a consciousness without racial prejudice, stereotypes, and racism.

It is necessary to create all the conditions for educating girls and boys in this process and we need others in the area of culture, of empowerment and economic quality. Between you and me there could be economic equality but not social equality, there could be legal equality but not social equality. Social equality is something much more complex.

The fact that we were all born in the same hospital, that we go to the same recreation centers, to the same schools, has no fixed meaning. From the social point of view it is deeper, a phenomenon that passes from generation to generation, which implies being conscious that equality is the goal. The difference is what we run up against every day. Social equality is an integrated system in which individuals have to deal with their identity. "I'm Cuban, an intellectual, a party militant, and black, that's who I am." All mixed together.

# 14—Affirmative Action: An Incitement to Debate?

Race or skin color must never be the ultimate premise for a person's right to certain social benefits. Whoever starts from such a premise in Cuba is no doubt a racist individual acting behind society's back. But as long as racism exists, "race" will be considered a premise to favor some individuals over others who are in all cases members of a "race" deemed inferior. Even the destitute will always be discriminated against just because they're poor.[1] For more than fifty years Cuba has practiced remarkably humanitarian social policies that have pushed all disparities and inequalities to the very edge of egalitarianism. Much has been achieved by this policy as far as the improvement of people's standards of living is concerned, especially in the case of the usually underprivileged.[2] Never in all these years, however, has skin color been taken into account as a strong variable for social distinction, even in today's Cuba. Some obstacles remain unchallenged, as acknowledged by Fidel Castro himself in the notion of "objective discrimination."[3]

Throughout history, some people in Cuba have been discriminated against by society on account of their skin color. Others have too, regardless of the said feature, since you did not have to be black or mestizo in pre-1959 Cuba to be treated as they were. White people were also discriminated against if they were lower class, poor, workers and, particularly, poor peasants. And for black women the problem was two- and even three-fold, as they were discriminated against by men, for being female, and for their skin color.

All the types of people who have been discriminated against for so long are in great need of affirmative action, that is, social policies that take into account their differences and make provisions to eliminate them. We inherited so many structural disadvantages from colonialism that any action to set things right in the average person's lifetime is all but impossible, high as our life expectancy may be in Cuba today. If we fail to implement new policies, many will die without seeing these evils tackled and removed from our society.

Cuban blacks and mestizos have been particularly affected by racism and discrimination because, for starters, their social and economic standing has been the lowest and most insecure since colonial times as a result of their cruel exploitation. All the more reason, then, to put forward sociopolitical actions specifically designed for their benefit, because in light of the current disparities any set of egalitarian measures would only reproduce the problem at another level.

Nevertheless, there are other Cubans who suffered from capitalism's exploitation and a certain degree of discrimination too—based on class rather than race—and as a result sometimes had to cope with the same kind of socioeconomic difficulties as many black people do, even if the latter were also discriminated against for their skin color. They all must be helped, especially the black and mestizo Cubans, to overcome their many social, economic, and cultural disadvantages.

Facing us is a juncture not unlike that of the African Americans and Hispanics in the United States. A Hispanic there would be considered as white in Cuba, not so in the United States, and therefore they suffer from racial discrimination in that country. However, "affirmative action" as we know it has been fiercely attacked in the United States, where they have called it "reverse racism" on grounds that "the minorities have enjoyed such advantages over white people or at least achieved a proportionate parity with their peers in society."[4] Even if unsupported by the facts, this hypothesis has many followers.

Indeed, since it came into being together with the Civil Rights Act of 1964, and mainly after Reagan's mandate, affirmative action has little by little faded away into a big discussion that changes and gradually erases its guidelines.[5] It is particularly targeted by middle-class blacks, who hold that it brings discredit on them by placing them lower than the whites. Of course, coming from the blacks themselves, this harsh criticism pays no attention at all to the interests of the vast majority of their number, still weighed down by poverty, discrimination, and inequality in present-day America, even under a black president.[6] But debate has made it clear now that affirmative action can be dealt with from a different angle.

What is more often in the crosshairs is the fact that affirmative action gave precedence from the outset to blacks, Hispanics, and other minorities, using a race-based quota system. That's why after 1964 certain groups had some right of way to get jobs, enter universities, etc.

Such methods mold the attitude of those who use them and end up highlighting the disadvantages supposedly hanging over the black population and other minorities, and it is what the black middle class complains of on grounds that they have worked very hard to get to where they are today and do not want to be seen anymore as less capable than whites. In other words, owing to this mechanism, "race" would be an argument to offer advantages.

It is true that making a race-based preferential treatment institutional is morally unjustifiable, but we cannot overlook the fact that some people, because of their race, suffer from certain structural disadvantages originated in and multiplied by U.S. capitalism. We must try to eliminate these disadvantages if we expect to have an egalitarian society where everyone can look forward on equal terms and enjoy the same possibilities.[7]

A quota system does not do the trick. We had one in Cuba around the second half of the 1980s and it did not work. But no method based on giving direct priorities to people of a certain color will solve our problems, either. We need the kind of affirmative action that recognizes a disadvantage—come from where it may—without raising it to a privileged position, much less when it comes to the race issue: the kind known as "Affirmative Action for Development."

Whereas Affirmative Action for Preference until very recently recognized and used the differences as an element to allot quotas, Affirmative Action for Development evades neither the need for action nor the differences that justify it. Instead it has a plan aimed at redressing the balance in performance and providing the targets of the action—workers, students, etc.—with the abilities they need to be on a par with any other group. It is about using affirmative action to bring the disadvantages down to zero and then evaluate individual performance according to standard parameters common to everyone.

This kind of affirmative action based on the needs that justify its use pays heed to potential disadvantages but it is not morally reprehensible. Nor does it get in the way of scientific-technical progress, as it gives everyone the same opportunities to participate, whether or not they are at a disadvantage.

Accordingly, we can use affirmative action for our own good, as long as we start from the premise that we need it to polish the differences we inherited from the past and never manipulate those differences to distribute advantages, but instead into a reason to work for improvement. Simply put, it is about helping those who are burdened with disadvantages so that they can eliminate them before they are evaluated (for a job or entrance into school).

At any rate, our social policy has to provide resources to work on these disadvantages, and with Affirmative Action for Development it would be possible without compromising any healthy, balanced, and ethical search for equality.

A study of whether this kind of affirmative action could apply to Cuba's situation is well worth the try, considering that the Cuban-trained social workers contributed a number of ideas in this regard that are now being implemented through our solidarity programs in foreign countries. A study should also keep in mind that Cuba's is not the only society still affected by the remnants of colonialism, and certainly not the only one with firsthand experience of slavery.

# 15—The Challenges of Race within the Socialist Context

Nowadays there are many challenges we must face in Cuban society, what Fidel Castro referred it as a "social disgrace": racism. And we must deal with racism in the context of an era of economic challenges. During the period 1989–94, when the economic crisis took hold, followed by the Special Period, we could notice that in spite of extraordinarily humanistic social policies and a long struggle for justice and social equality, bordering on egalitarianism, there were many people not able to achieve a stable life. It was also shown that most of those people were black and mestizo. Even those we can consider "middle class," that is, top professionals, doctors, university professors, highly skilled workers and members of the intelligentsia, saw their standard of living severely affected. We can't say that these conditions have been completely overcome.[1]

The economic measures discussed widely today to modernize the economic model, measures having to do with labor issues, are most complicated and dramatic. They also represent an important challenge for the workforce as a whole, and specifically for the black and mestizo workers.[2] Then, it is not a secret to anyone that the latter have been always, historically, less skilled—the most disadvantaged in the labor force, holding the worst jobs, receiving the lowest salaries, and the lowest retirement benefits. As a result, they were the least absorbed by this so-called new economy, and finally, those least able to balance their family income by remittances coming from abroad, since this population is the least represented in emigration. For instance, in the 1980s there was a massive migration to the United States, without family support and with the stigma of being labeled "*marielitos*," representing only 15 to 16 percent of the emigrants to that country.[3] Therefore they do not hold the best jobs in the United States; they don't receive the best incomes; and as a result they are in the worst situation to travel and send money to their relatives in Cuba. They also have to face the racial discrimination permeating North American society, particularly in Miami, where they emigrated.

Neither blacks nor mestizos are easily hired in the sectors of the Cuban economy where the dollar currency is more common. So, some seek refuge in *santería* for profit, illegal activities, pimping, and prostitution, illegal resale of products, etc. Therefore, out of the total prison population today in Cuba, blacks and mestizos represent almost 57 percent, compared with 43 percent of white representation.[4] Demographically speaking, they are overrepresented within the prison population (according to the 2002 census, 65 percent identified themselves as white, 10.1 percent as black, and 24.9 percent as mestizos).

Some problems will demand a lot of time to solve; others will demand more political will than time. All, however, demand that we work with utmost strength, as radically and aggressively as possible, without rushing or improvising. Because in the midst of the extremely complex situation of our country, alternative solutions are not always socially convenient.[5]

### Different Positions
### about the Racial Problem

Not everybody concerned today about the race issue in Cuba shares similar political visions. Some openly question the ability of the Cuban political system and its leadership to solve it.

For others, the problem does not even exist, therefore it is not worthwhile to be concerned nor even to speak about it. In reality there are two basic positions on the race question.

One position considers the race problem in Cuba to be the responsibility of the Cuban government, as it is allegedly due to the absence of a human rights policy, democracy, and civil freedoms for the black population. In this way of thinking, the leaders of the Revolution are racist, particularly Fidel Castro, who has not dealt with the racial problem by trying to resolve it. They share the race issue, within more general political positions, with so-called dissidents, who mount criticism of the treatment of racism in Cuba based on the same pillars of criticism of North America toward the island. There is a tendency on their part not to recognize the work of the Revolution toward blacks and mestizos and to link the solution of the race problem to change in the political system in Cuba. This essentially makes them part of the political confrontation that the United States deploys in its quest for a regime change in the island.[6]

The other position, beginning with the advances achieved by the Revolution, criticizes its errors in the treatment of the issue as lacking a broader debate; in the absence of the topic in education; not considering the "color of the skin" as a variable of social differentiation in Cuba, which would allow a more closely attuned policy to lingering inequalities; the lack of a statistical system reflecting the social and economic problems of black people, allowing us to conduct better studies. However, this group considers that black people have advanced a great deal and if the Cuban Revolution had not occurred, blacks would have been compelled to make a revolution in order to achieve what they have had until today. They believe that solutions lie in deepening socialism, developing debate within it in which race problems are part of perfecting today's Cuban society. They do not accept that a political change in Cuba could benefit black people, because they do not think that a paradigm exists to justify such a political position.

The new battle against racism in Cuba carries implicitly the fight between these two positions and the intent of each of them to find and to create changes in Cuban society benefiting the black and mestizo people. It can be said that both positions seemingly pursue similar objectives, but differ radically in the way of reaching it. The former position contends that the Cuban Revolution should make way for a different political situation; the latter contends that the Revolution should stay, rectifying the errors made in the treatment of the race issue, but deepening the work that began in 1959.

Both positions display their actions within a framework of political tolerance by the Cuban government, so the confrontation is not violent, but peaceful. Nevertheless, both positions face objective challenges vis-à-vis the race issue. The main ones are to eliminate the internal prevailing ignorance on the issue, followed by the need to strengthen racial conscience, which is still lacking within the current society; and to stimulate the self-esteem of black people, to have the race issue occupy the place it should have at all levels of Cuban education, and to gain a level of institutional attention. Achieving those things, we could say that there is only one political battle to wage, which is not substantially different from the struggle going on in Cuba for the improvement of society and the well-being of black and mestizo people within it.

However, it is clear that the first position departs more and more from the interests of a social struggle against racism in Cuba to quickly become part of the political confrontation between Cuba and the United States. It requires taking a position separating them from the fight for socialism, a system that has allowed blacks and mestizos in Cuba to have a position within society unlike any non-white groups in other societies of the Western Hemisphere. This position is led by Carlos Moore, author of several books on Cuba's race issue, among others, *Fidel Castro, Blacks, and África* and a book called *Pichón*.[7] Moore was one the individuals who promoted the declaration by a group of North American artists and intellectuals against Cuba, in the *Miami Herald*, December 1, 2009.[8] Therefore, those of us who believe that the problems can be solved from within the Revolution must work boldly to promote and advance our alternative solutions.

*Some Concrete Challenges to Overcome*

I am not going to name all of the challenges, nor even most of them, but nevertheless we will mention some that, for their importance, threaten to hinder our efforts to solve the problems of discrimination and racism in today's Cuba.

Among such challenges, it is useful to highlight the following:

1) We must strengthen cultural and racial identity, especially in our children and youth. To do that it is necessary, among other important tasks, to firmly restructure teaching, specifically of history. Try to take the study of slavery out of the box we have built, keeping it in the nineteenth century, and bring it to our times. This will allow us to assess seriously its consequences in today's Cuban society. The official abolition of slavery in 1886, only 124 years ago, is very little time indeed to say that its deadweight and consequences no longer coexist with us.

   At the same time, it is imperative that the study of race and skin color enters Cuban schools, at all the levels of the system; otherwise we will never obtain an understanding of the roots of the Cuban culture that our students and youth need. Because without racial awareness, there is no ability to fight against stereotypes, discrimination, and racism.[9]

   Studies about Africa, Asia, and the Middle East must have an important place in our programs of world history, literature, geography, social and philosophical thought, among others. It is necessary in our universities to broaden ethnic-race studies and research the underlying phenomena behind color in Cuba, delving deeper into its history, its consequences in the shaping of the Cuban nation and in the national features that these phenomena assume today in our country.

   How is it possible that in a multicolored nation like Cuba, that there is no scientific study of those issues in our universities?[10] What development of science can we speak of if the core of that development is, to identify ourselves as a people and as a nation, ignored, nor approached, and given a biased treatment? What general and holistic culture can we speak of today in Cuba, with such neocolonial baggage in our teaching?

A scientific approach to the issues of race and color must enter in Cuban schools, at all levels, so that they can definitively transfer to the culture, thus making it possible to thoroughly combat the negative edges that allow room for racism, racial stereotypes, "whitening," and the existing racial discrimination in our country.

Our higher education, the fundamental springboard to the scientific and research development of any nation, is plagued with prejudices on the racial issue, institutional inaction, ignorance, and even fear to address it. We are repeating the same errors made in the former Soviet Union with sociology in the 1950s, and displaying the same prejudices that anthropology suffered for many years. For that reason today, sociology studies in our country do not have the experience it could have had, over more than forty years, while in Cuba there are few anthropologists.

An environment is created within the university, almost unconsciously, that favors racism, which for the most part identifies Cuban culture with Western culture, and marginalizes cultures and religions of African origin. Cuban history and Latin American history are presented as an exclusive history of whites, underestimating the protagonist role of blacks and mestizos. Western civilization is presented without denouncing its latent racism.[11]

2) Our statistical system should improve considerably so that color can be factored into the socioeconomic measurements we generate. It is not enough to count our population, it must be recorded in all of its features, and particularly color, a variable of important social differentiation in a country like Cuba. Not taking into account this variable, it leaves out of the population analysis an important group of indicators. This impedes characterizing in a real way the people's socioeconomic situations, introducing inaccurate biases affecting the social politics and the direction of the society as a whole.

Economic and socioeconomic categories such as unemployment, quality of employment, entrance levels, wages, state and quality of housing, marginalization, family violence, remittances, access to higher education, internal migration, external migration, life span, child mortality, maternal mortality, general population mortality, levels of retirement, access to recreation, appliances and other goods, should be quantified in the context of statistics on the color of the skin.[12]

Not all in the Cuban population enjoy equally the advantages that the social policies put at their disposal. For many years, social distribution was equitable, but the population is not homogeneous, for reasons that can also be racial, and not all citizens reach the opportunities at their disposal. That issue is seen very clearly in education. It is not the same to come from a family with a university education as to come from a working-class family, without contacts with intellectual life. Regrettably, it is not the same thing to live in Nuevo Vedado than in Parraga or Pogolotti. During the economic crisis, the first students who began dropping out of the university classrooms were black and mestizos. The new students were almost all white women. The blacks and mestizos reappeared years later, under the thrust of the Social Workers project.[13]

The idea that "we all are equals" was a slogan of pre-1959 Republican demagoguery. No, all Cubans are not the same. It must be recognized that on average, depending if we are white, mestizo, or black, although equal under the law, we have had different historical starting points that transfer from generation to generation. For that reason, the only way of erasing such a complex reality is to base social policies on still existing inequalities. Therefore, it is necessary to quantify and identify those inequalities and to attack them where they exist.[14]

Our statistics, either demographic or socioeconomic, should reflect the color of the skin, because they have to reflect the nation. Cuba is not Sweden or Holland. We are in the Caribbean region. When we do not reflect color, we are tossing 500 years of history into the wastebasket of forgetfulness. We are ignoring the inheritance of colonialism from which all of us still suffer today. I wonder how anyone can understand and scientifically direct Cuban society without taking color into account. Of what town are we speaking? To what nation are we referring when we do not take color into account?[15]

3) The multicolor feature that characterizes our nation has to be present everywhere the population develops. And when it is not there, all of us who are aware of its importance—white, mestizos. and blacks—should demand it. Our society cannot be definitively democratic, educated, and for all without considering that component. Democracy, social justice, human rights and racial balance are inseparable.

4) Affirmative action should have its space among us. Otherwise it will be impossible that, in a fairly acceptable time, we can balance the historical different starting points of the racial groups composing our society today.[16]

5) A social problem, even when it is not yet resolved, always adopts concrete expressions that often are political. We live today in very difficult and complex times. These stand out because the problems tend to become institutionalized. That is the reason why in today's Cuba civil society is gradually generating an institutionalization regarding the race issue at the fringes of the state, its devices and mechanisms. This means that there are sectors of society that are especially affected by the race issue for which institutions do not provide answers to their new needs, worries, and concerns.

The debate on race is not promoted on institutional levels. The race issue is not in the agenda of any of the political and mass organizations, neither in the National Assembly or the Popular Power at the municipal level. The race issue does not appear in any of the documents opened recently for public debate. It was not debated in the Congress of the Union of Communist Youth, nor by the Committees of Defense of the Revolution. Nor does it appear on the agenda of the union movement.

Except for a very limited number of institutions, such as the Ministry of Culture, UNEAC, and the Fernando Ortiz Foundation, along with other foundations, community projects, and informal groups, the race issue does not have an explicit presence in national life. Media mention it on a very limited basis and without any systematization, and do not report activities that touch on the topic. However, the framework of concerns regarding the race issues broaden and its expression in cultural work is taking a larger role. A consensus around the issues has taken shape mainly in the midst of the complex current economic situation. But except for some statements of the country's main leaders, in speeches by Fidel and Raúl, the government and political institutions have never addressed it openly. Nor are there signs of creating potential measures and policies concerned directly with the race issue.[17]

Hence, we must work firmly to institutionalize the issue and its possible solutions from a perspective that contributes to and is part of the set of policies that the country is debating to advance socialism. This is especially important because other groups are focusing on race as an issue demonstrating the absence of democracy, human rights, and civil freedoms for the black population, with positions linked to counterrevolutionary elements.[18] These forces take advantage of the debate opened up by the Commission of Human Rights and Race, recently held in Geneva. It is happening exactly as we have warned so many times before. It is an issue of our reality that we ourselves do not address but is done by others, and not always with the best of intentions.

Mainly, it is a matter of politically opposed points of view. Our points of view are:

- It is necessary to open a public debate on the issue in the context of economic reforms occurring on the island.
- It is necessary to bring the race issue to the Conference of the Party and to the Party Congress.
- It is necessary to deal with the details of the issue at all levels of the Popular Power, including the National Assembly.
- The issue has to be part of the agenda in the political and mass organizations and, in particular, inside the union movement.
- It is necessary to adopt immediate steps allowing us to advance in a holistic way in the area of education.
- It is necessary to create a specific institutional device, at the provincial or national level, or both, to address the race issue.

Lastly, we Cubans cannot limit ourselves to being merely spectators, using the excuse that in Cuba there is no indigenous population or that in Cuba we all are Afro-descendants. In each one of the three continental meetings of the campaign "500 Years of Indigenous Resistance, Black and Popular," there was a declaration of solidarity with Cuba. A movement whose axis is the recovery of the right of self-determination of nations perceives the Cuban people as a symbol of the continental resistance in the defense of its sovereignty and dignity. Hence, how could Cuba not identify with this movement? How could Cuba not consider it an important ally in the anti-imperialist struggle, that is to say, in the fight for liberation of the continent?

# Glossary of Names and Terms

*Ajiaco*—A Cuban stew that consists of many vegetables and spices from Amerindian, African, Chinese, and Spanish culinary traditions. The Cuban scholar *Fernando Ortiz* (see below) once defined the country as an "ajiaco" owing to the impact that these cultures had on Cuba's national identity.

*José Antonio Aponte* (?–1812)—A free black who led in 1812 a pro-independence and anti-slavery rebellion—the first nationwide attempt to unite blacks, both free and slave, and Cubans of Spanish and mixed descent in these two causes. Spanish authorities and their Cuban collaborators brutally suppressed the movement claiming that Aponte was organizing "a race war" as in the *Haitian Revolution* (see below). Aponte and several of his closest collaborators were hanged and their severed heads displayed in a cage at one of the principal entrances to Havana.

*Francisco de Arango y Parreño* (1765–1837)—Cuban lawyer, businessman, economist, and occasional official in the colonial government.

*Fulgencio Batista* (1901–1973)—A former army sergeant, he helped lead the Sergeants' Revolt in September 1933, a military coup by junior officers in wake of a popular uprising that had overturned the dictatorship of Gerardo Machado weeks earlier. He was promoted to colonel and chief of staff and organized a second coup in January 1934, unleashing repression against workers, peasants, and revolutionary forces. After dominating several governments as army head, was elected president in 1940. Did not run for reelection in 1944, but retained a power base within the army officer corps. Led coup on March 10, 1952, establishing brutal military dictatorship. Overthrown by advancing rebel army and popular uprising and fled to Dominican Republic, January 1, 1959.

*Battle of Ideas*—A series of programs instituted by the Cuban government at the end of the 1990s to address the economic and social inequalities—"marginality" as it was sometimes called—in the country exposed by the *Special Period* (see below) that disproportionately affected blacks and mestizos. Two of the most visible of the programs were those for training young people who had fallen through the revolution's social safety net to become social workers and the extension of the University of Havana to branches in all 169 municipalities.

*Bay of Pigs* (see *Playa Girón*)

*José Agustín Caballero* (1762–1835)—Cuban philosopher and theologian associated with educational reforms such as free primary education.

*Walterio Carbonell* (1920–2008)—Black Cuban intellectual, writer, and activist, who was one of the first individuals to raise the race question after the triumph of the Revolution in 1959 but was disciplined because of his criticisms. His numerous literary contributions have been belatedly recognized as suggested here.

*Fidel Castro: Speech of March 22, 1959*—To a mass rally of almost a million in Havana, two and a half months after the triumph of the Revolution, Prime Minister Fidel Castro addressed what he called the "four battles" of the revolution. Along with unemployment, low wages, and the cost of living, Castro said the other major problem was "the shameful practice . . . of excluding blacks from jobs." As well as describing the forms this took in both the workplace and broader society, Castro explained how the new government's policies would end such practices. This was the first time that he or any of the other leaders addressed in any kind of detail the problem and proposed solutions and had a major impact on the entire population. It was immediately followed by television interviews in which he detailed and clarified his remarks. Soon afterward racial segregation in public and private spaces was made illegal as well as discrimination in employment.

*Carlos Manuel de Céspedes* (1819–1874)—A Cuban planter (see below, *Creole*) who freed his slaves on October 10, 1868, and declared the Republic of Cuba, which launched Cuba's *Wars for Independence* (see below). He was killed in battle in 1874 and is widely seen as Cuba's Father of His Country.

*Salvador Cisneros Betancourt* (1828–1914)—Cuban politician who was the president of the Republic-in-Arms, 1873–1875. He freed his slaves once the Ten Years' War began (see below, *Wars of Independence*).

*Club Atenas*—In Havana, the most prestigious and influential of the black and mestizo "societies." Founded in 1917, it catered to the black elite and promoted cultural activities, some with political implications, during the Republican era prior to the 1959 Revolution. The "societies" had their roots in the African-based fraternal organizations called *cabildos de nación* that served mutual aid and recreational needs for slaves and free persons of color before the Republic in 1902. Club Atenas was taken over, as was true with the other "societies," by the government in 1961 and made into a children's center.

*Coup d'état of 1952* (See *Fulgencio Batista*)

*Creoles*—Term used for native-born Cubans of Spanish descent during the colonial period. A Creole landowning class developed in the nineteenth century, but Spanish colonial policy reserved positions of government and administration for Spanish-born colonists, known as *peninsulars*.*

*Cuban Communist Party Third Party Congress, 1986*—At the end of the congress Fidel Castro elaborated on the underrepresentation of blacks and mestizos in the leadership of the party and the need to take measures to increase, along with women and youth, their presence in its upper echelons. The congress, in response, elected a new Central Committee that doubled the number of blacks and mestizos to twenty-eight percent.

*Cuban Missile Crisis (Called the October Crisis in Cuba)*—In October 1962 U.S. President John Kennedy was told that the Soviet Union had secretly installed in Cuba nuclear armed strategic missiles. The Cubans agreed to their presence as a deterrent against an expected U.S. invasion. Kennedy's demand that the missiles be removed led to a confrontation between the United States and the Soviet Union, the most intense and dangerous moment of the Cold War.

*Escambray*—From 1959 until 1965 the Cuban Revolution waged a battle against CIA-armed and -financed counterrevolutionary bands centered mainly in the Escambray mountains of central Cuba. During these opening years of the Revolution, there were at one time or another 299 bands with 4,000 members that carried out assassinations, sabotage, and other terrorist actions. They were defeated largely through the mobilization of peasants and workers from the affected areas themselves.*

*Girón* (see *Playa Girón*)

*José Miguel Gómez* (1858–1921)—General in Cuba's Second *War for Independence* (see below), Liberal Party leader, and president of Cuba from 1909 to 1913 during the *"Little War of 1912"*(see below).

*Juan Gualberto Gómez* (1854–1933)—Cuba's most influential black leader in the early years of the Republic. An ardent defender of black and mestizo rights, he collaborated with *José Martí* (see below) before the Second War for Independence, rose to the rank of general during the war, and consistently opposed U.S. neocolonial designs after the war.

*"Guerra Chiquita"* (see *Wars for Independence*)

*Nicolás Guillén* (1902–1989)—Often called Cuba's national poet, Guillén, a mestizo, was also a journalist, political activist, and writer. He helped found the National Union of Writers and Artists of Cuba, of which he became president in 1961.

*Haitian Revolution*—Inspired by the French Revolution, slaves in France's most profitable colony did the same from 1791 to 1804. The victorious outcome had a major impact on Cuba, inspiring slaves there and frightening their slave masters who feared Cuba would become another Haiti—an opinion that lasted well into the twentieth century.

*Independent Libraries*—As part of its decades-long effort to undermine the Cuban Revolution, the U.S. government began in 1998 a project to promote "independent libraries" on the island in the name of fostering "civil society." In fact, they served as a conduit for U.S. government policy positions toward Cuba. About the individuals funded by the program, an investigation by the American

Library Association concluded that, "They aren't librarians at all. They are paid by the United States government . . . who try to buy dissidents in Cuba."

*Independent Party of Color*, or *Partido Independiente de Color (PIC)*—a political party founded in 1908 mostly by veterans of Cuba's independence wars who were black and mestizo. The party had thousands of members and supporters nationally. It advocated an end to racial discrimination, land distribution, free and compulsory education, the right to a trial by a jury that included blacks, opposition to the death penalty, an eight-hour workday, and other social demands in the interests of working people irrespective of skin color. The party was banned under the Morúa Law (see below, *Martín Morúa Delgado*) and its leaders arrested in 1910. It organized an armed protest in 1912 that was brutally suppressed by thousands of well-armed soldiers and paramilitary groups in what is sometimes called the "*Little War of 1912*." Estimates vary that from three to five thousand of its adherents or presumed sympathizers were killed.

*Ku Klux Klan*—In 1933 a branch of the notorious anti-black U.S. terrorist group was founded in Cuba, Ku Klux Klan Kubano. In many ways it was a right-wing response to the *Revolution of 1933* (see below) but was never able to attract a significant following.

*Esteban Lazo Hernández* (1944–)—First secretary of the Communist Party in the City of Havana province, 1994–2003. Vice president of Council of State since 1992. A member of the party's Central Committee and Political Bureau, he is Cuba's most senior black leader.

*Liberation Army* (see *Wars of Independence*)

*"Little War of 1912"* (See *Independent Party of Color*)

*Antonio Maceo* (1845–1896)—Military leader and strategist in Cuba's nineteenth-century wars of Independence from Spain. Popularly known in Cuba as the Bronze Titan, Maceo, a mestizo, led 1895–96 westward march from Oriente that culminated in Pinar del Rio Province. At conclusion of first war in 1878 (see *Wars of Independence*) became symbol of revolutionary intransigence by refusing to put down arms in an action that became known as the Baraguá Protest. Killed in battle.

*Gerardo Machado* (1871–1939)—Led brutal U.S.-backed dictatorship in Cuba 1927–33. Elected Cuba's president in 1924. Forcibly extended term in office in 1927, unleashing protests across Cuba, which were brutally suppressed. August 1933 revolutionary upsurge brought down dictatorship and sent him into exile.

*Mambises*—Fighters in Cuba's three wars of independence from Spain between 1868 and 1898. Many were freed slaves and other bonded laborers. The term "mambi" originated in the 1840s during the independence fight from Spain in nearby Santo Domingo. After a black officer in the Spanish army named Juan Ethninius Mamby joined freedom fighters there, colonial forces began calling guerrillas by derogatory name "mambies." Later "mambies" was applied to the Cuban fighters, who adopted it as a badge of honor.

*Mariel*—In 1980, Fidel Castro announced the opening of the port of Mariel to alienated Cubans who had stormed the Peruvian embassy in Havana desperate to leave the island, and he informed exiles in Miami that they could pick up relatives as well. Some 125,000—among them criminals and mental patients—arrived by boat in South Florida in five months.

*José Martí* (1853–1895)—Cuba's national hero. A noted revolutionary, poet, writer, speaker, and journalist. Founded Cuban Revolutionary Party in 1892 to fight Spanish colonial rule and oppose U.S. designs on Cuba. Organized and planned the 1895 War for Independence (see below, *Wars for Independence*). Killed in battle at Dos Rios in Oriente Province. His anti-imperialist program and broader writings are central to Cuba's internationalist traditions and revolutionary political heritage.*

*Moncada Program*—Following an unsuccessful attack on the military barracks of Moncadain Santiago de Cuba on July 26, 1953, to overthrow the *Fulgencio Batista* (see above) dictatorship, Fidel Castro delivered at his trial his now famous "History Will Absolve Me" speech in which he detailed the aims of his actions and vision for a new Cuban society. Smuggled out it became the founding document for the July 26th Movement that led to the Cuban Revolution.

*Martín Morúa Delgado* (1856–1910)—Cuba's first black elected senator in 1901. As President of the Cuban Senate, he introduced in May 1910 a law that banned political parties based on race or class. The Morúa Law was a direct attack on the *Independent Party of Color* (see above) and helped set the stage for the *"Little War of 1912"* (see above).

*Carlos Moore* (1942–)—Black Cuban writer and academic who broke with the Cuban revolution over the race question in the early 1960s and lives abroad. A longtime critic of the Revolution, he is the author of several books including *Castro, the Blacks, and Africa* (1988), and an autobiography, *Pichón* (2008). Moore was the intellectual author of "Acting on Our Conscience: A Declaration of African-American Support for the Civil Rights Struggle in Cuba," of November 2009, signed, initially, by sixty prominent African Americans that accused the Cuban government of abusing a supposed fighter for black rights and responded to by numerous defenders of the Cuban Revolution in the United States and Cuba.

*NED*, or *National Endowment for Democracy*—A U.S. NGO funded by Congress "dedicated to the growth and strengthening of democratic institutions around the world." Its Cuba program, in place since 1984 and intended to undermine the Cuban Revolution, targeted in 2010—the most recent public data—2.4 million dollars to various projects including the "Afro-Cuba Alliance . . . to encourage greater discussion and academic analysis about racial issues in Cuba."

*Operation Mongoose*—Code name given to a series of actions that the U.S. government initiated to overthrow the Cuban Revolution seven months after the mercenary invasion it backed was defeated at *Playa Girón* (see below). It included the arming of groups to carry out assassinations, sabotage, and subversion and was administered from the White House by Attorney General Robert Kennedy. It precipitated what the Cubans call the "October Crisis" or the *Cuban Missile Crisis* (see above).

*Fernando Ortiz* (1881–1969)—Renowned Cuban essayist, ethnomusicologist, and scholar of Afro-Cuban culture. He coined the term "transculturation" in 1940 to describe the phenomenon of merging and converging cultures and once called Cuban culture an "ajiaco" after the island's famous stew that incorporated all of its culinary traditions.

*Pact of Zanjón*—Treaty that ended the Cuban First War of Independence, February 10, 1878 (see below, *Wars of Independence*). *Antonio Maceo* (see above) and his brother José refused to sign the treaty because it did not agree to complete abolition of slavery and independence and kept on fighting until he went into exile, to return later.

***Tomás Estrada Palma*** (1832–1908)—Served as the first President of Cuba between 1902 and 1906, inaugurating the Republican period and, effectively, Cuba's neocolonial status in relation to the United States.

***People's Power,* or *Poder Popular***—Cuba's popularly elected government bodies at the municipal, provincial, and national levels, established by the 1976 constitution. National Assembly of People's Power, elected every five years, is the highest legislative body and elects Council of State and its president, who is head of state and of government.*

***Platt Amendment***—Named after U.S. Senator Orville Platt (Republican, Connecticut), this provision was imposed on Cuba in 1901 during the U.S. military occupation. Under the terms of the amendment—incorporated in Cuba's new constitution—Washington was given the "right" to intervene in Cuban affairs at any time and to establish military bases on Cuban soil. The Platt Amendment was eliminated from the Cuban constitution in the wake of the 1933 revolutionary upsurge (see below, ***Revolution of 1933***), but Washington continued to claim "rights" to its naval base in Guántanamo, and institutionalized other forms of political and economic exploitation of Cuba.*

***Playa Girón***—On April 17, 1961, 1,500 Cuban mercenaries organized, financed, and deployed by Washington invaded Cuba at the Bay of Pigs on the southeast coast. In less than seventy-two hours of combat, mercenaries were defeated by Cuba's revolutionary militias, armed forces, and police. On April 19 remaining invaders were captured at Playa Girón (Girón Beach), the name Cubans use for the invasión and battle.*

***Regla de Ocha***—Another name for Santería, also known as La Regla de Lucumi, or Lukumi, is one of the religions of West African origin practiced in Cuba. It combines Yoruba and Roman Catholic traditions.

***Republic-in-Arms*** (see ***Wars of Independence***)

***Revolution of 1933*** (see ***Fulgencio Batista, Gerardo Machado***)

***Holden Roberto*** (1923–2007)—Leader of the National Liberation Front of Angola, or FNLA, a U.S.-backed armed group in Angola that opposed the more popular Cuban– and Soviet Union–supported Popular Movement for the Liberation of Angola, or MPLA.

***Tomás Romay y Chacón*** (1764–1849)—Distinguished Cuban doctor who is considered to be the founder of medical science in Cuba.

***José Antonio Saco*** (1797–1879)—Cuban statesman, writer, social critic, publicist, essayist, anthropologist, historian, and one of the most notable Cuban figures from the nineteenth century. He supported abolition and encouraged white emigration from European countries to counterbalance the demographic effects of the slave trade. While he opposed annexation to the United States and championed a Cuba free from oppressive colonial mandates, Saco could not conceive of blacks and mestizos as equal to whites and part of the emerging nation.

***Second Declaration of Havana***—Proclamation presented at and approved by the Cuban people at a mass rally of over a million on February 4, 1962. A response, in part, to Cuba's expulsion from the Organization of American States, it declared that the road opened by its revolution was now open to all the people of Latin America and, thus, a challenge to U.S. hegemony in the hemisphere. In listing the gains of the Revolution it stated that Cuba had "suppressed discrimination due to race or sex" and that a change in public consciousness had taken place which was "incompatible with . . . discrimination against women, Negroes, Indians, and mestizos."

***Special Period***—The term used in Cuba for the extremely difficult economic conditions the Cuban people faced from the early 1990s on, and the policies implemented in the face of them to defend the Revolution. With the disintegration of the regimes of Eastern Europe and the Soviet Union that previously accounted for 83 percent of Cuba's foreign trade, the island was brutally thrust back into the world capitalist market from which it had been partially sheltered for more than twenty-five years. The sudden and unilateral break in trading patterns, exacerbated by Washington's economic blockade, led to the most severe economic crisis in Cuba since 1959. In 1993 and 1994 a number of measures were adopted to address the worsening economic conditions. Even though shortages of food and other essentials remained, by 1996, through the efforts of Cuban working people, inflation was brought under control, and a recovery began.*

*United States "transition documents"*—A detailed policy statement in 2004 of more than 400 pages commissioned by then secretary of state Colin Powell for the George W. Bush administration and then later supplemented in 2006 by a directive from his successor, Condoleezza Rice, for reintroducing capitalism into a post-Revolution Cuba.

*Wars of Independence*—From 1868 to 1898 Cubans waged three wars for independence from Spain: Ten Years' War (1868–1878), "Little War" or "Guerra Chiquita" (1879–80), and war of 1895–98 leading to end of Spanish rule. The military command of the first war was known as the *Republic-in-Arms*. U.S. military occupied Cuba after Spain's defeat and imposed the so-called Platt Amendment on the constitution, authorizing Washington to "exercise the right to intervene" in Cuba and to establish naval bases on the island.*

*Entries with an asterisk were taken from the very informative glossaries in various publications of Pathfinder Press about the Cuban Revolution. We would like to thank Pathfinder Press for permission to use them.

# Notes

## FOREWORD

1.   The letter of the sixty and the counter-declarations can be found at http://
     www.minnesotacubacommittee.org/race-in-cuba.
2.   Carlos Moore, *Were Marx and Engels Racists?* (Chicago: Institute of Positive
     Education/Third World Press, 1972).
3.   One of the most telling aspects of Moore's autobiography, *Pichón, A Memoir:
     Race and Revolution in Castro's Cuba* (Chicago: Lawrence Hill Books, 2008),
     is that his opinion about the Cuban Revolution on the race question stands in
     sharp contrast to that of the members of his family who remained in Cuba.
4.   I have long suspected that the decision of the Clinton administration in 1994
     to permit a significant increase in the amount of remittances that Cuban-
     Americans could send to their relatives on the island was consciously done to
     promote racial inequality there. The economic racial disparities that Cuban
     immigrants after Mariel experienced in the United States would, therefore, be
     reproduced in Cuba itself.
5.   Jack Barnes, *Malcolm X, Black Liberation & the Road to Workers' Power* (New
     York: Pathfinder Press, 2010), 299–328.

## PREFACE

1.   Morales keeps a blog at http://www.estebanmoralesdominguez.blogspot.
     com/, the best venue for staying current with what he has to say.

### 1.CHALLENGES OF THE RACIAL QUESTION IN CUBA

This essay is a summary of *Desafios de la problematica racial en Cuba* (Havana: Editorial de Ciencias Sociales, 2008). It originally appeared in Spanish in *Temas* 56 (October–December 2008): 95–99.

1. It is worth mentioning the books of Tomas Fernandez Robaina and Sandra Morales, useful attempts to try to place the race question within the context of present Cuban reality. See also: Juan Antonio Alvarado Ramos, "Relaciones raciales en Cuba. Nota de investigacion," *Catauro* 6 (July–December 2002): 52-93; Maria Magdalena Perez Alvarez, "Los prejuicios raciales: sus mecanismos de reproduccion"; and Maria del Carmen Calio Secade, "Relaciones raciales, proceso de ajuste y politica social," *Temas* 7 (July–September 1966): 37, 44, and 58.

2. Esteban Morales, *Desafios de la problematica racial en Cuba* (Havana: Editorial de Ciencias Sociales, 2008).

3. *Temas* has published portions of the results of these studies. See Rodrigo Espina and Pablo Rodriguez, "Raza y desigualdad en la Cuba actual," *Temas* 45 (January–March 2006); and Pablo Rodriguez, "Espacios y contextos del debate racial actual en Cuba," *Temas* 53 (January–March 2008).

4. The following research papers can be found at the Anthropology Center (Centro de Antropología) of CITMA (Ministerio de Ciencia, Tecnología y Medio Ambiente), Havana: Pablo Rodriguez, Ana Julia Garcia, and Lazara Carrazana, "Relaciones raciales en la esfera laboral," n.p., 1999; Rodrigo Espina, Estrella Gonzalez, and Maria Magdalena Perez Alvarez, "Relaciones raciales y etnicidad en la sociedad cubana contemporinea," n.p., 2003; Ana Julia Garcia, Estrella Gonzalez Noriega, and HernanTiradoToirac, "Composicion racial en la estructura de cuadros," n.p., Havana, 2003.

5. Institutional racism does not exist in Cuba, meaning it is not built into the sociopolitical system or the institutions, as was the case before 1959. The revolutionary process, with its anti-discriminatory ethos, drove racism back into what are now its principal niches: the family, the individual consciousness of many people, the so-called emergent economy, and some exclusionary groupings, where it still exists because the definitive battle against racism did not take place. This shortcoming led to its concealment, only to reemerge now, when more contacts with the market economy, the reemergence of inequalities, and the whole economic and social deterioration that resulted from the crisis of the 1990s are being felt.

6. See Rebecca J. Scott, *Slave Emancipation in Cuba: The Transition to Free Labor, 1860–1899* (Princeton: Princeton University Press, 1985), published in Cuba by Editorial Carninos, Havana, 2001; Alejandro de la Fuente, *Una nacion paratodos: Raza, desigualdad y politica en Cuba. 1900–2000* (Madrid: Colibri, 2000); Carlos Moore, *Castro, the Blacks, and Africa* (Los Angeles: Center for Afro-American Studies, University of California Press, 1989);

Robin Moore, *Musica y mestizaj: Revolucion artistica y cambio social en La Habana, 1920–1940* (Madrid: Colibri, 1997).

## 2. RACE AND THE REPUBLIC

1.  The Vietnam War is a modern-day example of historic distortion. Judging by the message sent by many of the films about that war, new generations will end up knowing nothing about what really happened in Southeast Asia.

2.  Wood to McKinley, Havana, April 12, 1900; LC, Papers of Leonard Wood, 28. Quoted in Alejandro de la Fuente, *Un anación paratodos: raza, desigualdad y política en Cuba, 1900–2000* (Madrid: Editorial Colibrí, 2000), 67.

3.  Ibid., 67–68.

4.  Ibid., 68.

5.  Ibid.

6.  Ibid., 69.

## 3. A MODEL FOR THE ANALYSIS OF THE RACIAL PROBLEM IN CONTEMPORARY CUBA

1.  See Esteban Morales, "Cuba–Estados Unidos: un modelo para el análisis de la confrontación hacia finales del siglo," *Temas* 18–19 (julio–diciembre 1999): 80–89.

2.  This brief essay does not allow for a thorough presentation and description of these stages. In any case, our historians have produced brilliant analyses that still leave room for amplification and debate.

3.  It is not a variable but a constant, which has been articulated throughout the Cuban historical process, subjecting the racial problem to the priorities of maintaining national unity. This will be explained in detail further on.

4.  It should be clear that we do not pretend to offer a history of our object of study but rather to synthezise at the structural and socioeconomic level the key moments that may help us explain the current situation of the racial problem in Cuba. We do aim to offer conclusions from our analysis that may contribute to the formulation of policies that may help us finally overcome the problem.

5.  Two clear examples of this are (1) in the colonial period, when England and Spain were jostling for the abolition or continuation of slavery in Cuba; (2) during the 1898–1902 period when North American intervention dramatically changed the internal Cuban dynamics.

6.  It means that there is a close relation among the component units, for being and belonging to the same whole, determined by the object and design of the study. Common traits promote interactive and indissoluble relations.

7.  We will return to this complex problem under the heading "Unity within Diversity" later in this essay. In Cuba, for more than thirty years, cultural identity was of little relevance for the process of the construction of socialism. Concrete circumstances prioritized class struggle and responses to external aggression as essential ideological resources for national identity. See Rolando

Zamora Fernández, *Notas para un estudio de la identidad cubana* (Havana: Centro de Investigación y Desarrollo de la Cultura Cubana Juan Marinello, 2000), 187.

8.  Due to space, we will not consider all the variables here, except for those that are indispensable for the objectives of this essay.

9.  Once racism is no longer exercised by the structures of formal power, that is, no longer institutionalized, it seeks refuge in the family, the individual consciousness, and some social groups to await a propitious time to manifest itself again. This is the social phenomenon in Cuba today, to which we will refer in this essay.

10.  Reasons for which, neoliberal globalization, racism, and xenophobia go hand in hand. Globalization is intrinsically discriminatory and excluding.

11.  For further treatment of this topic, see E. Balibar and I. Wallerstein, *Raza, nación y clase* (Madrid: Editorial Iepala, 1988), 313–29.

12.  According to statistical studies, blacks and whites today are almost at the same level of education. See Eduardo San Marful and Sonia Catasús, *Dinámica de la población cubana por el color de la piel* (Havana: CEDEM, Universidad de La Habana, 2000), 14–18. In a project carried out by the Centro de Antropología de la Academia de Ciencias in Havana and Santiago—two of the most representative provinces—serious imbalances were discovered regarding access to the same level of position in employment. See Pablo Rodríguez, Ana Julia García, and Lázara Carrazana, *Relaciones raciales en la esfera laboral* (Havana: Centro de Antropología, CITMA, 1999).

13.  To amplify further, see Eduardo Torres-Cuevas, "En busca de la cubanidad," *Debates Americanos* 1 (1995): 2–17.

14.  Regarding this process, there is an obscure area that requires more research. It is the role the indigenous group played in the process of creolization, considering that its early and total extinction has been disputed based on the scrutiny of, and doubts about, the data preserved. It is a matter of great importance because it recognizes a more complex process of creolization. See José A. García Molina, "Los aborígenes cubanos: leyenda de una extinción," *Temas* 7 (July–September 1996): 28–36.

15.  For additional considerations, see Jesús Guanche, *Componentes étnicos de la nación cubana* (Havana: Fundación Fernando Ortiz, 1996), 135–36.

16.  Ibid., 118–30.

17.  Ibid., 130.

18.  See Fernando Ortiz, "Los factores humanos de la cubanidad," in *Estudios etnosociológicos* (Havana: Editorial de Ciencias Sociales), 10–43. Cited by Pablo Rodríguez, *Catauro* 2002: 103.

19.  See Guanche, *Componentes étnicos de la nación cubana,* 129.

20.  In the United States a person with a drop of black blood is considered black, regardless of the white color of the skin.

21.  See Norma Suárez, *Fernando Ortiz y la cubanidad* (Havana: Fundación Fernando Ortiz, 1996), 9. (Colección La Fuente Viva.)

22. Such seems, lamentably, the case in Russia and other Eastern European countries.

23. Quoted in Rolando Rodríguez, *Cuba: la forja de una nación* (Havana: Editorial de Ciencias Sociales, 1998).

24. See Aline Helg, *Lo que nos corresponde. La lucha de los negros y mulatos por la igualdad en Cuba, 1886–1912* (Havana: Editorial Imagen contemporánea, 2000), 217–313.

25. See José A. Tabares del Real, *La revolución del 30, sus dos últimos años* (Havana: Editorial de Ciencias Sociales, 1973), 21–62.

26. The last U.S. ambassador before 1959, Earl T. Smith, supported Batista until his final hour, even hiding information from the Eisenhower administration. See Esteban Morales, *La política de Estados Unidos hacia Cuba, 1959–1961* (Havana: CESEU, Universidad de La Habana, 2002).

27. In another essay, "Racismo y discriminación racial en las estadísticas," I include the data to justify these assertions.

28. We now have seventy ongoing social programs, led by the Unión de Jóvenes Comunistas, under the personal guidance of the Presidente del Consejo de Estado, whose charge is to offer solutions to a set of existing social imbalances. For example, programs to rescue young people who are neither studying nor working. In addition, the Ministry of Culture collaborates with the UNEAC and its members to develop "Programas Comunitarios" in different districts of Havana. The theoretical approaches for these programs are being developed in the field with symposia, meetings, and numerous coordinating activities.

29. For statistics, see section on "Racism and Racial Discrimination."

30. See Morales, "Cuba–Estados Unidos," 80–89.

31. Different organizations created by the Revolution played an important role in these activities. They were mass organizations formed on the basis of a shared set of objectives and work plans that made no distinctions based on class, gender, or race.

32. We refer to the state of affairs until the end of the second half of the eighties when the economic difficulties in European socialist countries surfaced. Cuba had constructed socialism between two walls: (1) economic relations with socialist countries, and (2) the United States economic blockade. The first wall protected us and the second one affected us but also isolated us from the imbalances of the capitalist system. Henceforth, the island was plunged into a sort of double blockade.

33. As we all know, the revolutionary leadership selected the road to alleviate the economic crisis, a road full of strains and bends that, nevertheless, avoided the so-called shock therapy, a well-worn solution in other latitudes. The state carried the burden of the essential cost of the crisis, and the people were protected from suffering during the most dire and dramatic circumstances between 1989 and 1994.

34.   According to research by the Centro de Antropología, the remittances, in addition to concentrating on the white population, play an even more significant role in the emergent sector of the economy. Intellectuals receive more frequent remittances than workers. Workers in the "new economy" tend to receive more remittances. See Rodríguez, García, Carrazana, *Relaciones raciales en la esfera laboral.*

35.   We do not have the actual figures, but it is generally accepted, both within and outside official circles, that the data for blacks and mulattos are well above their demographic percentage. This should not surprise us, if we consider all the situations faced by these social groups during the Special Period.

36.   See Censo Nacional de Cuadros del Estado, La Habana, 1987. This is demonstrated in the sale/trafficking of products on the black market, which are only available there after they are stolen from the state-owned warehouses. An obvious example is the case of powdered milk. All of this presents a close correlation with the large percentage of black mulattos who are in prison for having engaged in black market activity.

37.   See *La población de Cuba, según el color de la piel*, special supplement to Censo de Población and Viviendas de 1981, 7–10.

38.   See María del Carmen Caño, "Relaciones raciales, procesos de ajuste y política social," *Temas* 7 (1996): 58–65.

39.   Evidence of this phenomenon can be found in the belief, fairly widespread among the Cuban population, that, in order to obtain employment in the tourist sector or with the corporations, there is nothing better than having a personal connection or sponsor. See Pablo Rodríguez Ruiz, et al.,. "Las relaciones raciales en Cuba. Una aproximación a la realidad actual," Centro de Antropología de la Academia de Ciencias de Cuba, 23 (n.p.).

40.   We have already referred to these disadvantages, which affect the lack of people of color, such as the underrepresentation of blacks and mulattos in economic leadership positions, especially in the emerging sector of the so-called "new economy."

41.   No great effort is required to prove what we are saying here. One needs only to review state structures at their highest levels: ministries, national organizations, social organizations, non-governmental organizations, and academic and scientific institutions, etc. Except for the armed forces, sports, and certain cultural sectors, in particular music, what we express here is totally valid.

42.   See Fidel Castro's speech of March 22, 1959. Fidel broached the issue with intensity by observing that it was a damaging social legacy that had to be eliminated. The silence that followed did not mean that these concerns had disappeared.

43.   *Investigación sobre desarrollo humano y equidad en Cuba* (Havana: CIEM, 1999), 6.

44.   This implies a sort of "affirmative action" that, because of its novelty and complexity in our social space, will require much debate and research.

45.   *Investigación sobre desarrollo humano*, 7.

46. Ibid. Such awareness perfectly captures the situation for blacks and mulattos in the group still considered poor in Cuba.

47. This means that a socioeconomic analysis such as ours is not sufficient to comprehend the social situation, the economic differences, and social inequities, that blacks and mulattos encounter at their different points of departure. It would be necessary to complement it with anthropological, sociological, and cultural perspectives, and a historical assessment of the issue. Only several sciences working in unison may provide an integral answer.

48. The issue of affirmative action, about which there is much debate nowadays, especially in the United States, a country with a long trajectory in these matters, is complex. It seems that the concept has been considered and implemented not to create different requirements for blacks but to create policies that would place them in conditions to meet the requirements, which would be the same for all racial groups.

49. See Caño, "Relaciones raciales," 64.

50. Carlos Marx said that in times of revolution society would be able to see in days that which centuries would have passed in waiting. That is, centuries of accumulated exploitation cannot be overcome in only a few decades.

## 5. UNDERSTANDING THE CUBAN RACIAL QUESTION

1. This is true of any social theme that is left unattended by scientific study. Such a problem tends to fester and can become a chronic condition within the social body.

2. Recently, the Cuban Color Project has been reconfigured, through a Permanent Working Commission of the UNEAC, whose objective is to fight against racism and racial discrimination by carrying out solid cultural work on the theme.

3. This commission emerged from the Department of Culture of the Party Central Committee, where its initial impetus was provided under the direction of Esteban Lazo, member of the Politburo of the Communist Party of Cuba (PCC), with assistance from Eliades Acosta, then head of the aforementioned department, and from Gisela Arandia, coordinator at the time of the Cuban Color Project.

4. Esteban Morales has published a dozen or more essays, which can be found in national publications and on the Internet.

5. This attitude on the part of our press received a public rebuke when in early December of 2009 a group of North American artists and intellectuals headed by Carlos Moore issued a statement accusing Cuba and the Cuban government of racism. Using the pretext of a person imprisoned in Cuba and manipulating the situation, the former collaborator of the Angolan mercenary Holden Roberto gathered signatures from a group of sixty intellectuals and artists on a racist, counterrevolutionary, and provocational document. The newspaper *Granma*, which had never bothered to reflect on the theme in its pages, imme-

diately published a statement in response by a group of Cuban intellectuals
and an article written by the journalist Pedro de la Hoz.

6.   In America slavery was based on color: the slave was Indian or black. In clas-
     sical slavery, the slave could be white and that allowed him, if he was able to
     escape, to blend in as afforded by his skin color. But in America that situation
     never existed.

7.   Behind all of the racial categories, especially of whiteness, there is a good dose
     of social hypocrisy, because after 800 years of Arab colonization of the Iberian
     Peninsula, which whites are we talking about?

8.   In the study "Reforma económica y población en condiciones de riesgo, en
     Ciudad de La Habana," conducted by Ángel Ferriol and Maribel Ramos y
     Lía Añé, of the INIES, one can see clearly how blacks and mestizos are the
     people most impacted by the Special Period. See Esteban Morales. *Desafíos
     de la problemática racial en Cuba* (Havana: Fundación Fernando Ortiz, 2007),
     161–96.

9.   See Pablo Rodríguez, Ana Julia García, and Lázara Carrazana, *Relaciones
     raciales en la esfera laboral* (Havana: Centro de Antropología, CITMA, 1999).

10.  Sadly, television at times adopts the most prejudiced attitudes toward certain
     cultural products, for example, never airing Eric Corvalán's documentary
     *Raza*, or delaying the showing of *Las raíces del corazón*, Gloria Rolando's short
     film, dedicated to the so-called Guerrita del Doce. Recently Cuban television
     has started to air a few spots dedicated to the theme of race, but in my opinion
     neither expert nor of great quality.

11.  Our statistics, by not taking color into account, fall into the absurdity of mis-
     sing an opportunity to display the true work of the Revolution.

12.  We do not know if at present measures are being adopted to solve the situation,
     but the problems already exist and have accumulated.

## 6. THE METAPHORS OF COLOR

1.   In March 1959, when Fidel Castro said that racial discrimination was one of
     the defects that had to be overcome in Cuba, some people didn't support him
     and even predicted difficult, unpleasant situations. Now, when this problem
     is considered to have been solved many years ago, it is hardly surprising that
     those same attitudes persist.

2.   The measures that were adopted in 2005 to raise pensions and minimum
     wages and to increase the distribution of subsidized basic products are part
     of a social policy that has always had a deeply humanistic content and that
     unquestionably benefits blacks and mestizos—the racial groups with the larg-
     est proportions among the poor.

3.   Isaac Barreal, *Retorno a las raíces* (Havana: Fernando Ortiz Foundation, a
     Fuente Viva Collection, 2001), 154–55.

## 8. SKIN COLOR, NATION, IDENTITY, AND CULTURE: A CONTEMPORARY CHALLENGE

1.  Some authors and other people speak of "residual racism." a term that somehow implies that this evil has beaten a retreat. Actually, I think racism is only hiding away, if weakened after so many years of revolutionary struggle. Nor can we deny that the fight against racism was dissolved into the struggle to beat poverty, inequality, and every form of discrimination. Therefore, this complicated issue has never been directly and specifically acted upon, despite its distinct influence on our economic, cultural, social, and all other ways of life. That it was officially pronounced dead out of someone's personal obstinacy rather than certainty helped no more than the social pressure to hush it all up as if it were a taboo subject. That's why we're so behind in the struggle against this social scourge, as Fidel defined racism in 1959. Accordingly, we must show our appreciation to those who always alerted us to the danger of a problem that is now making a comeback and proving that what was once said to be settled never really was.

2.  In recent statements during an interview, Mr. José María Aznar said that Muslims had invaded Spain and stayed there for over 800 years. That such a stupid thing was said by someone who until very recently was the prime minister of that country makes this assertion all the more unreliable.

3.  It's no coincidence that we were the second-to-last country in the hemisphere to abolish slavery. Spain clung to it, devising a whole legal maze to undermine the efforts of the abolitionists, whose claims were being strongly noticed in Cuba, particularly after the first war of independence. As an example of these attempts we could mention the execution by firing squad of the eight medical students in 1871, the continued refusal to sell Cuba, *el manejo de la autonomia*, Spanish captain-general Valeriano Weyler's concentration camps, and the sacrifice of Admiral Cervera's naval squadron in 1898.

4.  Abolition entailed freeing the slaves so that they could join the Cuban independence war and that blacks, until then enslaved, would become citizens. This means that among the reasons behind the supporters of Cuban independence was also the idea of a nation that welcomed black people. However, before that idea becomes a reality, all of us Cubans still have a lot of battles to wage.

5.  The notion of race in its modern meaning has no recorded history before America. With time the colonizers used color codes for the phenotypical features of the colonized and took them as the emblematic traits of racial profiling. Thus they legitimized the dominant position imposed by the Spanish Conquest. The notion of race, by no means in keeping with a human being's biological structure, is literally an invention.

6.  The issue of racism took shape through the attitudes shown by Calixto García, Estrada Palma, Cisneros Betancourt, and others who, both during the Little War and the 1895 war, twisted the role played by Antonio Maceo in a number

of events, including the unjust replacement of his brother, General José Maceo, in eastern Cuba and his continual refusal to reinforce the second stage of the east-to-west invasion that José was supposed to lead.

7.  See Joel James Figarola, *Fundamentos Sociologicos de la Revolucion Cubana (Siglo XIX)* (Santiago: Editorial Oriente, 2003),16.

8.  A shameful, unfortunate episode involved the opinions expressed by Flor Crombet (a mestizo), as requested by Calixto García (a white), in a letter to Maceo accusing him of being a racist. This gave rise to promises of a duel that never took place.

9.  Thirty years later, however, he expressed his support for the abolition of slavery.

10. See Jose Luciano Franco, *Documentos para la Historia de Haiti* (Havana: Archivo Nacional, 1951). Quoted by Joel James Figarola *Fundamentos Sociologicos de la Revolucion Cubana (Siglo XIX)*, 10.

11. Three key thinkers were left out of this discussion: Felix Varela, Jose de la Luz y Caballero, and José Martí, since they all became pro-independence supporters, unlike Saco, although he lived through the whole period of the first Independence War. For further details see Isabel Monal and Olivia Miranda, *Pensamiento Cubano del Siglo XX* (Havana: Ed. Ciencias Sociales, 2002), 1:1–43.

12. For further information see Raul Cepero Bonilla,"Racismo y Nacionalidad," *Catauro* 11 (2005): 148–57. For men like Arango y Parreño, Saco, Del Monte, and even the presbyter Varela, the color black was a symbol of shame.

13. It's impossible to forget Narciso Lopez's annexationist expeditions between 1850 and 1852, thwarted by his own death and the subsequent American Civil War. The notion of annexation has seen substantial change ever since, and nowadays the extreme right-wingers involved in U.S. policy on Cuba say it would be an (undeserved) "honor" to appear on the star-spangled banner. The idea today that annexation would turn Cuba into another full-fledged U.S. state is simply inconceivable. At best, a southern Florida district sounds more like it.

14. See Carmen Barcia, *Catauro* 4 (July-December 2001): 36–59.

15. There was a kind of "involuntary" annexationist feeling displayed even by some leaders of the independence movement who took on a one-sided racist, arrogant stance, as in the unfortunate case of Calixto Garcia, whose extraordinary patriotism is beyond question. He adopted a very negative attitude toward the brothers Antonio and José Maceo during the Little War and the 1895 War and, acting behind Maximo Gomez's back, facilitated the entry of the U.S. Army in Cuba.

16. Spain made this decision perhaps because Cuba's surrender to the Liberation Army would have brought about the fall of the Spanish Crown, so they had no choice but to give it to the United States. It was Calixto Garcia himself who, naively and without consulting anyone, made things easier for the U.S. troops, who first thanked him by banning him from Santiago de Cuba and then by

letting him die, soon afterward and in very strange circumstances yet to be established, without a chance to correct his mistakes as the only Cuban general with sufficient rank to avoid, or at least hold up, the American intervention.

17. There are various views on this process among the Cuban intellectuals. See Esteban Morales, "Cuba: algunos desafios del color," which shared Third Prize in the 2005 "Pensar a Contracorriente" competition. A version of this article is published in this volume as chapter 2.

18. Those who did formed an alliance with the U.S. administration of the moment, the U.S. Army, a bunch of opportunists, the *criollo* bourgeoisie in western Cuba, a group of Spanish traders, the autonomists, and a not inconsiderable number of Cubans who had fought in the Liberation Army.

19. That's why we hold that the inception of a truly Cuban nation for all its citizens did not take place until the triumph of the Revolution in 1959. Cuba was never complete before that year.

20. Many people refuse to accept this fact, some because they couldn't care less and others for lack of firsthand experience, but most of them because they feel embarrassed to admit that they have always gotten a lot out of it.

21. See Ana Cairo, Aputes Sobre los Chimos, *Revista Catauro* (2002) No. 2, 167–174.

22. For further information, see Esteban Morales, "En Cuba lo que rige es la llamada 'linea del color,'" *Catauro* 6 (July–December 2002): 52.

23. Unlike traditional slavery in Greece or Rome, in America it was color-based. Natives, blacks, and slaves were the same thing; hardship was suffered not only by blacks but also by poor people, except that it was harder to avoid in the case of the black and native population.

24. See Fidel Castro, *Revolucion*, March 26, 1959.

25. For further information see Morales, "En Cuba lo que rige es la llamada 'linea del color.'"

26. This is a real danger we can't afford to disregard.

27. This issue is widely covered in Esteban Morales, *Cuba: los retos del color* (Havana: CEBSH, University of Havana, 2005).

28. Not that we haven't made a great deal of progress in both fields. We have, but the development of our nation still has many unsolved problems ahead.

29. Read about the latest attempts to address this issue in the so-called *Transition Report* and in statements made by then secretary of state Condoleezza Rice.

30. See *El Pensamento Politico de Fidel Castro*, Book 1, vol. 2, January 1959–April 1961 (Havana: Editora Politica, 1983), 393–97.

31. See Morales, "En Cuba lo que rige es la llamada 'linea del color,'" for an alternative explanation about why this topic, taken up in 1959, was shelved and turned into a taboo subject by 1962.

32. An interesting thing often takes place when it comes to the race issue: many people can't really get around it, but they just keep it out of any argument that we still have discrimination and racism.

33. There were many gladiators in the arena of literature and the arts—too nume-rous to mention in this brief essay—whose praiseworthy efforts to fight for the race issue often crashed into the wall of silence build around this subject in those years. Now it's just being reintroduced in Cuban social sciences thanks to figures like Don Fernando Ortiz.

34. The formation of a national culture is an objective process that no one can escape, even if some take a bossy attitude, as if only one ingredient of the dish were enough for them to have the final say. National culture is a stew made with many foodstuffs impossible to separate even when it's still in the oven. And like it or not, we're all mixed in the casserole.

35. From a Marxist standpoint, the question of whether there's a theory of cul-ture, politics, or economy is an epistemological mistake. Marxism's topmost achievement, where it went one better than the bourgeoisie's so-called social sciences, is precisely that it went beyond the watertight compartments of those bourgeois views on society and gave us a cosmogony and a holistic vision of social phenomena. That's why it would be wrong to look at any topic exclusi-vely from a cultural perspective.

36. We must bear in mind that since it was established by the Founding Fathers, the United States has seen Cuba as part of its continental territory and there-fore as part of American culture. That's why our confrontation with that coun-try has always gone beyond the political arena and reached the cultural.

37. How can anyone imagine that any social process in Cuba can take place over and above the current political system?

38. I would say that this is not exclusive to Cuba. We also see it in the process of cultural formation across Latin America and the Caribbean. As for the United States, we would have to go deeper into the limits that colonization imposed on the natives and blacks, since no resemblance to the above-mentioned pro-cesses is observed. Although they also received this influence, there's no com-parison with the "Cuban melting pot."

39. Currents like Black Nationalism arose in the United States, something unthink-able in the case of Cuba.

40. Suffice it to learn about the conditions imposed on Afro-Cuban religious practitioners and the discrimination these religious suffered for many years.

41. Part of this source of knowledge is being fiercely attacked. Imperialism steals not only oil but also culture.

42. We'll see further how the development of national culture is affected by the same factors that affect the race issue.

43. Make no mistake, the slender chances of participation available to blacks and mestizos are also a consequence of the great differences in their status when the Revolution took over back in 1959, which can't be eliminated in such a short time. It's clear that every existing statistical report shows the same arran-gement: whites, mestizos, and blacks, from top to bottom, which shouldn't come as a surprise.

44. It's not just inherited burdens, but faults our society could still reproduce. See Rodrigo Espina and Pablo Rodriguez, "Raza y Desigualdad en la Cuba Actual," *Temas* 45 (January–March 2006): 44–54.

45. Here I say "black person" in the sense commonly used by our people.

46. However, there's always the danger that our institutionalization is affected. Find more details about this controversial issue in Morales,"En Cuba lo que rige es la llamada 'linea del color.' "

47. In my essay "Cuba: los retos del color" I explain how racism could still make a comeback in the institutions of our civil society as a result of the dynamics imposed by the relations between formal and informal power, even though it's not practiced by our state and government, whose members don't live like a Praetorian Guard.

48. All social measures adopted in the last few years in the fields of health, education, social security, food production, employment, housing, material supplies, etc., are a clear indication of a process to consolidate what we could call policies of social benefit for the whole Cuban people.

49. See Espina and Rodriguez, "Raza y Desigualdad en la Cuba Actual,"and Morales, "En Cuba lo que rige es la llamada 'linea del color.'"

50. For further information see Esteban Morales, *Desafios de la problematica racial en Cuba* (Havana: Fundacion Fernando Ortiz, Collection La Fuente Viva, 2007).

51. Outstanding attention is paid to this subject at all levels of the Communist Party of Cuba.

52. Unfortunately, the attitude adopted by some teachers known to have tried to bridge this gap and save the day tends to push things out of the frying pan into the fire.

53. No racial group is excluded, but the truth is that blacks and mestizos are poorly represented in our syllabi.

54. We take on such classification as valid, since it's the one that better describes our population.

55. Why is it that every time the top leader of the Revolution speaks at length on the race issue his words are not widely publicized?

56. This is a fact, despite the very critical approach taken by cultural currents such as rap music and its alternative discourse of denunciation. Cuban TV has also started to make some restrained attempts along these lines.

57. An example of this can be found in some of the reports presented by Cuba in the last few years: *Research on Human Development and Equality in Cuba*, 1999 (CIEM-UNDP, Havana, 2000); *Statistical Profile of Cuban Women on the Threshold of the 21st Century* (ONE, Havana, 1999); *Cuba: 10 years after the Conference on Population and Development* (CEPDE-ONE-UNFPA, Havana, 2005); *Cuba: Millennium Development Goals*, 2nd Report (INIE, Havana, July 2005). In these reports it's possible to verify Cuba's great progress in every order. However, any chance to flaunt the Revolution's work for

the sake of specific strata and social groups who are the hardest hit by poverty falls through with the absence of the variable skin color. Moreover, their scientific worth can be questioned on grounds of their failure to take into account as key a feature of the Cuban population as skin color.

58. I'm talking about the books written by Aline Helg, Carlos Moore, and Alejandro de la Fuente. Black and mestizo families hardly ever appear on Cuban TV.

59. Sadly, this already happened in the case of human rights. We took forever to have our own discourse about it, and we're still paying dearly for it. Only recently did journals such as *Temas*, *Catauro,* and *La Gaceta* publish works on this highly topical subject.

60. UNEAC is home to Grupo Color Cubano, whose members regularly discuss this issue, albeit in very a limited and scarcely disseminated context, largely unheeded in our media.

61. Unfortunately, this topic appears in the so-called *Transition Report* and is being manipulated to cause the Cuban Revolution as much trouble as possible.

62. The vindicating, dignifying work of the Cuban Revolution was no doubt extraordinary, but this is about rooting out negative stereotyping, prejudice, and racism out of Cuba's social body once and for all. Until that happens, we'll be living in danger of going backward.

## 9. STATISTICS AND THE COLOR OF SKIN

1. None of this would make any sense if we were talking about the United States, where no Cuban would be considered as white, because of his/her Hispanic heritage, and where the sociodemographic structure is quite different.

2. When non-equal persons are treated homogenously, it reproduces inequality at another level. In this state of affairs, it is very difficult for those trailing behind to reach those ahead of them. This forces a change in the social policies that takes into account the differences from the starting point of each racial group, and specifically within such groups. Even the same racial groups are not homogenous internally. This is more so in Cuba, which has traveled a long road in the dialectics between opportunities and possibilities in the use of the advances created by the Revolution.

3. Fidel speaks about objective discrimination in Fidel Castro, "Speech in the closing session of the 2003 Teaching Congress" (Havana: Oficina de Publicaciones del Consejo de Estado, 2003), 27–30.

4. The Oficina Nacional de Estadísticas (ONE) and the Centro de Estudios Demográficos (CEDEM) of the University of Havana are doing a lot of work to advance in this direction.

5. The most important human right is the right to exist, and the indigenous and Afro-descendant population, lost in generic and impersonal numbers, makes them invisible, and cancels its existence.

## 10. SHOOTING WITHOUT A SCOPE: AN INTERVIEW

1. Address given by Comandante Fidel Castro Ruz, prime minister of the Revolutionary Government, in the Presidential Palace, March 22, 1959. His speeches and interviews on this and other topics of the moment are collected in the two volumes of thematic selections of his thoughts. See Fidel Castro, *El pensamiento de Selección Temática*, 2 vols. (Havana: Editora Política, 1983).

2. Esteban Morales Domínguez, *Desafíos de la problemática racial en Cuba* (Havana: Fundación Fernando Ortiz, collection La Fuente Viva, 2007).

3. *Mil artistas cubanos, Mil deportistas cubanos, y Mil mujeres cubanas,* photographic exhibition by Pierre Maraval, 1996, 1997, and 1998, Pabellón Cuba, ExpoCuba, and the Habana Libre Hotel, respectively.

4. Closing address delivered by Fidel Castro Ruz, "Seguire moscreando y luchando," 8th UJC Congress (Havana: Office of Publications, Council of State, 2004), 18.

5. Ibid.

## 12. RACISM IN CUBA, AN UNRESOLVED ISSUE: AN INTERVIEW

1. Introduced by then-senator Martin MorCia Delgado, it was intended to prevent parties from standing in the political elections on the basis of their racial sympathies or as representatives of a given race group. For further details, see Martin MorCia Delgado, *Integracion cubana y otro sensayos* (Havana: Publicaciones Comisión Nacional del Centenario de Don Martin MorCia Delgado, 1957), 241–45.

2. Fidel says: "I call it objective discrimination, a phenomenon associated with poverty and a long-standing monopoly of knowledge." Fidel Castro, *Las Ideas son el Arma Esencial en la Lucha de la Humanidad porsu Propia Salvación* (Havana: Oficina de Publicaciones del Consejo de Estado, 2003), 28–29.

3. A reference to Darsi Ferrer, an opponent convicted on July 21, 2009, of buying allegedly stolen construction materials on the black market. In their declaration, the African American intellectuals call him a civil rights leader and demand his immediate release.

4. We should not let this happen. Rather than an ethical issue, which is no less important, we must unequivocally consider this as a political matter worth fighting for in order to finally attain to a society "with all and for the good of all" as José Martí advocated. Nevertheless, we need to come to terms with the fact that racism, stereotyping, and racial discrimination do exist and have to be eradicated from our way of life if we ever want to succeed.

5. Nowhere in the statistical yearbooks that Cuba sends to the United Nations with data on social issues are the Cuban people classified according to skin color. The height of absurdity, since such an arrangement would clearly show how much headway Cuban non-whites have made as a result of the Revolution's course of action by comparison with the social progress of the whole popula-

tion. The overall reluctance to bring the color issue to the fore is so deeply ingrained that it keeps us from exhibiting the achievements of the Revolution.

6.    Name of both the seafront wall and the avenue that go along several miles of the coast in Havana.

## 14. AFFIRMATIVE ACTION: AN INCITEMENT TO DEBATE?

1.    That "race" is a social invention is beyond question. There's no such thing as race, but people's outer differences have always been used by the exploitative elites to make value judgments in order to keep certain individuals constantly subjugated. That's what they did to the black slaves and the Native Americans, and today, five centuries later, remains a matter yet to be resolved.

2.    See Fidel Castro's speech in the Closing Session of the Congress "Pedagogy 2003," February 7, 2003.

3.    *Ideas are an essential weapon in the human race's struggle for its own Salvation* (Havana: Oficina de Publicaciones del Consejo de Estado, 2003), 27–30.

4.    Ricardo Fernandez, *Exclusion e inclusion: El impacto de la acción afirmativa, Public Interest* 127(Spring 1997).

5.    As president, William Clinton tried to prevent the elimination of affirmative action and even launched an initiative called *A Single America for the 21st Century,* eventually consigned to oblivion by George W. Bush.

6.    Actually, Mr. Obama has done nothing for his own for fear of being criticized by his supporters.

7.    That the ruling elite in the United States cares little about this problem is beyond question.

## 16. THE CHALLENGES OF RACE
## WITHIN THE SOCIALIST CONTEXT

1.    See Esteban Morales, *Desafíos de la problemática racial en Cuba* (Havana: Editorial Fernando Ortiz, Colección Fuente Viva), 157–93. Today, blacks and mestizos have advanced. Yet quite a few, after reaching higher education and professional levels, are in better conditions to adapt to the changes. Many of them can be self-employed, but many others need help finding suitable employment, especially in the industrial and construction sectors, taking into account their importance among the proletarian class. Nevertheless, affirmative action must be very much present to help those left at the periphery of the solutions that will  be generated. Because, throughout those years, the crisis has affected the gains of the social support levels.

2.    President Raúl Castro, in a meeting of the broad Council of Ministries, announced a postponement of the timeline to execute that measure. *Granma,* March 1, 2011.

3.    This emigration via Mariel harbor was composed of a mass of non-white people, most of them with low educational level, some had been in prison, and showed behaviors deemed unacceptable. Moreover, practically none of them

had a sponsor in the United States; they were rejected and shunned from the beginning. Many were considered excludables and kept in detention centers, and finally labeled as "different Cubans., undesirable persons. Very few were able to insert themselves into American society with some degree of recognition. In the United States, "marielitos" became synonymous with undesirables.

4. See Cuba's Declaration in the United Nations Committee on Human Rights and Race Discrimination, Geneva, January 2011. Not all of those practicing *santería* are driven by the profit motive: the majority demonstrate an honest and ethical behavior, and simply practice their religion.

5. To get more information, see "Raúl Castro, Meeting of the Council of Ministries," *Juventud Rebelde*, March 1, 2011. See also speech given at the closing of the 4th Session of the National Assembly of Popular Power, December 20, 2009, in *Granma*, December 21, 2000; and speech by Raúl Castro Ruz, at the closing of the 9th Congress of UJC, Havana, April 4, 2010, in *Granma*, April 5, 2010.

6. See *Negra Cubana tenía que ser*, CIR FEEDS (Committee for Racial Integration), *"Mujer Ante el Espejo,"* posted: February 15, 2011. CIR FEEDS *Por una Revolución Ética*, posted: December 1, 2010.

7. For futher information visit http://afrocubaweb.com/carlosmoore.htm.

   The Alianza Afrocubana of Carlos Moore, the Asociación Encuentro de la Cultura Cubana, and Bibliotecas "Independientes" por Cuba have been recipients of funds from NED, which was created to channel what previously had been CIA funds. The problem was that their funding sources kept on creeping into the media, and the U.S. Congress decided to provide financing more openly.

   The relationship of Carlos Moore with U.S. official circles has always been an object of speculation. It is said that the book *Fidel Castro, los negros y África* was published with CIA funds. A document published in the 1980s revealed that funds given to Moore during his residence in Southern California came from the FNLA, which was financed by the CIA. During Holden Roberto's exile in the United States, Moore spent a lot of time with him, because Roberto traveled constantly between Washington and Miami, acting as an assistant and translator, which reveals the kind of circles Moore was frequenting.

8. See Cuba's reply, *Granma*, December 9, 2009.

9. One of the most serious problems we face today in the fight against racism is the lack of racial awareness and self-esteem among Cuban blacks and mestizos. Quite a few of them inherited and became accustomed to accept, almost passively, race discrimination, since they often considered themselves inferior. Education has made a negative contribution, lacking debate. Also, there is the attitude in many people that since they are not whites, they don't try to be white: a ramification of the old legacy of "whitening."

10. Regrettably, there are not many experts in these subjects in our universities. Very few professors would be capable of lecturing about the history of Africa,

Asia, or the Middle East. Unfortunately, the person who without a doubt was our best expert in the history of Africa and the Middle East, Dr. Armando Entralgo, with a well-known body of work, died a few years ago. High schools and universities do not pay enough attention to these subjects.

11. This situation resulted from the assimilation of an imported Marxism with many limitations for focusing on our own problems. Anthropology was considered a bourgeois science, sociology a response to historic materialism, the mathematic economic model a subjective-marginalizing deviation of the theory of value in the Marxist political economy. In summary, a phenomenon of dogmatization and ideologization of science, which fortunately we have begun to overcome. See Morales, "Ciencia y Política: un dúo complejo," *Revista Bimestre Cubana SEAP* 27 (2007): 27–36.

12. It is amazing the amount of statistical data that Cuba sends to the United Nations in which the population is not classified by the color of the skin. Therefore, the true social work of the Revolution loses the opportunity to show it. What are the reasons for this enormous absence? Cuba is a multi-colored society, and this is not simply a matter of pigmentation, but of history. See Morales, *Cuba: color de la piel, nación, identidad y cultura. ¿Un desafío Contemporáneo?* (Havana: Editorials Ciencias Sociales, 2008):163–89, esp. n. 58. Also, our census does not consider linguistic differences, the underlying mix in our population of those descendants of the Antilles islands (Jamaicans, Haitians, etc). The Chinese population represents less than 1 percent, so are eliminated from the census. Places of origin are not taken into account. For those reasons, the census is culture deficient.

13. The experience of the Social Workers was, without a doubt, an affirmative action, planned by Fidel Castro who identified the problem, and helped many young people, mainly blacks and mestizos who had became marginalized in the workforce and university education. Now many are in university classrooms, creating a racial make up more akin to the Cuban population, and more similar to the makeup of the first years after the triumph of the Revolution.

14. Only fifty-one years have elapsed since the radical Revolution decided to attack the inequalities generated by Cuban society, stemming from a colonial slave system, and later from a neocolonial Republic, which advanced only a low percentage of the population. The rest was made up of a meager middle class, and a great mass of salaried workers and poor farmers *(campesinos),* whites, mestizos, and blacks who, with few exceptions, had never had access to wealth. Before 1959 in Cuba, poverty was also white, but wealth was never black. To deny that reality, not overcome yet, and made worse by race discrimination, would lead to a lack of political realism, which would end up impacting not just the social project of the Revolution, but also the nation's political stability.

15. See Morales, "Estadísticas y Color de la Piel," *Jiribilla* (2010).

16. See Morales, "Cuba Acción Afirmativa: ¿Invitación al Debate?," *Jiribilla* (January 2011).

17. Only Fidel Castro and Raúl Castro have openly spoken about the issue on multiple occasions, demonstrating their concern. No other political leader at the national or state level has ever mentioned it.

18. See *Declaración del CIR*, posted February 24, 2011, in *Negra Cubana tenía que ser*, to find documents and statements in solidarity by Orlando Zapata, Guillermo Fariñas, and Oscar Elías Bicet. Since they are black, this was an attempt to label them as fighters for race and human rights in Cuba.

# Index